P9-BJP-379

Scandalous Mercy

When God Goes Beyond the Boundaries

Published in France by Editions des Béatitudes. February 2017
Original title: "Scandaleuse miséricorde. Quand Dieu dépasse les bornes"
Translated from French by Anne Laboe
Editor: Christine Zaums
Grafic design of the cover: Nancy Cleland
Painting of the front cover: "Forgiveness", by Daniel F. Gerhartz
Printed by Grafotisak, Grude, BH. August 2017
ISBN: 978-0-9860453-9-4

Sister Emmanuel Maillard

Scandalous Mercy

When God Goes Beyond the Boundaries

TABLE OF CONTENTS

To our amazing Father of Mercy,

To my dear assistants Ann–Marie, Chrissey,
Laurence and Pascal
Who added to this book a touch of beauty,

To the good thieves of today and the bad ones,

To all those who are thirsty of happiness.

Preface

When the history of evangelization is written – and it can only be written after the Lord's return, when we can finally see things as they really are – all the Lord has done, directly in souls and through many of his servants and most especially Mary – will have proven to be overwhelming in both its extent and its efficacy. In this book sister Emmanuel has given us a remarkable glimpse into the wonders that God is doing in our own day, generously pouring out mercy and redemption throughout the world. These stories of God's amazing mercy should give us hope for the most distant of souls.

Sr. Emmanuel has been given a special vocation to both understand and effectively communicate the wonders of grace being poured out to all – both from her "home base," living in Medjugorje as she does, and through her extensive travels throughout the world where she has a chance to see and hear many wonderful stories of what God is doing and has done.

This book is another extraordinary gift to the Church from the pen – and even more so, from the heart and spirit, of Sr. Emmanuel. Anyone who has read her previous books knows that she is an extraordinarily sensitive interpreter of the heart and mind of the Lord with a special sensitivity to the mission of Mary as she wins grace for souls in truly amazing ways. After all she has already recounted of the extraordinary working of grace all these years one may wonder – is there still more to tell? Yes! Amazing wonders still happen and seem to be multiplying and this book provides a particularly rich feast where we all can taste and see that the Lord is good, so good, so amazingly good.

This book has the capacity to awaken faith in those who have lost it, strengthen it in those who have it, and call to deeper conversion and great holiness anyone who reads it. What indeed, can we return to the Lord, in gratitude for all he has done and is doing and is willing to do – if a soul merely says yes to the grace and mercy that he always stands ready to pour out.

In gratitude, we can read this book slowly, as Sr. Emmanuel counsels us, and yes, with handkerchiefs at the ready – I can witness to that – and share it with as many people as we can.

Thank you Sr. Emmanuel for this book. Thank you Mary for your mighty prophetic and evangelistic mission in our time. Thank you God, Father, Son and Holy Spirit, for being so kind to us as to shower us with your merciful graces in such abundance.

Given the fierceness of the spiritual battle that is raging for our eternal destinies, may none of us miss this special hour of visitation from heaven!

Ralph Martin, S.T.D.
Director of Graduate Theology Programs in the New Evangelization
Sacred Heart Major Seminary
Archdiocese of Detroit

Introduction

Your writer is a survivor, thanks to God's mercy! Of course, if I compare my journey with that of certain witnesses in this book, Raphael, Nivaldo, Natalie, or even Bruno, who wanted to assassinate Pope Pius XII, my own descent into the netherworld seems less spectacular. Yet, I have to attest to the fact that in that distant epoch of my youth, Jesus saved my life in extreme circumstances, and I was able to taste – just as I still taste – the immense joy of plunging myself into the arms of my Creator and Savior, even after looking longingly at ways of … leaving this world.

But you don't have to pass within a whisper of death to encounter mercy, to discover the maternal womb of God, which bursts with love when faced with the depth of our human poverty! Every one of us carries in the deepest part of himself an intrinsic thirst, visceral and inescapable, for communion with Love. This book is here to announce good news to you: it is possible to find it and live it! I wasn't attempting to write a dissertation on mercy here; rather, I was trying, like a seeker of pearls, to recognize it in the everyday life of those dear to me, in the course of my missions, and in the amazing stories which were reported to me, like the one of Maïti.

Before you begin your reading and before discovering the love that emanates from these stories, I have two pieces of friendly advice to give you:

1 – Don't devour the chapters too quickly, as you undoubtedly did with "The Hidden Child of Medjugorje." You risk not drawing from them all their benefits. Instead, force yourself to read just one chapter per day. In each reading, you will be

captured by the story itself (like a movie), and you will be tempted to turn the pages quickly. But at the heart of each story there is a message for your life, unremarkable though it may seem, words that seek to penetrate you, so as to give you strength, to enlighten you, to console you, and to enable you to choose life with enthusiasm. Stop, and allow these words to fill you up!

2 – Get your handkerchiefs out, just in case!

For many of our contemporaries, life is very difficult; for some, it is even cruel. So, without masking the shadows which hover over our future, I have attempted to show you some pathways to take, so that you can say, when closing the book: "Oh, how good God is; I could never have imagined He'd be so good!" My goal (secret) is to make you fall into His arms! To invite you to live there in happiness! All the persons I selected for this book cry out for you to obtain that happiness. Also, whoever you are, there is a Heart which is madly in love with you. Listen to the humble echoes of the pressing call from the One with the greatest thirst for love.

His name? King of Mercy!

1
MY GIFT IS YOU!

Raphaël and his family. © *Photo Alleanza di Misericordia*

In the spring of 2015, while I was in Rome, I had the joy of finally meeting and being able to talk to the man I had been told was a hero. His name is Raphael Ferreira de Brito. He is a young Brazilian with an angelic face, not very tall, curly hair and a lively demeanor. His eyes were filled with joy and life, not to mention his humor. However…

Raphael's mother Ruth was raped at the age of sixteen by a twenty-five year old man from Barretos near São Paulo, Brazil. And that is how the child was conceived, in violence. His father then disappeared without ever knowing his son. A few months later, her uncle... who had drunk too much alcohol, started beating Ruth with a broom, saying: "If you don't have an abortion, I'll take care of it myself!" Ruth was seriously injured and rushed to the local hospital, which was dangerously lacking in hygiene. Almost none of the premature children born there survived. The doctors said: "It's the mother or the child!" They couldn't save them both. Ruth, who considered her own life to be a disaster, decided to let the child live.

Her little boy was born at five months and twenty-nine days. Doctors gave him no more than a few hours to live because some of his vital organs like his lungs were not yet fully developed. A nun, sister Brigida, who died a few years later with a reputation of sanctity, worked in this maternity ward and asked the dying mother if she could baptize the boy. "Whatever you do, the important thing is for him to live!" Said Ruth. He was supposed to be named Marc Aurelius, but the nun insisted that he receive the name of Raphael so that he could enjoy strong angelic protection. She took a syringe and poured a few drops of water through the incubator where the child rested, and baptized the boy. For six months she took care of the newborn baby. To everyone's surprise, Ruth survived the surgery and was able to go back to work in the cotton fields. Eight months later, Raphael came out of this adventure unscathed, and was entrusted to his grandmother for four years, then to his aunt until the age of eight. At his aunt's, he was instructed by the Jehovah's witnesses who instilled in him a straightforward dislike for Catholics and the Virgin Mary. He was eight years old, and sold ice cream in the streets to make a living. These were Raphael's "charming" first steps in the world.

He was happy enough, until the day when tragedy struck that changed his whole life.

That day was Father's day, and Raphael was nine years old. At school, he saw his friends preparing drawings for their fathers and he was deeply unhappy that he didn't have a Dad to whom he could give the drawing he had made for this occasion. "It must be so wonderful to have a Dad!" He said to himself. That evening, when it was time for prayers (with the Jehovah's Witnesses), he opened the book of the Prophet Jeremiah and read:

"Before I formed you in the womb, I knew you; before you were born, I set you apart; I appointed you as a prophet to the nations," (Jer 1: 5).

As he read the passage Raphael said to himself: "So God is my father! He has known me since I was conceived." That night, he asked the Lord to come and collect the gift he had prepared for Fathers' day. His child's heart was certain that God would come in person. But nothing happened: God did not come, and in the morning the gift was still there. At that precise moment, deeply disappointed and hurt, Raphael decided to no longer pray, convinced that God, like his father, abandoned him. As time went by he started to go out with friends and use drugs, and he experienced all kinds of destructive behavior. For three years he plunged headlong into the world of drugs, alcohol and sex. Ecstasy made him go completely crazy during the parties.

Yet, on August 11, 1998, at 5 in the afternoon, his life turned upside down in the middle of a party full of alcohol and drugs, a party that lasted for three days. This was the moment God chose to flood the life of Raphael with His mercy, and He did it in record time. Despite his young age – he was about 15, Raphael was already completely high on drugs. Suddenly, one of his friends suggested they leave the place. Strange! Even more bizarre, the friend said to him: "Come with me to church, I'm going to receive my first Holy Communion." Raphael was wide-eyed, because with his Jehovah's Witness upbringing, he had never set foot in a church. But he ended up going. Drunk and high on drugs, he sat at the very back of the church. Suddenly at the pulpit, a boy asked the assembly to pray for fathers both present and absent, because Father's Day was celebrated that day.

Raphael was in shock and started to shake. He thought to himself, 'Father's day, an accursed day! Pray for fathers? No way! Never! Didn't my father leave me and completely disappear? I don't even know if he is still alive!' For Raphael, this day was definitely the most sinister day of the year.

The boy continued to speak at the pulpit, but this time he pointed to the assembly, giving Raphael the feeling that he was addressing him personally. The boy began to read the passage from Prophet Jeremiah: "Before I formed you in the womb, I knew you."

Raphael fell to his knees and burst into tears. This was the second time he had heard the words of Jeremiah and they echoed deeply inside him. After so many years these words came back like a boomerang. Raphael saw his entire life flash before his eyes like in a movie, and especially that moment when God didn't come to collect His gift. Then, while he was still kneeling, he heard a loud voice speaking in his heart, telling him: "Raphael, you are my son! I did not come to take your present that day, because my gift is you: you are my greatest desire! Get up, change your life and follow me!"

Then everything stopped and Raphael realized that Mass had ended. It all seemed to have lasted just a few seconds. He got up and, to his great surprise he didn't feel any effect from the drugs. He immediately looked for a priest to tell him what had just happened, and the priest told him: "Rejoice, my child, because today you have been visited by God!"

After that day, Raphael neither took drugs nor abused alcohol. He began to attend catechism to prepare for Confirmation despite the fact that his godfather, who was linked to a cult practicing black magic, was strictly opposed to it. But Raphael held out.

Shortly thereafter, the second part of the prophecy echoed within him in a special way: it was time for the mission!

The highlight in this sequence of events took place on December 31, 1999, on the eve of the third millennium. Since Raphael was insisting on going to church, his godfather violently beat him. Bloody, upset and very angry, Raphael begged the Lord to help him.

To his amazement, the first reading of the day was again the verse from the Prophet Jeremiah:

"Before I formed you in the womb, I knew you; before you were born, I set you apart; I appointed you as a prophet to the nations." (Jer. 1:5)

The Gospel that followed included an exhortation: "Love your enemies and pray for those who persecute you." Raphael understood the message and when he got back home, he took his godfather in his arms and began to pray for him, laying his hands on him. At that precise moment, his godfather collapsed on the floor. He had just experienced an instant conversion. All night Raphael told him about God. His uncle wanted to go to confession as soon as possible, but before going to the Church, he collapsed again, whispered words of gratitude to Raphael, and died from a massive heart attack.

Throughout all these events Raphael understood that God was calling him to something greater. He was eighteen years old. Then he met the Community Alleanza di Misericordia (The Covenant of Mercy.[1] "Here, he thought, I can live out my calling as a lay missionary and announce this great love of God with which I myself have been gifted."

Am I Dreaming or What?

He spent a year in this community without seeing his mother. Then came the time when the missionaries returned home to visit their parents. Raphael went to see his mother in Barretos. He took advantage of his stay to do some pastoral work in the streets, including visiting the homeless. He planned to arrange for accommodation and meals for them. One day, his mother went out to visit a sick aunt. During her absence, he went to the central square in town, and there he saw five beggars whom he invited. To his great surprise, only one of

[1] Alleanza di Misericordia is an ecclesial movement founded in São Paulo in Brazil, which cares for street children. They are present in Brazil, Italy, Poland, and Portugal. alleanzadimisericordia@gmail.com 39 070 285 393 - www.alleanzadimisericordia.it

them accepted his invitation. And he was even more pitiful than the other four!

After having carefully washed, shaved and dressed him in new clothes, Raphael invited him to the table for a good meal, just the two of them. He was very affectionate with his guest, so that the man found the courage to open his heart. And this was indeed a wounded heart!

During the very joyful and trusting conversation, Raphael almost fell over. He asked the man to repeat what he had just said, word for word.

"Wait a minute… is this a dream or what? Her name was Ruth? And this happened in Barretos, at that time?"

"Yes," said the man. "That's exactly right!"

Raphael stood in silent stupor and then burst into tears. He had understood. The young woman this man had raped was his mother! And this poor beggar he had in front of him, this was his father! His heart skipped a beat. He didn't know whether to laugh or cry. In shock, he began to kiss his father and kept thanking God for this unimaginable gift he had been given. After having introduced Himself as a Father, the Divine Father, who deeply loved him, The Lord granted Raphael's wish as a nine year-old child with a broken heart, which was to know his Dad.

Needless to say, on that day, Raphael's father received some robust evangelizing from his new found son! It was about time, because this man's deteriorating health didn't leave much time for him in this world.

Today, Raphael continues his mission with his wife Lilian and their son Daniel in Sardinia (Italy), with a single goal: enable as many people as possible to know and experience, as he did, the infinite mercy of God. Raphael was on mission in Poland May 15, 2013, at a large retreat for priests in the diocese of Koszalin, when he heard that his father had passed away at the very moment he was giving his testimony. His father had died two days earlier, on May 13, 2013 (anniversary of the 1st apparition in Fatima!). Mass was about to begin, but he had time to tell the priests about his father's death, so that during the Eucharistic prayer the celebrants could pray for him in person. By "The priests" we mean the huge crowd of priests present around the altar that day. There were eight hundred priests with three bishops and all committed to offering their mass on the next day for this man. What other deceased person has ever been this blessed?

Will the wonders of God's mercy stop there? To think that, would be to misunderstand our Creator!

Yes, Jesus had indeed come to collect the gift from this little broken-hearted orphan and had given him a gift as well, a gift which was a hundredfold greater!

2
Pearl's Breathtaking Climb to Holiness

Mother Teresa of Calcutta

Outcries, blood-curdling screams, insults, blasphemies, the most abject obscenities, and continual threats… What an unbearable racket! Those who are cared for at Mother Teresa's Home can endure it no more. It's impossible to escape this torment. Too much is too much. Dealing with their own miseries is enough for them. Who on earth is this woman who yells and screams, breaking their eardrums day and night? It's a very young voice. It sounds almost like a child.

Pearl arrived among the patients several days earlier very bad off and in a wheelchair. Since her arrival she has been violently spewing her despair on anyone who approaches her. Mother Teresa's sisters – Missionaries of Charity – found her in the street. They gathered her up half dead, just as they did for most of the residents of this poor shelter. For years, Pearl, had been living with the deadly effects of the AIDS virus.

One might expect that this home is in an underprivileged area of Calcutta; but it's not. Is it in the squalid neighborhoods of Cairo? No, again. Could we be, then, in one of the steamy favelas of São Paulo? Not at all. Against all expectations, this new home, already swarming with busy bees in white saris, is tucked into the heart of one of the most prestigious cities in America: Washington, D.C.! Did Mother Teresa, champion of the poorest of the poor, change her tune and begin to deal with the richest societies of the world? What is she doing here with her little cotton veil and her worn-out sandals?

With a handful of sisters, she came precisely for people like Pearl. Those in the capital city who are being softly killed because they were born in squalor and are unable to come out of it.

Mother Teresa's sisters are not faint of heart! They have seen and heard it all, and learned how to get beyond the horror with a smile. For them, it's a matter of sowing love wherever the opposite reigns. It's a matter of stemming the tide of evil in all its forms by using the methods of their Divine Master: gentleness, love, patience, mercy, and joy. An extremely acrobatic feat!

Every single day, every single hour, the sisters take turns at the side of Pearl who is condemned to death far too young. They feed her, they nurture her, bathe her, change her clothes and bedsheets, cut her toenails and show her great kindness. For her part, this young girl never stops spitting and spewing out her despair and cursing the sisters, as though reeking vengeance on them for the accumulated failures of her miserable life. But the sisters remain unstinting in their service and nothing alters their smile. Not even a shadow of a smirk ever appears on the beautiful faces of these young Indian women.[2]

It didn't take many days before a little light appeared in this antechamber of death. Faced with the inexplicable perseverance of their goodness toward her, Pearl's heart began to soften. One day she asked one of the sisters, "Why are you always nice to me, when I'm constantly insulting you, insulting you and cursing you?" The sister was just waiting for that! Finally, the ice had begun to break, and they could not miss this chance!

"Because our God told us that you are the body of Christ. We want to treat your body with reverence and love," the sister said.

Pearl was in shock. She thought she was dreaming. But the sister was not kidding! Never ever in her life had anyone spoken to her in this way! After a moment of silence, Pearl's tone completely changed. She asked, "Wait a minute… You mean your God told you that?"

"Yes," answered the sister.

"Well, then, I'd really like to know your God! If this God tells you to treat me like that, I want to know that kind of God!"

The sisters hurried to call a priest who was the chaplain of the Home. He visited a number of times and without hesitation (let's not forget that Pearl was dying) proclaimed the Word of God to her. He described in particular the most striking episodes in the life of Jesus. Pearl didn't miss a bit of it. She was all ears, fascinated. Her eyes wide with wonder, she kept asking

---

[2] "Smile at Jesus in your suffering," advised Mother Teresa. "For to be a real Missionary of Charity you must be a cheerful victim. There is nothing special for you to do but to allow Jesus to live His life in you by **accepting whatever He gives and by giving whatever He takes with a big smile,"** (*Come Be My Light*, ed. Kolodiejchuk, Brian, 2007).

for more! Then the priest spoke to her about the Eucharist. He had barely explained the Last Supper with Jesus and the celebration of Mass when she cried out, "If that's what it's all about, then I want to have the body of Christ! Will you give me Communion?"

There was no time to lose. The priest baptized her, confirmed her, and had her make her First Communion. After receiving Jesus in her heart, she declared, "That's the first time a man came into me, not to take from me, but to give me everything!"

Then she revealed the secrets that had made her life a tragedy. "My mother was a drug addict, she always was. When I was 10 years old, she put me out into the streets to work as a prostitute. She needed the money I earned to buy her drugs. How many men, and, at times, women, have passed over my body and abused me over these last ten years… I can't even count them! So I got the AIDS virus and now I'm going to die. I'm only 20 years old… But I am so happy to have Jesus!"

From that moment on, for the first time in her life, Pearl discovered what inner peace was. The residents of the hallway where her room was located began to whisper among themselves, "Maybe she died. We don't hear her anymore!" While others said, "No, she is in her room, she is resting. Something might have happened!"

The next day, Pearl exchanged a few more words with the nuns. She asked them about their lives because she was so moved by the special quality of their behavior. Then, noticing that they were wearing a ring, she asked them, "Are you married?"

"We are not married to a man," they answered. "But we are the spouses of Jesus."

"What? You can become the wife of Jesus? Is it true? Is that possible? But I want to become the spouse of Jesus, too! But… why would he want to marry a loser like me, who was a prostitute for ten years? And who is going to die of AIDS?"

The sisters had tears in their eyes. They looked at each other in silence, overcome with emotion. They couldn't hide their feelings!

At night they asked each other, "How can we do it? How can we give her what she wants? We need to call Mother Teresa immediately! She will tell us what to do in this situation. The little one is going to die soon …"

Mother Teresa's answer tumbled down upon them like ripe fruit. She had understood everything in a fraction of a second. No discussion, no time lost.[3]

Discretion obliges me here not to reveal what will always be for the sisters, at their request, a kind of family secret. The fact remains, however, that a few days later, Pearl rendered her beautiful soul to God, clothed in the habit of the Missionaries of Charity.

---

[3] In *Come Be My Light,* Mother Teresa is quoted as saying, "Everyone and anyone who wishes to become a Missionary of Charity, a carrier of God's love, is welcome; but I especially want the paralyzed, the crippled, the incurables to join for I know they will bring to the feet of Jesus many souls," (*Come Be My Light,* 147).

3
The Woman Lost on the Hill

Apparition Hill in Medjugorje, © Photo EDM

This story takes place in June of 2001, at the time of the 20th anniversary of the apparitions in Medjugorje. Soon after arriving in Medjugorje from her homeland, Colombia, Juanita was stuck on the hill called Podbrdo, which overlooks the little hamlet of Bijakovici. She followed her group of pilgrims to the hill and prayed with them in front of the big wooden cross just above the second Joyful Mystery. Because her husband had just died, she was inconsolable there. Deeply engrossed in her memories, she lost her awareness of time for a little while, and, when she opened her eyes, the group had left, and she was completely alone on this foreign hill. Her moment of panic didn't last long because almost at that same instant, a Franciscan friar came up near the cross. She asked him: "Good Father, could you show me the path to get back onto the road down below?" "Don't go down right away, Madame, pray." "But I've already prayed!" "Pray some more. Stay a little while!"

Observing the gentleness of that priest and his luminous expression, she took advantage of the moment by asking him some deep questions that were of vital importance to her. "What did the Blessed Virgin say about death, Heaven, Purgatory, prayer, and suffering?" The Franciscan launched into a marvelous catechesis, and delivered point by point the very heart of the teaching of the Blessed Mother. Recognizing that this priest was undoubtedly inspired by the Holy Spirit, she opened her heart to him and poured out in a few sentences the very grievous situation in which she found herself. Married for 20 years to a man who had already been married in the Church, she was at first estranged from the Sacraments before finally leaving the Church altogether. She was aware that she was immersed in sin, to which was added the infinite sadness of having lost the man she considered the love of her life.

This Franciscan spoke Spanish fluently, which worked out well for her! He gave her some precious advice and invited her to make Jesus her top priority in life from that moment on, and he said that it would give her peace of heart. Two hours passed by during this unexpected conversation, and Juanita now had to find her group again. She asked the priest if he could hear her confession after 20 years of estrangement. "Go instead to the confessionals near the church," he told her. "In the second confessional near the statue of Saint Leopold Mandic there is a priest who speaks Spanish, and who will be able to hear your confession. Then go to Mass and receive Holy Communion. Jesus will be so happy you have returned to Him!"

Juanita already experienced a major interior transformation. She hurried down the mountain enthusiastically, leaping from stone to stone with the lightness of a liberated heart. Her whole being burned with a joy she had never known as she headed toward the church.

She found the priest, made a profound, heartfelt confession, received absolution, and entered the church where she experienced the most beautiful Mass of her life. When she returned to the hotel, she found the group of pilgrims she came with and ate dinner with them. How could she ever hide the marvelous experience she just had on Apparition Hill? So Juanita launched into a detailed account of her conversation with the Franciscan, her voice shaking with emotion. Her life had certainly taken a new turn!

"If anyone wants to understand the messages and receive counsel for his life, I recommend that Franciscan," she told them. "He was awesome, and he even spoke our language perfectly, and that's so rare!"

"What's his name? asked Pablo, the group leader.

"Oh, gosh, I'm so sorry. I completely forgot to ask him! But since he's a Franciscan, you're bound to find him around the church tomorrow."

When the meal was over, there was an atmosphere of great happiness, because Juanita had opened the eyes of the group to the beauty of certain messages they had not yet understood. Then it was time to say the final prayer before going to bed. The group gathered around into a circle and prayed the final mysteries of the rosary. Then Pablo handed out to each of them a small picture on which was written a very beautiful prayer of adoration. They planned to recite it together to conclude the evening. Juanita recited the prayer and turned the card over to see the picture.

"That's him!" She cried, her eyes open wide. "That's the man who was with me on the hill. It's absolutely him. I recognize him!"

That very instant, Pablo, shocked, ran into the kitchen, unable to contain his tears. Everyone wondered what on earth had happened to him. Juanita noticed the expression on his face and said to herself, "What did I do? Who is this priest? What's the problem?" She turned towards her sister with a questioning look. Her sister answered with a voice full of emotion: “Juanita, that’s Father Slavko Barbaric. He died six months ago!” She couldn’t say anymore, because her throat, too, had closed up and her eyes filled with tears. In the face of such a miracle, she didn’t know whether to laugh or cry from joy.

Everyone understood, and a profound silence fell over the group. Even today, so many years later, they remember that remarkable sign Heaven gave them: a saint had appeared to Juanita, the lost sheep they had brought with them out of mercy, in order to alleviate her sorrow.

4
The Maternal Womb of the Father

Mercy, that marvelous divine reality, constitutes the greatest attribute of God. Let's bypass the Latin etymology of the word mercy and concentrate instead on its Hebrew roots, the building blocks of the Bible, because they introduce us to a more profound insight on mercy.

In Hebrew, the word "mercy" is *rahamim*, which is the plural form of the word *rehem*, the maternal nexus, the uterus. *Rehem* refers to the most intimate and most noble part of the woman: a protected nest, where life takes form and where the embryo grows. It is in this wonderful little tabernacle that the Creator descends in order to accomplish a new miracle: the spark of life. How extraordinarily beautiful this biblical language is, because through it profound mystical concepts are explained using the most concrete realities on earth! For example, to make the intensity of His Mercy comprehensible, God has chosen this word which makes reference to the uterus. Note that the form is plural (*rahamim* and not *rehem*) to better describe the immensity of His own depth. It is not that God has many wombs; rather, the word is plural to signify intensity. What is produced in the womb of God is even greater than the miracle that happens in the womb of a woman who becomes a mother.

In the Gospel of Luke, chapter 15, Jesus offers us a marvelous image of the Heavenly Father in the parable of the Prodigal Son. It's the story of a son who, all at once, demands his part of the inheritance, asserts his independence, and leaves the paternal home. In a moment of imprudence and blindness, this young man imagines he can find in this independence his true happiness: unfortunately, it's only a mirage, a subtle trap laid by the Devil. The father's heart is overwhelmed by sorrow. It wounds him to see his son under the spell of such a terrible illusion. How could he choose to lead his life without structure, away from the gaze of his father, just to feel autonomous and free? What actually happens is just the opposite! The son falls into the slavery of sin and gets caught up in the concupiscence of human nature, and becomes contorted and blind in a way. Jesus tells us next about the young man's descent into misery; he finally ends up at the point of wanting to eat the scraps fed to pigs, so he won't die of hunger. Not exactly kosher for a Jew!

Why this misery for the son? Because he wanted to behave like a free electron, a satellite with no orbit! He hadn't understood that it was in living near his father, in deep, heartfelt communion with him, that he would find not only happiness but also his true autonomy.[4] Here, surely, the figure of the father represents the Heavenly Father.

This parable deeply concerns us, because the closer we approach the Holy Trinity, the more we enter into the embrace of communion with God. That embrace is the most profound desire of man. The more we distance ourselves from it, the more we leave its orbit, the more we lose all peace. It is precisely the distance we establish between God and ourselves that makes us lose peace.

God has taken a great risk: He has chosen to allow us complete freedom to decide either to live with Him or live without Him, because true love must be free. In the parable, it is the son who decides to leave his father and not the father who

[4] See "the Dialogue of Saint Catherine of Sienna" and "The Diary" of Saint Faustina who write that to achieve autonomy, the objective finally attained by the Prodigal son, there are, for us all, four stages to pass through. You must go from 1) dependence (like that of a child) to 2) anti-dependence (revolt, adolescent rebellion), to 3) independence (the son who lives far from his father and from authority) to arrive, finally at 4) true autonomy and health, which permits free interdependence and choice between persons.

abandons his son. Inside the heart of the father, an emptiness remains without his beloved son, who has left him. It is a gaping wound. Day and night, like a sentinel, in unwavering hope, the father waits for the son to let him regain his unique place in his heart. Notice that the father could have surrendered to bitterness and chosen to abandon his son. "If he wants to leave, then let him pay the consequences!" No, it was nothing like that! The father was at the corner of the road each day, ardently on the lookout for the return of his son. Doesn't that illustrate magnificently the divine mercy of God the Father? Is it not the maternal womb which keeps returning to that single idea that the little one has gone astray and thus lost happiness, peace, joy, communion? Divine mercy resembles the most pure maternal love that exists. All mothers understand that by instinct!

When the son in the parable is reduced to wanting to eat the scraps fed to pigs to survive, what does he begin to think about? "The servants in my father's house are better fed than this," he says to himself. So he decides to return home. Is this a fervent outpouring of love for his father? No, he is tormented by hunger and he knows where to find bread. We must admit that it is in that state of mind, one of total self-interest, that he goes back again along the path to the paternal home.

How does his father react when he sees him in the distance? Even though his son is filthy, in rags, and smells awful (pigs don't smell like roses!), he runs toward him, welcomes him with open arms, embraces him tightly for a long time, and covers him in infinite tenderness with kisses. The heart of this father overflows with joy, and he orders his servants to quickly prepare a feast, to bring him a beautiful robe, to dress him in it, to put a ring on his finger and sandals on his feet, to kill the fatted calf, to rejoice and feast.[5] Jesus emphasizes this point in

[5] The white robe/vestment symbolizes purity regained; the ring has on it a seal which confirms the ratification of contracts; the sandals symbolize newfound freedom because slaves at that time always walked bare foot.

another passage of Scripture: “There is more joy in Heaven over one sinner who repents and returns to God than over 99 righteous ones who have no need of repentance,” (Luke 15: 7).

Let’s consider a great friend of God, Saint Faustina Kowalska of Poland, who had committed a sin: she experienced great shame because of it, profound distress, and was humiliated before God: “Oh, my God, I beg Your forgiveness; I regret having wounded You. I have sinned.” And how did Jesus answer her? “My daughter, the humility with which you have repented for your sin has obtained for your soul a glory and a beauty superior to any you have already earned without having committed it.”

It’s simply proof that God is so good He takes our sin upon Himself. Instead of condemning us and punishing us, He transforms it into something positive, as long as we return to Him. Certainly, sin always has a bad smell to it; it stinks, even. But if we demonstrate true contrition out of love for Jesus, He transforms this foul odor into perfume. That is an astonishing truth, confirmed by many saints, notably Catherine of Sienna in her Dialogues with the Heavenly Father.

Let us enter, without delay – just as we are – into the embrace of the Father and jettison our sin into His heart burning with love! The maternal womb of the Father is waiting for us.

5
THE ANONYMOUS MAN FROM BOGOTA

Gloria Polo

Her nose was bleeding. She tried in vain to hide the stains which were accumulating on her handkerchief, and she was limping a little. But what a gaze she had! There was a softness and strength; light and joy. That's what I saw when I met her for the first time in Desio, Italy, at the opening of the Bi-Annual Marian Convention in 2011, attended by 7,000 people. Her name was Gloria Polo. Her translator whispered in my ear the reason for her bloody nose. The problem is that if I tell you the reason right now, you won't believe me. So, I'll let you know about it later in the story.

Actually, Gloria shouldn't even have been in Desio the day we met. She should have died a long time ago. She owes her life and the unbelievable experience she spoke about to a man she has never met in her life, and whose name she doesn't even know. This anonymous man from Bogota is the true heart of Gloria's story; he is one of those many saints we only discover in Heaven. Like all saints, he is humble and his presence is powerful but hidden. Before we get to him, we have to first ask who Gloria is!

Originally from Bogota (Colombia), Gloria has become more and more well- known in Europe. I do not want to paraphrase the magnificent testimony of this woman. You have to see her and hear her in person if you don't want to miss a single bit of all she transmits. Gloria belongs to that very rare type of witness who viscerally relives her experience while telling it to others. Her Latin American charisma adds even more to her amazing story. [6] Rather, I want to highlight a part of her testimony which powerfully reveals the extreme mercy of God!

At the age of 25, Gloria could really only boast of being a first class brat. Young, rich, beautiful, seductive, sexy, intelligent, gifted, well-married, she thought the world revolved around her and made it known to those around her, especially those who, according to her, were not on her level. In fact, she openly scorned them. An avowed feminist, Gloria defended abortion (she had undergone one herself at the age of 16) as well as euthanasia. She also encouraged women to get rid of their husbands: "If your husband cheats on you, leave him! Never be submissive again to a man!" She admits that she destroyed a lot of families that way.

And what's more, and perhaps even worse, she encouraged those around her not to believe in God. She loudly and with passion affirmed that those who believe in God are pitiful ignorant people. For her, neither sin, the devil, nor even Hell existed. She attacked the Church, showed her contempt for it, counseled everyone against confession, and even mocked priests. It goes without saying that she was blind to her own faults.

---

[6] Gloria's website is: www.gloriapolo.com.

She lied through her teeth, (she was actually a dentist!) and after a typical lie, voluntarily added: “If I lied, may lightning strike me!”

Now, no one provokes Heaven in vain. One day, Gloria met her nephew at the National University of Bogota to attend a dental seminar. Suddenly a huge storm blew up out of the blue, and the two of them ran for shelter under a portico. Out of nowhere lightning violently struck both of them. It was May 5, 1995. Gloria’s nephew died on the spot, but Gloria had a different fate. The copper IUD (Intrauterine Device or a contraceptive coil) she had implanted drew the lightning into her body and left her half-dead. That’s when the amazing adventure began in which that anonymous man from Bogota would play a decisive role.

Transported to the hospital, between life and death, she had an out-of-body experience, much like the ones recounted by others who have also had near-death experiences. But for Gloria, there was something more, and it was intense! I’m giving you here only the shortened version of her story, so I can get to my point more quickly.

At the precise moment when the lightning struck, Gloria was transported into a magnificent light, a very powerful light, like a white and radiant sun. Then, while approaching this light, she understood that she was in the arms of Jesus.

“Know that when we die, Jesus takes us into His arms like tiny infants, and, with a great deal of love, He lifts us up and presses us against His heart,” she often says in her talks.

Jesus embraced her with all His love, and when she found herself against His heart, she realized that this Heart was open, pierced by a deep wound. Then, she saw a door. There were two living trees on either side of this door, and, in the distance, she saw a garden with flowing water, vibrant flowers, and love all around. Great peace and immense love reigned over all. Gloria wanted to enter the garden at any price, but she couldn’t, because only people in the state of grace were admitted there.

In adolescence, she basically separated herself from the love of God by falling into very serious mortal sin, which she never confessed. For her, it was out of the question to confess to men whom she considered "worse than others." It was certainly this most subtle and fallacious argument of the devil which had pushed Gloria into pride, thus preventing her from seeking the mercy of God. Jesus loved her so much that He had respected her freedom.

After seeing the garden she wanted to enter but couldn't, Gloria felt trapped in a descent, passing one by one through successive levels leading to an abyss. There she saw a crowd of creatures coming at her with expressions full of hate. Hate that terrorized her. Their ugliness was intolerable. She cried out: "I'm a good Catholic! I have nothing to do here!" Then she heard a gentle voice say to her, "If you're a good Catholic, tell us, what God's 10 Commandments are?"

Where was the brilliant Gloria who always got out of everything? Lamentably, she froze. She stammered that everyone had to love one another, something she vaguely remembered her mother saying during her childhood, but her knowledge stopped there. Then, the voice described to her in purest truth and with stunning precision how she had trampled on every one of God's Ten Commandments, and how she had exhorted others to do the same. Not a single detail escaped this enlightened inventory of the actions she took throughout her life. Even in the face of all she had done wrong, Gloria had no shred of repentance. As far as she was concerned, she had done everything right!

That is what is known as stubborn pride. Gloria persisted in arguing that she had not committed any errors. She had arrived at the pinnacle of blindness.

She continued to descend, descend inexorably. She passed through various levels of Purgatory, meeting there people she had known, in particular her father. She suffered more and more and cried out desperately that she didn't belong in this terrifying chasm. Then the gates of Hell were at her feet. Since, after death, nothing but the naked truth is revealed to the conscience, she knew that if she crossed the threshold of this infernal abyss, she would remain there for all eternity.

It was like a flash of lightening, an old memory came back to her mind. When she was a dentist, she had a client who prayed a great deal and who had murmured to her in private: "Doctor, you are very materialistic, and one day, you will need this: when you find yourself in imminent danger, ask Jesus Christ to cover you with His blood, because He will never abandon you. He has already paid the price of blood for you."

How did the memory of that client come back to her at that exact moment? She thought she had completely erased it from her memory! Now here she was, plunged precisely into that terrible peril, that very "imminent danger." She began to scream, as though she were insane: "Jesus Christ! Lord! Have pity on me! Forgive me, Lord! Give me a second chance!"

The result was not long in coming: she felt herself ascending again until she stood before Jesus Himself, Who was beaming with light and love. She was fascinated. He welcomed her with tenderness, the way He would a prodigal son who had come back, and He distinctly spoke these words: "You are going to come back, Gloria. You're going to have a second chance. Know that if you have been saved, it was not because of the prayers of your family, but because of all those people, who, without your knowing it, sent their whole-hearted prayers up to Me out of immense love for your soul."

Gloria then saw a multitude of tiny lights appear, like flames of love. They represented all the people who were praying for her while she was in the hospital. And among those flames, there was one which radiated the most intense light and from which the greatest love was emanating. She tried to see who this person was. The Lord then revealed to her in detail how she had received her second chance and to whom she owed this escape-by-a-hair from Hell.

The Poor Peasant

Among the most fervent souls in Colombia was a saint who was resplendent in a particular way. It was him! He to whom Gloria owed her second chance. A poor peasant who lived at the foot of the Sierra Nevada of the Saint Marta Mountain Range. Jesus described the heart of this man as the greatest flame in the country! He added: "This man whom you see loves you enormously, without even knowing you."

This poor farmer had just seen his entire harvest burned at the hands of the guerrillas. He had not even one morsel of bread on his table, neither for him, nor for his family. Moreover, the guerillas wanted to take his oldest son to serve in the guerrilla army.

However, that particular Sunday, the day after Gloria's accident, he put on his finest clothes and made his way to the village with all his children. He entered the church to attend Mass and prostrated himself on the floor. As he began to pray, he was overcome with immense joy. The Lord invited Gloria to listen to his prayer: "Lord, I love You. I thank You for my life! Thank You for my children! Thank You for giving me the grace to love You. Please, let my children love You; let Colombia love You; let Colombia become good!" It was a prayer of praise and of altruistic supplication. What a beautiful soul! There was a true Christian!

Then the Lord showed Gloria what this man had in his pocket: a 10,000 peso note (around 3 euros) and another of 5,000. It was his entire fortune. When the collection basket passed in front of him, he put in the 10,000 pesos. Gloria was ashamed. What had she ever given to the collection? The counterfeit bills she had received at her dentist office!

When this man received Holy Communion, Gloria experienced an explosion of light in his heart. The Holy Trinity had entered him and he was radiating light.

After Mass, the man left the church. With the 5,000 peso bill he had left, he bought a panela (a type of honey cake) and some salt. The sales clerk wrapped the panela in newspaper. It was a half-sheet of the newspaper "El Espectador," in which there was a description of Gloria's lightning strike accident, and a photo showing her burned body. When our peasant saw this picture, he was overcome with such emotion that he began to read the article. Since he didn't know how to read very well, he had to put a lot of effort into it, and Gloria heard him recite each word, "Den-tist …" What tenderness! With each sentence he read, his compassion toward her increased, as if she were his own daughter.

Then he began to cry, and with his face on the ground, he begged the Lord: "Father," he said, "take pity on my little sister! Lord, save her! Lord, save my little sister! I will make a pilgrimage to the Sanctuary at Buga.[7] But save her, Lord!"

He didn't even have enough to eat, and he was promising to travel across the whole country for her! In other words, five days of travel for a stranger! He called God "Father" and her, "little sister." That profoundly touched the Lord, Who, when pointing out this humble peasant, said to Gloria: "You see? That's love of neighbor!"

What a marvel a humble soul is! The Lord did not resist him.

Gloria asked the Lord to reveal this man's name and tell her how she could meet and thank him. But that wish was not granted to her. "You will never know him on this earth," He told her, "because I don't want to remove anything from his glory!"

After talking to her about the saintly peasant, the Lord, in His infinite love, entrusted to Gloria a great mission: "What you have seen and heard, repeat it, not a thousand times but a thousand times a thousand times; and woe to those who, after listening to you, will not change. They will all be judged more severely – whether they are consecrated priests or the simple faithful, as

---

[7] This Sanctuary is located at the far end of the country.

you yourself will be when you return here, because there's no worse deaf person than the one who doesn't want to hear, no worse blind person than the one who doesn't want to see."

Gloria added in her testimony: "This, brothers and sisters, is not a threat! On the contrary, it's the exhortation of a God who loves us, who wants to prevent us from falling into this terrible hole which is Hell, because He wants us with Him in eternal joy. When each of you sees the book of your life open before His eyes at the moment of death, He will see everything, just as I saw everything. Do you know what causes the greatest pain at the time of personal judgment? It is knowing that our God was calling us and seeking us throughout our lives with ineffable love and tenderness, and seeing the miserable response we gave Him."

Today, Gloria continues to speak with the Lord for several hours a day, when she goes to Adoration of the Blessed Sacrament. He instructs her about many of the realities of our present society. He has also entirely restored her burned body. Science cannot explain why Gloria is doing so well. The experts slump in astonishment over the many medical files that have accumulated since her accident. Gloria is a living miracle and a magnificent example of the Divine Mercy: her ovaries were burned, because the IUD she was wearing attracted the lightning to her, yet three years later, she brought a new little daughter into the world!

Satan is not at all happy with her, and he looks for ways to prevent her testimony.

On that day when I met her, why was her nose bleeding? Because, when getting off the train, in the little station of Desio, he punched her in the face! Why was she limping? Because he struck her in the legs! Gloria's reaction? "It's a good sign for tonight's mission. It will be blessed!"

Several years ago the Lord revealed to Gloria that the peasant from the Sierra Nevada had just been killed by the guerillas, along with his entire family. On that day, she could see the face of the man for the first time. He came to visit her in a vision while she was at Adoration. He didn't say a word. There was a profound silence between the two of them, but, in her soul, Gloria knew that it was him. His eyes opened wide, and he seemed utterly stupefied to find himself face to face with Gloria and to see his little sister alive, after he had seen her at the gates of Hell and had pleaded so hard for her. They smiled at each other. Gloria described him tenderly in the following way: "He had swarthy skin, a beard, and an expression of infinite gentleness." Everything between them had been communicated to one another in an exchange of gaze.

From that day on, each time Gloria gives her testimony, or whenever she finds herself in a delicate situation, she feels the presence of this extraordinary friend, who accompanies her because of his own solicitude, like an extra guardian angel on a special mission. The Lord revealed to her that it would always be that way, even as far as Heaven, where he would be waiting for her.

This holy peasant, the most luminous soul in all of Colombia, the very powerful conduit of the mercy of God and magnificent example of charity, will remain for us the anonymous man from Bogota.

6
BEWARE OF FALSE MERCY!

When Gloria Polo was an adolescent, although she had been raised Catholic, she slowly slid into a dissolute way of life, wanting to act like her friends, who – left to their own devices on their spiritual journey – were not aware of the consequences of what they were doing. Sheep without a shepherd! When Gloria became pregnant at the age of 16, she was frightened. What should she do? It was impossible to announce this news to her parents! It was also impossible to hide it from them. So, there she was, cornered, and in a state of immense anguish. But it didn't take her good friends long to give her the magic key to get out of her impasse!

"Do what we do!" They said. "Don't be stupid, it's nothing. In an hour, you'll be rid of your problem! And besides that, it's free!"

Gloria made an appointment with an abortion provider. She found it necessary to bend the way the wind was blowing and conform to the trends of the youth in her town. Gloria, taken to the operation room and lying under the artificial lights, wanted only to run away. After moments of heartbreaking deliberation, at the last moments she changed her mind and thought to herself, 'There's no way they're going to kill my baby!' But it was too late. The scalpels were already beginning their gruesome work. Just like that, her first child disappeared without a trace.

But really, without a trace? What a lie! Even today, 30 years later, Gloria can't even talk about that experience without her heart twisting into knots.

A short time after her abortion, Gloria's conscience was pounding with misery, because a deep discomfort in her heart had seized her. She knew deep down that her lifestyle was not right, and was not leading her to true happiness. A crucial question came to mind: 'Living like this, just where am I going to end up? My behavior is no good. I'm making a mess of things. I'm sinking in too deep. There's something not right. I'm going down a slippery slope!'

She decided to find a priest and tell him all she had been doing, hoping to receive some advice for her life and to be able to start again in a better direction. She wanted enlightenment! She decided to open her heart to a priest and follow his direction, whatever it was.

The priest listened to her as she reviewed her choices, her failures, and her profound doubts about the quality of her life. Then he smiled at her and told her to put herself at ease:

"Stop worrying!" He said. "You're young; take advantage of that, and do as your friends do. Why single yourself out? God is good. He always pardons. Don't fret about it. Go in peace!"

From that day on, as she herself testifies, Gloria dove headlong into immorality. Why deprive herself? After all, God is good, and hadn't she received the approval of the Church? Besides, did the devil and Hell even really exist?

A Fatal Formula

Gloria Polo's story is part of what we might call "false mercy." Basically, our generation sometimes has a tendency to equate mercy with leniency, which is more about being good-natured and cool with those whose conscience is piqued than reflecting the reality of the Mercy of God, which led Christ to the Cross. The contrast is tangible. To free us from sin, Christ endured unimaginable suffering in His body and even more intense suffering in His soul. How can we think or say that sin is not serious in our own lives, if it caused that kind of torment within Jesus, Himself? How can we take God's Commandments lightly, if their transgression required the atrocity of the Passion and Crucifixion of the Word Made Flesh to spare us from eternal damnation to Hell?

Can you imagine a doctor who, to put someone at ease, would tell one of his patients sick with cancer: "Don't be afraid, it's not that serious. People don't die from it; continue to smoke and drink, there's no need for a particular treatment." He would be depriving that sick person of any chance of survival, or alleviation from suffering while alive.

Yes, sin is serious. It is even more serious when people decide to be obstinate and persevere in it. Sin leads to the loss of the soul. When we become aware of that, the Mercy of God can act in us. That's what Pope Francis tells us in his book, "The Name of God is Mercy". He speaks about the necessary shame which must accompany the awareness of having committed a sin. It is the feeling of shame which compels us to turn ourselves towards the infinite Mercy of the Father, manifested in Jesus.

False mercy consists in denying the reality of sin and its seriousness, and, as a result, denying our need to be saved. In doing so, we render the cross of Christ useless! It's the subtle trap of the Enemy, because he disguises himself in goodness, understanding and compassion. It's a clever imitation! The formula "it's not serious, everybody does it" is fatal. It deprives us of the Mercy of God and of His forgiveness, just as our cancer patient is deprived of treatment and sees his illness aggravated. That's the problem with "lenient" advice before absolution, it conveys a false mercy to the penitent who must recognize that his sin was against God and decide against it in the future.

Let's really understand it: we shouldn't go looking for an excuse for our sin, even if there is one – and often there is. Why? Because our excuses only offer us a short period of illusory peace, they are a justification. They may give us a certain psychological comfort, but since we have already absolved *ourselves,* they prevent us from sincerely asking for God's pardon! God's pardon goes infinitely beyond the meager and ephemeral psychological relief that our excuses give us. God's pardon puts a balm of tenderness over our wounds. It restores our dignity and gives us back our faith in Him and in ourselves. It fortifies us for the next battle against our erroneous tendencies; and often, confession after confession, that pardon liberates us from these tendencies and heals us. In those cases, it is the Precious Blood of Christ which flows over our infected wounds and transforms them into sources of blessing.

Do you want to know something? I'd prefer to fall into the hands of the Merciful God ten thousand times rather than get out of trouble using my own excuses once!

Why Don't You Come with Me and See Marthe?

At some point in the 70's, a man arrived at the Foyer of Charity in Châteauneuf de Galaure, France, to make a 5-day retreat.[8]

On that Thursday, the third day of the retreat, this man declared to Father Finet that his stories about Satan were old-fashioned, because Satan did not exist. He questioned why Fr. Finet would waste time speaking about beliefs from the Middle Ages. Father Finet simply smiled at him and didn't try to convince him otherwise. He knew that the man was so sure of himself, and so totally puffed up with the disastrous ideas that saturated France since the "Age of Darkness," erroneously called the "Age of Enlightenment," that he would not take heed of his words.

"Hold on," Fr. Finet said. "Before you go further with your questions, come with me to Marthe's house. Tonight she's

---

[8] At that time, Father Finet, co-founder of these retreat centers and spiritual director of Marthe Robin, was still living, and at his peak. He excelled in the art of speaking to those on retreat and winning their hearts for Christ.

going to enter into the Passion again, and I will be praying beside her at that crucial time. I hope you know I'm doing you a favor!"

The man was very happy. He had heard extraordinary things about Marthe, and this unexpected favor allowing him to approach her overwhelmed him with joy! He got into Father Finet's tiny car, and the two of them took off along the stony roads and savage hills of the Drôme. There was almost no conversation during the 10 minute journey. The priest made his way along, avoiding the potholes; his mind seemed to be elsewhere, undoubtedly moved by the profound mystery of what he was going to again witness. The man himself was more concerned with holding onto his seat during the sharp turns, than on what awaited him at Marthe's house.

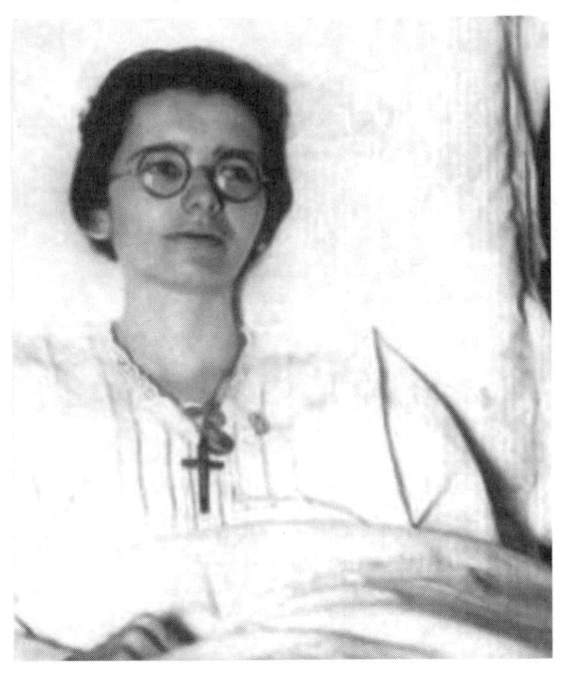

Venerable Marthe Robin.
© Photo Foyer de Charité-Châteauneuf-de-Galaure, France

The car had barely parked in the courtyard of the Farm (Marthe's tiny house) when the atmosphere turned sour. A deafening noise could be heard! An infernal din, ugly, terrifying laughter, howling animals and unbearable screaming greeted them. The priest was totally composed. He was used to it! He simply murmured to his passenger:

"It's Satan! He always shows up before Marthe's Passion to prevent her from saying yes. Don't get upset."

But the man was trembling all over; his blood was curdling in his veins... He could only think about getting out of there, because mortal terror had overtaken him.

"Let's get out of here," he begged the priest. "Okay, okay! I get it! Now, let's leave right away!"

"So, then, you heard it with your own ears! All this was necessary to make you understand that Satan exists, that he is completely real."

During his retreats, Father Finet always recounted that memorable episode. I heard it from his own mouth, and I saw the impact of that story on those at the retreat. Today, even in Catholic homes, people smile condescendingly at those poor, "backward" people who dare to say that Satan exists and that he is working on our downfall. If they only knew.

7
Scott Returns from Afar

Scott Sayer, United Kingdom

In a forest near Manchester in 2013, Scott was terrified. For two years, he had been practicing all the disorders promoted by the New Age movement, and today, in the middle of the woods, it was suddenly turning dark all around him. He could no longer see anything. But he perceived a feminine voice, unknown to him, which was murmuring something. He asked her to speak louder so he could understand what she was saying. This voice then whispered into his ear: "I can teach you a multitude of secrets and instruct you in knowledge that has been hidden from humanity." At that time she did not reveal exactly what those secrets were. Then she showed him his future: he would have lots of money, a beautiful house, etc. She added that in order to obtain all that was predicted she had to enter inside him. Scott resisted. He perceived that this proposition was very strange, and faced with his resistance, the feminine voice identified herself: her name was Baphomet.[9] She was trying to enter into his body by force, thus revealing herself to be a truly horrible creature. When Scott came out of this meditation, he realized that the experience had lasted 3 hours![10]

Who is this Scott? I was able to interview him, and here is his testimony:

"I grew up in a Catholic family from birth. I'm 27 years old and have one brother, one sister, and two half-brothers. When I was a child, my whole family went to church and prayed the rosary together at home. When I turned 11, I don't know why, but my family stopped praying together. Two years later my parents separated and then divorced.

Already devastated by these events, I also felt rejected by my father. I wanted to ignore him completely. He and I didn't speak for several years.

I developed a great deal of resentment inside, and, along with that, I turned away from God. My mother and grandmother did everything possible to get me to pray the rosary with them, but I refused and demonstrated a complete lack of interest. On top of everything else, I was in the full crisis of adolescence. I stopped going to church completely by the age of 16.

---

[9] Baphomet is a name given by some of the occultists in the 19th century to the mysterious idol that the knights of the order of the temple were accused of venerating, whether it was true or not. She was often represented with a head of a man with a beard, she was venerated as such, but she was also scary because of her ugliness. Her breasts and head were those of a goat. Satan or a demon, a member of the hierarchy of Hell. Goat headed idol named Baphomet. See USA Today July 24th 2015 Satan Temple's goat-headed statue debuts Saturday

[10] The rosary of the family during his childhood is very probably what protected him at the time of his encounter with Baphomet and what permitted him to resist her, because if he had joined with her …Imagine the result! How many young people today, unfortunately, do not resist.

Following the slippery slope of the culture of death offered to our young people, I began to smoke pot, then to take ecstasy and cocaine. I loved going to parties and getting drunk.

I left my home country to study in Australia for a year. An overwhelming feeling was devouring me inside, along with a certainty that something important was missing. But what? Whatever job I envisioned myself doing, there was always something that wasn't right about it. I knew deep inside that I wouldn't be satisfied. At 23, I turned toward several types of meditations: transcendental meditation, Hindu meditation, Buddhist meditation, Egyptian meditation, any meditations that I found on the internet and which would allow me to shut myself away with my headphones. I even became interested in Reiki but without actually practicing it. The most serious episode had me in the clutches of that mysterious woman, the one named Baphomet, whose voice I heard. I was ignorant then of the fact that Baphomet was the name of a demon, and I came to realize that she had tried to seduce me with her lies."

At that moment in the interview, I could sense that Scott was overcome with emotion and that he was nowhere near forgetting the horrible encounter he had which almost made him fall into a profound darkness.

During the years that followed those devastating experiences, Scott suffered greatly from "sleep paralysis," without realizing at the time that his symptoms were due to his New Age practices.[11]

---

[11] Sleep paralysis: a syndrome where one awakens and is unable to move. The brain is conscious, but the body is in total paralysis and will not respond to commands. This condition can generate a great deal of anxiety. The phases can be short or long. The symptoms of "sleep paralysis" recall one of the aspects of Gelineau disease known as the narcolepsy catalepsy syndrome. It is either a symptom of a more complex disease, or the expression of a neurological impairment which may be of toxic origin (drugs, infections, psycho-emotional or spiritual). There is a disconnection between the physiological control of the body without any alteration in consciousness.

The mercy of God was waiting for him along his most dangerous path. Scott's grandmother, who prayed constantly for him, dreamed of a way to keep him connected to the Lord. She invited him to accompany her to Medjugorje, arguing that she couldn't go alone because of her age. She hit the nail on the head! Scott was happy to go, because he had already been to Medjugorje when he was little and remembered that he had a good time there.

When he arrived at the home of the Gospa, the forces of evil which were still living in Scott without his knowledge, became unleashed. Because the Virgin Mary is the one who crushed the head of the serpent, his malaise became unbearable in her presence. At the very beginning of his stay, Scott woke up in the middle of the night, and to his horror, his body was completely paralyzed. His limbs were not responding to his commands and only his eyes could move. But that wasn't all. He sensed a dark presence in his room and it had the effect of emptying him of all life. There was nothing he could do! He had to endure this state and wait until it came to an end.[12] At that point he remembered the existence of God and sought to call upon Him. But he couldn't cry or even move his lips. However, in his spirit, he began to cry out: "Please help me Jesus Christ!" At that precise moment, as though Jesus was just waiting for the cry of His child before He intervened, the dark presence disappeared. When he was no longer under the hold of the enemy, two thoughts came to Scott's mind, surprising even him. Even though he had abandoned the Lord for years he thought to himself, 'I want to become a priest, and I have to go to confession to a Priest.'

---

[12] I myself had this experience during my adolescence after séances of spiritualism, using a ouija board, when we called down the spirits. There was also divination through cards and astrology, which I practiced with my friends. At the time, I couldn't understand why I felt so devoid of all energy. It was as if my whole life had been absorbed by something terribly low, and I lay prone on my bed. My mind could no longer command my body. I couldn't move. See Chapter 4 of The Hidden Child, where I give my testimony.

Because of the New Age practices to which he had given himself over, Scott had the feeling that he would have to find a priest capable of understanding his confession and understanding his wanderings into occultism. Several days went by, and, during the homily at Sunday Mass, he heard the celebrant describe the dangers of the occult. 'That's the one!' Scott said to himself. 'He'll know how to hear my confession.'

He said to me, "My grandmother jumped for joy when she saw me in the line of pilgrims who were waiting their turn in front of those famous confessionals. We call them "sin boxes" and there are many in Medjugorje."

Scott went on to explain: "I made a very sincere confession. The priest seemed to ask just the right questions and I was able to reveal to him easily all the suffering I had endured in my life. A great number of my spiritual wounds had been caused by my relationship with my father, then with my mother. To add to it all, after living with my girlfriend for 3 years, I found out that she had cheated on me and had lied to me, and that was a new and painful blow. Finally, because of a bad knee, I was refused to enter the army. This accumulation of failures made me think I was a living failure. But after that confession, what inner freedom I experienced! I had never felt that before!

It was then that I realized all the potential joy and peace I had squandered because of my bad choices. The good Father who had listened to my confession was very inspired when giving me my penance. It was to climb to the top of Cross Mountain, Krizevac, and to stop at each of the 14 stations. At each one, I was to think again about a specific moment in my life when I had been wounded and offer it up to Our Lord. That is exactly what I did. When I got to the top, I prayed the whole rosary and descended again, continuing to pray with all my heart. It was during that descent that I was again gripped strongly by the conviction that I had to become a priest. I said to Jesus then: 'I know that You are there; I know that I have done wrong in my life; but if You want me to become a priest, You'll have to give me a sign. I will do all that You wish.'

"When I got to the bottom of Krizevac, I began to walk along the little path which leads back to the village. It was at that time that the face of the Merciful Jesus (the one revealed to Saint Faustina) appeared before my eyes. It was not a 3-dimensional apparition but a simple vision. His face was radiant. He was shining with a golden light that does not exist on this earth. He looked me right in the eyes. That vision was all I could see, so much so that all that was to my left and to my right had disappeared from sight. At the same time I found myself enveloped in immense love, and I sensed that Jesus was saying to me, 'What more do you want?' Several seconds later, His face disappeared."

I hardly need to tell you that since his experience in Medjugorje, Scott has radically changed his life. He became one of those pilgrims who, through the mercy of God, has passed from death to life. A pillar of his parish, he attends Mass and Adoration daily and his relationship with Our Lady has had a resurgence. He has again taken up praying the Rosary, the tradition that his family taught him as a child.

One of the great miracles that Scott attests to is that the priest to whom he confessed revealed that he is an exorcist. Therefore, after Confession with this exorcist, Scott suffers no residual effects related to the New Age meditations he practiced before his conversion. In addition, he suffered no alteration of behavior, or symptoms of withdrawal after he stopped taking drugs.

At the present time, Scott does not yet know in what manner he will exercise his priesthood and serve the Church. Shortly after Medjugorje he found his bishop and the director of vocations in his diocese, because he couldn't imagine a life outside the priesthood. The director of vocations was a very good man who understood this new, potential candidate. Of course, it will take a good year of preparation before Scott can enter the seminary, so he remains open and is leaving his future in the hands of Christ, the great Priest, who is happy to share his own priesthood with His chosen sons. He is enthusiastic about being a conduit of grace in the New Evangelization. Surely, his testimony could move more than a few! Already he has met a Protestant who was also once involved in the occult practices of the New Age, but who has since abandoned that evil path. Since the Protestant's encounter with Scott, he has begun to pray a great deal, goes to Mass each day, and is preparing to become a Catholic.

If one day you should meet Scott near Manchester, he will tell you himself how grateful he is to Christ for the mercy He showed him. You will meet a joyful and satisfied man, with that quality of happiness that can only come from Heaven!

8
Confession of a Vampire

Father Antonello and Father Enrico. © Photo Alleanza di Misericordia

If you have never encountered true "fools for God", then let me tell you: I know a rather remarkable pair! Originally from Sardinia, Father Enrico Porcu and Father Antonella Cadeddu began their mission in Brazil, full speed, in the year 2000. Although they were from relatively well-off families, they moved into the middle of a slum, sleeping in a storage container, where comfort was impossible – in fact, pretty much non-existent, and the generous opening of their hearts to the world of the poor led them to unusual experiences.

One night, bedded down on the floor of their miniscule lodging, along with seven street people whom they had picked up in the Plaza Centrale of Sao Paulo, Father Enrico slept with one eye open. Because of his vast experience with persons on the street, he did not feel completely secure. Not to mention how difficult it was to sleep with the torrid heat, on a hard surface and in the dust.

Suddenly, Father Enrico saw a shadow approaching him. Despite a surge of adrenalin, he managed to keep calm on the surface. A young druggie was standing there, observing him, a box-cutter in his hand. It was Pedro, a 19-year-old in rags that our two priests picked up after they had a short conversation with him in the city several nights earlier. He simply said that he no longer wanted to sleep in the street and asked if he could be sheltered. He seemed so sad! How could our priests not think of the words of our Lord: "Whoever welcomes one of these little ones, welcomes Me," (Mat. 18:5)? That's how Pedro became one of the "guests" that night.

Father Enrico began to pray with all his might. The box-cutter didn't seem stable to him. How right he was! Pedro remained standing there for a while – minutes that seemed like hours to Father Enrico – then, strangely, the young man went to bed.

In the morning, very agitated, nervous, and seemingly out for blood, the young man went looking for Fr. Enrico with an angry face. When he found him, he told him a terrible secret: He had been attacked during the night by a compulsion, an almost irrepressible desire to cut open all his veins and drink his blood. However, something had prevented him from doing it. But he didn't know what it was. Actually, Father Enrico knew. It was his prayers of faith!

Pedro, observing that he was neither judged nor rejected by these priests, felt more at ease and little by little he regained his composure. He understood that he could reveal the terrifying secret which had been eating away at him since childhood:

At his birth, he was dedicated to the devil by his own family. Pedro learned of this during his adolescence. Since then Satan took him over and controlled him. He commanded Pedro to drink human blood, the blood of others or even his own. Inhabited by this irrepressible compulsion, he found it almost impossible to resist. It was the only way for him to find a pseudo peace, or rather, a short satisfaction. This false peace is typical of Satan, who always leaves us wanting more!

Our two priests, stupefied, realized that they were in the presence of … a vampire! Suddenly, it all became clear. They understood why Pedro's arms and several other parts of his body were covered with wounds: he had inflicted them on himself whenever he couldn't find any other prey whose veins he could cut to satisfy his thirst for blood.

Since he had become a drug dealer, he was detained in a prison for minors. There, he did everything possible to make his detention "buddies" fight one another. It was very calculated on his part, because after the fight, he could drink any blood that spilled. He confessed that often he ended up licking it off the floor. Pedro then revealed the whole drama of his short life and the suffering within his family who, in the end, abandoned him.

Our priests prayed for him, and Pedro almost immediately had an unparalleled demonic episode.

Several days later, he had another demonic episode, even more violent. Suddenly, his anger took over, it became very dark and his face contorted. He took a Gilette razor blade and rushed toward Father Enrico and the others. But a miracle happened. An image of the Virgin of Medjugorje was placed between him and Father Enrico. Pedro stopped mid-thrust and forgetting the priest, threw himself at the picture of the Blessed Mother. Howling with rage, he tore it to pieces. Soon the demonic outburst intensified. Satan was unleashed, and for hours everyone prayed for Pedro, imploring God to liberate him. Eventually he was liberated!

About one month later he was able to return to the world again, serene and peaceful, with a desire to begin a new life. In him, everything had changed: it was wonderful to see. Today, he is married, a happy man, and an unmatched witness to the faith.

Let us give thanks to God and to the Blessed Mother! What a miracle they accomplished to save Pedro through these priests! What new miracles do they have in store for him?

And we, who no doubt have not even come close to following Pedro's path in our own lives, will we know how to welcome the loving presence of God in our lives? Will we be able to recognize the presence of His mercy that embraces all His children with the same power?

The Courage to Evangelize

Our two priests went to the Central Plaza of São Paulo with the idea of rescuing for some lost and desperate souls. They found plenty of them, and, today these souls have found Christ and changed their lives. There are still thousands of men, women and children waiting for the Good News of salvation! There are all kinds of people, from the rich and well-off with extravagant houses, to the drug addicts living in the ghettos of our cities. Who is reaching out to them?

Our Creator has a life plan for each of us, a kind of divine dream to make all of us completely happy. But Satan too has his own plan, namely to shatter our lives into a thousand pieces. Padre Pio used to say that the greatest act of charity we can do for someone is to liberate his soul from the clutches of Satan.

Evangelizing takes courage. We must be ready to get slapped in the face (and receive the eighth Beatitude!). But how precious is the fruit when a lost sheep is found; when a soul that was dead comes back to life!

Young drug addicts in Brazil

A Man on a Bench

With Jesus at the helm, we are never short of surprises. Here is a beautiful example:

Two women had a great desire to learn how to evangelize, to make known the love of God to those who did not yet have any idea of it. Although they had no intention of actually doing it themselves, they decided to attend a class on how it works. Half way through the course, the students were required to go out two by two and speak about God to people they met on the street. The two women, who in the beginning were on fire with the notion of evangelizing, began to tremble with fear at the thought of undertaking of this mission. When they set out they saw a very secluded and quiet path and decided to walk down it in the hope and expectation that they would not see anyone.

But… rats! There, sitting on a bench, reading his newspaper, sat a man. The two women mustered up their courage and sat down beside him, one on the stranger's right and the other on his left. One of them plunged in and asked him timidly: "I'm guessing you don't have any desire to hear about Jesus Christ, right?" The man lowered a corner of his newspaper and rapidly scrutinized them. "As a matter of fact, yes!" he answered.

The two women forgot their fear, delighted to see that he was open and even desirous of hearing what they had to say. They launched into a warm monologue. Then there was silence, time to catch their breaths.

"May I talk now?" asked the man. "Let me tell you a story. Yesterday, my mother had a truly strange dream. 'Imagine this,' my mother said to me. 'I had a dream about you last night, and I feel compelled to tell you about it. I saw you standing in the middle of a lake of fire, but I don't have any idea what that means.' "A lake of fire?" I knew exactly what that meant.

"I am a professional swimmer, and I have lived a life totally centered on myself. My goal was to obtain all that I wanted, even to the detriment of my loved ones. When my mother spoke to me about her dream, I understood right away that she had had a vision of Hell. And I was in it! Standing right in the middle of the flames! My sister had always tried to bring me back to the faith and to the Church, but I continued my life without God. I was able to resist my sister's promptings, but last night, I took to heart the inspired dream of my mother, and I reflected on it. I decided to change my life and come back to God. But there's the problem… How do I go about this? I had no idea."

The man paused and said: "You thought I was sitting here reading the newspaper. . . The truth is that I was thinking about my life and praying to God, telling Him how much I wanted to change. I was explaining that in order for me to do that, He had to send me someone to help me, because I couldn't do it alone. It was then that the two of you came along…"[13]

That's evangelization: one day you get a kick in the teeth; another day you marvel at seeing that God prepared this heart to hear His Word. In both cases, we are surely great winners! When it's a kick in the teeth, we are the beneficiaries of the eighth Beatitude:

"Blessed are you when people revile you and persecute you and when people say all manner of evil against you falsely for my sake. Rejoice, and be glad: for great is your reward in heaven," (Matt.5:11-12).

When we stumble upon an open heart, we benefit from another type of joy: to have been the instrument of God in bringing back a lost sheep to the fold… Since there is more joy among God's Angels for a single sinner who repents than for ninety-nine righteous ones, we participate in this heavenly joy and our hearts dance with the Angels!

---

[13] Testimony given by Father Conrad CFR, a Franciscan Friar of the Renewal from the Bronx, New York, http://franciscains.free.fr/Communauté/Franciscains.php. www.franciscanfriarsoftherenewal.com. See also: Books written by Benedict Groeschel CFR.

9
WHY NOT GIVE EVERYTHING?

Let me mention here this wonderful parable of the great Indian poet, Rabindranath Tagore. He lived in the very poor state of Bengal, where Calcutta is located. He sets the scene for us with a beggar, who, in order to survive, puts his tin pot by the side of the road and waits for meager offerings for hours upon hours each day.

One day, the beggar saw, approaching in the distance, a magnificent chariot driven by a richly-dressed prince. He said to himself, 'Here is my golden opportunity.' The chariot stopped in front of the beggar in a huge cloud of dust, and the prince stepped down. He approached the beggar, and contrary to all expectation, asked him: "What do you have to give me?" The beggar, stupefied, began to tremble and started to rummage through his little knapsack, where he had gathered a handful of grains of wheat, his limited storage of food. He took out a single grain of wheat and offered it to the prince, who thanked him, and returned to where he came from. The beggar remained perplexed. Evening came, and the beggar returned to his little makeshift lodging and poured out his grains of wheat to eat. To his surprise, he found among them one grain of wheat made out of pure gold.

'Oh,' he thought to himself, 'if only I had given him all of it!'

The moral of the story? You only have what you give away...

Gandhi and the Diabetic Child

There are many ways to give. Blessed are those who give without counting! One of the most demanding word of Jesus in the Gospel is in Luke 6:30: "Give to everyone who asks of you!" But what a short and fast way to holiness it is! I chose from the Life of Gandhi (India again!) a beautiful and rare example of self-giving. We too may find in our daily lives the opportunities we have to help the poor, not only through words or material goods, but by identifying ourselves with them, as Jesus Himself did.

Ruya was being eaten away by worry, because her little 5 year-old boy was already diabetic, despite his young age. With a saddened heart, she applied herself to preventing him from eating sweets and cookies, but the urge was too strong for him, and he ate them in secret with his friends. What could she do?

During those times, the 1950's, Mahatma Gandhi was willingly receiving people in search of advice, because he was very close to his people. Although not a Christian, and never baptized, this remarkable man lived the Gospel in his own way, and it's beautiful to see how greatly the Holy Spirit can be at work in the heart of a man of good will. Ruya placed all her hope in him for her little Manoj. "I beg of you," she said to him, "speak with my child! If you tell him not to eat sugar again, he will listen to you. With me, it doesn't work!"

Ruya brought the little one to Gandhi, and after several minutes of intimate conversation, the child came back very happy and proud, but there had been no discussion of sugar. Ruya went home very disappointed: little Manoj continued to eat sweets.

However, several weeks later, not having found any other effective way to help her son, she returned to Gandhi's house and made the same demand. The head-to-head meeting with the child lasted again just several minutes. This time, the little one came back convinced not to eat sugar again. Ruya was radiant with joy! She enthusiastically thanked Gandhi and asked him this question: “How was it that, during your first meeting with my son, you didn’t talk to him about sugar?” An unexpected answer burst forth suddenly like a ray of light:

“How could I ask this child to deprive himself of sugar when I myself ate sugar every day? After my first conversation with him, I decided to deprive myself of sugar, and so, I was able to ask him to do the same.”

The venerable Marthe Robin knew Gandhi without ever having seen him, because she used to see certain persons in a mystical way, even those in far-away countries, and she prayed for them. Sometimes she even bi-located. One day, in the 1960’s, my friend Brigitte C., went to her farm. During their short conversation, Brigitte spoke about Gandhi. Having spent some time in India, she had been able to appreciate his qualities, particularly his remarkable disposition of mind and heart. To her great surprise, Marthe cried out suddenly: “But Gandhi, he’s like another Jesus!”

Beggar in India © Photo Paulo Tacchella

10
PETER AND JUDAS, CONTRITION OR REMORSE?

I have a question: How is it that some people are crushed down by the realization that they have sinned while others have the opposite reaction and use their sin as a diving board in order to plunge more profoundly into God's mercy? The best example to understand this dichotomy can be found in the Gospel.

The Apostles Peter and Judas both greatly sinned against the Lord during the time of His passion. One denied Him, the other betrayed Him. These were two cases of serious sin. However, the two men had completely different fates following their errors. How did it happen that Peter became the first Pope, Saint Peter, and Judas ended his days at the end of a rope, in despair? Would Christ have dispensed his mercy on one and not on the other? Didn't he have as much mercy towards one as he had for the other? Didn't he carry for both the same intense desire to save them and to take them with Him for eternity?

Some people are astonished that Judas, even after being seized by remorse, was not able, like Peter, to benefit from the forgiveness of Jesus and from His mercy, which should have saved him. What happened?

From that very first day when Jesus called him in Galilee, Peter followed his master with enthusiasm. He loved the way he spoke, the way he acted; he rejoiced at each miracle accomplished by Jesus and was jubilant when he saw Jesus silence His detractors with the power of the Holy Spirit. A very sincere love for Jesus was gradually born in his heart. Peter put his whole personality, his whole spirit, his whole heart into this relationship of love. Because of the strength of his love, he often reacted intensely and abruptly, at the risk of saying inopportune things. He was a sort of all-purpose blunderer in the group of apostles, which actually made him appealing to us, in a way.

With patience, Jesus corrected him, taught him, and showed him the path. Peter loved Jesus with all his heart, with all his soul, and with all his mind, despite his own failings. His good will simply wouldn't allow him to relent. When, before the Passion, Jesus foresaw the falling away of the apostles, Peter declared upfront and with force that even if the others abandoned Him, he, in any case, was ready to follow Him even to death. In short, Peter tried to convince Jesus that he was a strong man on whom Jesus could rely, even in times of trial. Peter couldn't be more sincere. However he lacked one very important dimension: he didn't yet recognize his own poverty. He had not probed the depth of the weakness he bore inside. He was blind about himself. After the agony of Jesus at Gethsemane and his arrest, he was the only one, along with John, to follow his Lord, even though from a distance, while the others hastened to flee.

Once inside the court of the High Priest, in the cold of that early April in Jerusalem, Peter began to weaken; his courage took a blow. Exhausted after a traumatizing night and the sight of a Jesus who had perspired blood and allowed Himself to be placed in chains without resisting, Peter no longer understood anything. Nothing seemed right anymore and fear flowed into him. His beautiful promises of valor collapsed. Without thinking, he allowed himself to be overcome with fear and realized that he had been a renegade in denying Jesus on three separate occasions. An hour passed between the second and third denials, an hour during which Peter felt deeply devastated. The cock's crow surprised him right in the middle of his complete fall from grace. It was at that exact moment that the miracle was accomplished: Jesus turned around and looked at Peter.

No trace of reproach, of anger, of indignation or of condemnation. Jesus remained this man overflowing with love and humility. Peter burst into tears. He had just denied the love of his life. But he had barely become aware of his utter weakness when the expressive gaze of Jesus penetrated him from top to bottom with infinite gentleness. He perceived then that this was Mercy. He was overwhelmed. What a contrast between the harsh sword of his three denial and the expression of Someone who is only love and mercy!

Peter came undone faced with this love. He was in pain because of his own sins, terrible pain! He wished he had never committed them. He had wounded the One who had become the very purpose of his life. That evening, Peter took the measure of his own misery. But because he loved Jesus sincerely and with all his heart, and because he had welcomed Jesus' gaze of love into his wounded spirit, he did not sink into despair.

What saved Peter at that moment? The exchange of gaze he had with Jesus. Peter understood that he was still fully loved by Jesus, not because he was strong and resolute, no! He was loved in his totality; he was loved in his weakness. Some mystics, like the Venerable Marthe Robin, tell us that he went to the Blessed Mother and that he melted into tears at her feet, confessing his triple denial and crying bitterly at having done such wrong to his Lord. On that day, the pain in the hollow of his heart was that magnificent gift from the Holy Spirit called contrition. It is that which causes someone to hurt after doing harm to a loved one. That night, the strong man called Peter fell from on high. He collided with his smallness. He let himself be covered in mercy. He became *Saint* Peter.

The Apostle Judas had also been called to be a saint, Saint Judas. How did he miss the opportunity for sainthood which was offered to him, as it is to each of us? We know from the Gospel that Peter loved Jesus with all his heart, despite his weaknesses, but it wasn't the same for Judas. Day after day, as he kept the purse for the apostles, he stole from this sum of cash and did not appreciate the love Jesus had for the poor. He had gotten used to violating an important commandment, "Do not steal", and he knew it. So he fashioned for himself a kind of double life. For all appearances, he was with Jesus, physically present at all His missions; but inside, he let himself be eaten away by the love of money and the pursuit of a plan that this money, he thought, would allow him to realize. We don't know what this plan was, but it seems that Judas was passionate about it to the point that, at his moment of great trial, he became easy prey for the enemy.

Basically, that long infidelity, of which he never repented, furnished Satan with an open door to get to his heart and inject it daily with poison. In the course of his three years of life in common with the apostles, how many times had he heard the words of Jesus about money, wealth, mammon and its disastrous dangers to the soul? How many times had Judas had the opportunity to fall down before Jesus and say to Him: "I am a scoundrel; for a long time I have been stealing the money of the community, I beg You to pardon me!" Jesus was waiting only for that. What a splendid feast would have been celebrated in Heaven for this sinner who returned!

But, no, Judas was obstinate. Jesus, who wanted at all costs to save him, gave him many signs of affection, but Judas didn't take them; his diabolical scheme had made him deaf and blind to the appeals of the Master. We know that during the Passover meal, the last supper with Jesus, Judas was placed very close to Him. Jewish tradition teaches us that the master of the Seder offers the first taste to the guest he wants to honor the most in the eyes of the others. That evening Jesus wanted to demonstrate in front of the eleven that he had designated Judas for the honor; but Judas didn't look at Jesus. As He had done for the others, Jesus had washed Judas' feet; He had even stated openly: one of you will betray me; letting it be known to Judas that He knew his secret plans. That ought to have made it easier to confess them. Judas should have been able to take Jesus aside and tell Him: "I was paid for having you arrested. Forgive me and flee immediately to Bethphage!" And Jesus would have forgiven him right then and there.

In the Garden of Olives, in order to point Jesus out to the

men he had gathered together, Judas gave Him a kiss. It was a kiss on the mouth. Now, at that time, such a kiss was, for the Jews, the sign of a contract of trust, sealed between friends. And Jesus said to him: "Friend, do what you must do!" (Matt. 26:50) Friend? That was the last lifeline Jesus threw to him while he lived. 'He called me *friend*?' Judas should have crumbled in front of such a proof of love. But, no, he was ruled mechanically by his passion, never understanding that in reality it was he, the wretched one, who had gotten himself arrested, tied up, and carried off to his death by another master to whom he had been submitting for three years.

Scripture speaks to us about Judas' remorse. Satan doesn't give any gifts. When he succeeded in tying up his victim, it certainly wasn't to give him peace and happiness but to manipulate him as he pleased. So Judas was then tortured interiorly by remorse. However, remorse has nothing to do with contrition. Judas, like Peter, had realized the depth of his spiritual poverty during that crucial hour of his trial, but he looked at his wretchedness with a lucidity that was remorseless and desperate instead of looking at Jesus, thereby giving Satan full satisfaction.

Remorse is born through contemplation of our misery. Watch out, though. We can have a clear look at ourselves and our misery without it being an inspired look. It is sometimes Satan who is torturing us. In that case, it is not about the pain of repenting, or the pang of love towards the other wounded person. On the contrary: it's about the pain of frustrated pride. Looking at one's self makes us sink downward, while looking at Jesus elevates and saves us. Looking at his own misery could do nothing but plunge Judas into despair. When he saw that Jesus had been condemned to death, he should have run to the Blessed Virgin, as Peter did and collapsed in tears at her feet. There, his tears of repentance would have kindled a beautiful star in the sky.[14]

[14] Listen to CD "No, Judas, it's not to late" available at www.sremmanuel.org

Today, many physical and psychological maladies or feelings of disquiet are due to remorse, which gnaws through the soul, inside us, often without our knowledge. But God, in His infinite mercy towards the sinner, invites us to true repentance and contrition.

How can we go from remorse to repentance, from despair to hope? It's a simple matter of gazing at Jesus. I stop focusing on myself, come out of my prison, and turn my eyes towards the Lord, who is extending His hand to me. Isn't it written in the scriptures: "Those who look to Him are radiant; their faces are never covered with shame," (Psalm 34). The enemy will always try to point out the evil that is in us and to imprison us in it, because he himself lives in a prison with no escape. He wants to capture us and tie us up next to him. But fortunately, Jesus came not for the righteous ones but for sinners, not for the healthy ones but for the sick. In other words, we're all on His list! His desire to draw the sinner towards Him is immeasurable. All we have to do to obtain mercy is simply to throw ourselves into his arms in complete sincerity. Therese, the Little Flower, explains that magnificently.

One day she had committed a sin, and she wrote: "right afterwards, I was invaded by great joy." How could such a saint be in a state of joy after having sinned? It seems she remembered right away the words of Jesus in the Gospel, "There is more joy in Heaven among the angels of God over one sinner who repents than over the 99 just who have no need of repentance." So, she said to herself, 'I'm that sinner,' and she threw herself into the arms of Jesus, totally confident of His mercy. She confessed her sin and added that in doing so, she triggered a great joy in Heaven and that she herself participated in the joy of the elect. That was the genius of Therese: she had not given in to negative thoughts about her culpability or to the temptation of discouragement after having sinned. She jumped into the arms of her Savior immediately, without allowing herself a single look at the ugliness of her misery.

A saint is not he who never sins; there was only one Immaculate Conception. No, a saint is one who has such confidence in the mercy of God that he doesn't hesitate to fall into His arms the minute he becomes aware of his error. The more he is a saint, the less he waits! But the temptation is always to look into oneself, to get discouraged after falling again, to feel guilty after having committed one more time the same mistake. One could spend hours, months even years dwelling on his misery without taking hold of the lifeline that Jesus extends to us, because He extends it to us always and at every moment. It is so easy to pass right by the treasure that is there for us! Our degree of holiness could be measured by the speed with which we grab hold of the mercy after a fall. Let's not give any time at all to the enemy to act and to ruin our souls by his deadly suggestions.

Every misery is an abyss that sucks us down and inside of ourselves, if we do not throw our misery in the heart of God.

It is worth noting that in the churches, the confessionals are more and more empty because there are no repentant sinners, and as a result, the more full we find the offices of psychiatrists. Instead, in dioceses where mercy is lived and preached we notice a shower of blessings and conversions. The toll of rapes and other crimes, suicides, divorces and abortions, and drug consumption diminish roughly at the same pace as the explosion of graces.

If the wage of sin is death, as St. Paul teaches, the gift of God is Eternal Life.

God and the Desperate Soul

Sister Faustina, the first saint canonized in the 3rd millennium, conveys this amazing dialogue between God and a soul that is sunk into despair.

Conversation of the Merciful God with a Despairing Soul, (Paragraph 1486, Diary of St Faustina).

> *Jesus:* O soul steeped in darkness, do not despair. All is not yet lost. Come and confide in your

God, who is love and mercy.

– But the soul, deaf even to this appeal, wraps itself in darkness.

Jesus calls out again: My child, listen to the voice of your merciful Father.

– In the *soul* arises this reply: "For me there is no mercy," and it falls into greater darkness, a despair which is a foretaste of hell and makes it unable to draw near God.

Jesus calls to the soul a third time, but the soul remains deaf and blind, hardened and despairing. Then the mercy of God begins to exert itself, and, without any co-operation from the soul, God grants it final grace. If this too is spurned, God will leave the soul in this self-chosen disposition for eternity. This grace emerges from the merciful Heart of Jesus and gives the soul a special light by means of which the soul begins to understand God's effort; but conversion depends on its own will. The soul knows that this, for her, is final grace and, should it show even a flicker of good will, the mercy of God will accomplish the rest.

My omnipotent mercy is active here. Happy the soul that takes advantage of this grace.

Jesus: What joy fills My Heart when you return to Me. Because you are weak, I take you in My arms and carry you to the home of My Father.

Soul (as if awaking, asks fearfully): Is it possible that there yet is mercy for me?

Jesus: There is, My child. You have a special claim on My mercy. Let it act in your poor soul; let the rays of grace enter your soul; they bring with them light, warmth, and life.

Soul: But fear fills me at the thought of my

sins, and this terrible fear moves me to doubt Your goodness.

Jesus: My child, all your sins have not wounded My Heart as painfully as your present lack of trust does – that after so many efforts of My love and mercy, you should still doubt My goodness.

Soul: O Lord, save me Yourself, for I perish. Be my Savior. O Lord, I am unable to say anything more; my pitiful heart is torn asunder; but You, O Lord…

Jesus does not let the soul finish but, raising it from the ground, from the depths of its misery, he leads it into the recesses of His Heart where all its sins disappear instantly, consumed by the flames of love.

Jesus: Here, soul, are all the treasures of My Heart. Take everything you need from it.

Soul: O Lord, I am inundated with Your grace. I sense that a new life has entered into me and, above all, I feel Your love in my heart. That is enough for me. O Lord, I will glorify the omnipotence of Your mercy for all eternity. Encouraged by Your goodness, I will confide to You all the sorrows of my heart.

Jesus: Tell Me all, My child, hide nothing from Me, because My loving Heart, the Heart of your Best Friend, is listening to you.

Soul: O Lord, now I see all my ingratitude and Your goodness. You were pursuing me with Your grace, while I was frustrating Your benevolence. I see that I deserve the depths of hell for spurning Your graces.

Jesus (interrupting): Do not be absorbed in your misery – you are still too weak to speak of it

– but, rather; gaze on My Heart filled with goodness, and be imbued with My sentiments. Strive for meekness and humility; be merciful to others, as I am to you; and, when you feel your strength failing, if you come to the fountain of mercy to fortify your soul, you will not grow weary on your journey.

Soul: Now I understand Your mercy, which protects me, and like a brilliant star, leads me into the home of my Father, protecting me from the horrors of hell that I have deserved, not once, but a thousand times. O Lord, eternity will hardly suffice for me to give due praise to Your unfathomable mercy and Your compassion for me.

The Prodigal Son. from Rembrandt. © Photo Museum of Vienna

11
A Surprise in the Confessional

At the beginning of May, 2010, an Italian family from Naples arrived in Medjugorje, in a state of profound distress. Spiritually, they had no peace, and physically they carried a heavy cross: not only was their little 5 year old Giulia almost completely deaf from birth, but their 8-year-old son, Antonio, suffered from epilepsy. His seizures were happening more and more often throughout the day, several times per week. His parents couldn't stand to see him suffer any longer.

One evening, along with some other pilgrims, they went to Apparition Hill. Our Lady would be appearing to the visionary Ivan, so they went to pray the rosary under the stars, while waiting for her. There, the family simply put everything into the hands of Mary. They expected powerful aid from Heaven during this pilgrimage.

The next day, the father, Vittorio, shared the grievous situation of his family with the group leader, hoping for a word of comfort from him; but the leader simply said: "Go to confession!" Surprised by this terse response, the man did an examination of conscience. Quite frankly, he had been living a life of sin and had not been to confession for many years! In other words, a long time ago he had fallen from the state of grace and now he has the audacity to come to where Our Mother is appearing and beg a favor from heaven for his children. Eventually, he understood that it was necessary to first make his own peace with God, just as the group leader who had a sense about these things had proposed, then ask for grace for his children. Recognizing in the words of the group leader a personal invitation from God, Vittorio decided that it was high time to go and make a good confession and sincerely renounce all his sins.

To the astonishment of everyone, following his confession, his son Antonio (who knew nothing about that confession) stopped his convulsions right away. Since then, he hasn't had a single one! As for his 5-year-old little sister, she began to talk when she returned from the pilgrimage, speaking intelligible words for the first time.

In his beautiful testimony, the father concluded this way: "I'm changed! My wife and I see life completely differently now. It's a great comfort to have found serenity and to see my wife regain her optimism. Ever since that confession in Medjugorje, I have been able to see the benefits of a life lived in the light of God."

A Remedy to Seize

Yes, Our Lady knows why she asks us to go to confession monthly. "When there is sin," Our Lady of Medjugorje tells us, "there is no peace. With sin, no one can be happy. Monthly confession will be the remedy for the Church of the West," (Message of 1982).

"Many have come to Medjugorje to ask for a physical cure, but at the same time, they are living in sin. No, Dear Children, that is not right. Let them first abandon sin and make a good confession, because the health of the soul is more important than the health of the body. Many more healings will be granted if people abandon sin… I can't help you if you don't follow God's commandments, if you don't go to confession, if you don't enter into the Mass," (Message of 10/25/1993).

"I wish to lead you all to my Son, your Savior. You are not conscious of the fact that without Him, you have no joy, no peace, no future, no Eternal Life," (Message of 7/25/2010).

"I expect you to look with sincerity into your hearts and to see how much you love the Father. Is He the last one to be loved? Think how many times, surrounded by material goods, you have betrayed, denied, or forgotten Him! My Children, don't let yourselves be deceived by earthly goods. Think about the soul, because it is more important than the body; purify it! Call on the Father; he is waiting for you. Return to him!" (Message of 11/2/2009).

12
Pascual Forgives the Priest

Pascual was a little boy, from Columbia, very well-behaved and very handsome. In school, he spent a lot of time with a certain priest who sadly, conceived the idea to abuse him. When the priest took him apart from the rest of the children and spoke to him of his plan, little Pascual had the excellent notion to run, thus escaping the hands of his predator. But the child was so traumatized by the attitude of this priest, which was unimaginable to his child's heart that he rejected, as a whole, the Church, priests, and the good God Himself. That day, he became a pure and hardened atheist.

As he matured, Buddhism attracted him and he immersed himself, body and soul, into this philosophy and its Eastern practices. It fascinated his mind, which was hungry for new ideas.

One day, his best friend proposed to make a trip to Bosnia-Herzegovina in the hope to bring him back to Christ and reconcile him with the Church. He explained with enthusiasm that he had heard of a village where a small group of children had extraordinary spiritual experiences with heaven. Piqued by curiosity and by the attraction of a long trip to another continent, Pascual allowed himself to be persuaded and went with a number of pilgrims to Medjugorje. There, Our Lady was waiting for him, and using her incomparable maternal skills, succeeded in winning over his heart and brought him back to Jesus.

When he returned to his native country, Pascual was a different person: a converted Christian, happy and fulfilled. He changed his life radically, and his wife followed him in this conversion. He began to organize pilgrimages to Medjugorje himself, and thanks to this, the Blessed Virgin transformed many other hearts.

But he never forgot the priest from his childhood. He received the grace to forgive him, and this forgiveness was so profound that he decided to find the priest again with the intention of speaking to him about that fateful event. He quickly located the priest, and he soon found himself in front of an old man who welcomed him warmly, without really recognizing him. After exchanging some formalities, Pascual spoke to him about a little boy, who in all innocence had placed his trust in a priest, but who, one dark day, had been betrayed by this man. This little boy had grown up, and, after rejecting the Church and its priests and even God Himself, he had been put back on the path of faith by the Virgin Mary.

Very quickly, the old priest read between the lines, recognized the incident in question, and began to tremble. Pascual hurried to tell him, "Be at peace! It is this little boy who comes to you today to tell you that he forgives you with all his heart. Not only does he forgive you, but Jesus has healed his wound so well that it no longer bears any trace of bitterness or revulsion."

The priest broke down sobbing with tears, then murmured in a voice breaking with emotion: "I have been haunted for 36 years by what I did; 36 years during which I searched for peace without finding it, 36 years during which I begged God to forgive the unforgiveable. And here today, He has granted that to me! I can die in peace, because you came to visit me." Pascual held the priest in his arms for a long time, until the shaking from his sobbing began to ebb away. The mercy of God had brought back victory!

The Flat Note

Imagine a man who loves music and most of all, his joy is complete when he can attend concerts in order to listen to the best composers. One day he went to a concert given by a very famous orchestra, he expected to hear a symphony fit for kings, with the best quality of musicians. To his great surprise he heard one of the violinist making a very loud flat note, damaging the entire concert! He left the theater with his fingers in his ears. He was very angry and swore that from that day forward music would not be part of his life, it would be his last symphony. 'How horrible. How dare a person play a flat note in a concert, and how dare the conductor allow that,' he thought to himself. 'I'm finished with music!'

When he returned home he threw his private collection of symphony music, including classics played by infamous artists, into the garbage.

Or… let's imagine a man who is treated by a doctor. This doctor, through a serious medical error, harmed the guy instead of cured him. Furious, the man cursed all the doctors of the world and decided to never consult another doctor for the rest of his life!

It is in this way that some people react when they have to suffer from a priest who commits a grave error either in his words or in his action. From that day on all the other priests receive the same hit and are ostracized for similar reasons. Often the entire church, and God Himself is thrown into the same package! How many men and women have fallen into this trap and have stopped practicing their Christian faith after such a bad experience that has happened to themselves or someone they know or heard of in the Church? They do not realize that they are severely punishing themselves. They deprive themselves from an indispensable source of graces for their peace of heart and way of holiness. They also punish God for a crime He has not committed, and from which he is the first to suffer!

That's when Satan rubs his hands together in excitement. He does not hesitate and often succeeds at injecting his own bitterness in a soul, separating this child of God from his Divine Father. Why should we forget the saints who swarm around the Church in their sublime friendship, bringing joy, consolation and precious help on the way to God?

A Catholic Priest Writes to the New York Times (March 2015)

Among the many priests who live with simplicity and holiness their priestly ministry to the people of God, there is one who had the courage to answer the attacks of the media against the Catholic clergy. What he writes will probably never be published by the media on a grand scale because in order to earn a lot of money, you have to tickle the public with scandals. You have to shock the public by a subtle mixture of money, sex and religion. Seeking the truth? You must be kidding! It doesn't pay enough.

A big thank you to Fr. Martin Lasarte who exposes, with simplicity, the true facts. Here is the letter that a Catholic priest sent to the New York Times published in the March 2015 issue.

Dear Brother Journalist:

I am a simple Catholic priest. I am happy and proud of my vocation. I've been living in Angola for 20 years as a missionary. I have read in a number of publications, especially in your newspaper, the amplified stories of pedophilic priests, always portrayed in a morbid way with detailed research into past errors in the lives of these priests.

There was one, in a city in the United States in the 70's, another in Australia in the 80's, and so forth, some more recent … Certainly, all these incidents were condemnable!

There were some journalistic pieces that were thoughtful and balanced, others hyped up, full of prejudices and even of hate. I feel enormous sadness about the immense harm that some men who should have been signs of the love of God have been swords in the lives of innocent children. There are no words to justify such acts. There is no doubt that the Church must be on the side of the weak and most vulnerable. For that reason, all the measures that can be taken to prevent these acts and protect the dignity of the children should be an absolute priority.

But isn't it strange that there is so little news and such lack of interest in the thousands of priests who are sacrificing their lives daily and dedicating themselves, body and soul, to millions of children, to adolescents and to the most disadvantaged of these in all four corners of the world?

I'm sure the following would be of no interest to your newspaper:

1) That I've had to transport many starving children along roads that were mined during the war of 2002 from Cangumbe to Lwenain Angola, because the government has been unable to do it, and NGO's have not been authorized;

2) That I've had to bury dozens of children displaced by the war;

3) That we have saved the lives of thousands of people in Mexico by running the only health center within a zone of 90,000 square kilometers and by distributing foodstuffs and grain;

4) That we have been able to procure education and schools for more than 110,000 children in the last 10 years;

5) It passes without interest that, along with other priests, we have had to rescue nearly 15,000 people in guerilla camps, after they were forced to give up their weapons because the United Nations and government food never arrived;

6) It's not an interesting news item that a 75-year-old priest, Father Roberto, traveled all across the city of Luanda, caring for street children, guiding them to safe houses, so that they could be detoxed from the gasoline they inhaled while earning their living as flame throwers;

7) Teaching literacy skills to hundreds of prisoners is no longer news;

8) That other priests, like Father Stephan, organize safe houses, so that the young, maltreated, beaten, and even raped can find refuge there;

9) Nor is it of any interest that Father Maiato, 80 years old, visits homes for the poor, one by one, comforting the sick and vulnerable;

10) Today, it's not news that out of 40,000 priests and religious, more than 6,000 have left their countries and their families to serve their brothers in leper colonies, in hospitals, in refugee camps, in orphanages for children accused of sorcery or whose parents who died from AIDS, in schools for the most poor, in job centers, in welcome centers for those testing positive for HIV, etc;

11) Or, especially, that most priests are spending their lives in parishes and missions, motivating people to live better and, more importantly, to love better;

12) It's not news that my friend, Father Marcus Aurelius, in order to save children during the war in Angola, transported them from Kalulo to Dondo, and that, when returning to his mission house, he was machine-gunned on the road; that Brother Francis, with 5 female catechists died in an accident on their way to help in the most remote rural areas of the country;

13) That dozens of missionaries in Angola have died from simple malaria because of poor sanitation;

14) That others have been blown to bits by mines while visiting their faithful; currently, in the cemetery of Kalulo, lie the tombs of the first priests who arrived in the area … none of them older than 40;

15) It's not news to follow a "normal" priest doing his daily work, experiencing his troubles and his joys, spending his whole life with no attention in the community he serves.

The truth is, that we are not trying to make news, only,

simply, to bring the "Good News"; this News which, with no fanfare, began on Easter morning. A tree that falls makes more noise than a thousand which stand and grow. A great deal more attention is paid to a priest who commits an error than to the thousands who give their lives for the myriads of poor and needy. I don't pretend to apologize for the Church and its priests.

A priest is neither a hero nor a neurotic. He's simply a normal man, who, with his human nature, seeks to follow Jesus and to serve Him by serving others. There is in us misery, poverty, and fragility, as there is in every human being; but there is also beauty and grandeur, as there is in every creature.

When you insist on advancing such a painful theme in an obsessive and persecuting manner, while ignoring the bigger picture of their work, you create truly offensive caricatures of Catholic priests, and these wound me.

I ask only, dear Journalist, that you look for the true, the good, and the beautiful. It would greatly elevate your profession.

In Christ,
Fr. Martin Lasarte, SDB

"My past, Lord, I entrust to Your Mercy; my present to Your Love; my future to Your Providence."

13
Lucia and the Most Impossible Forgivenenss

My very dear friend Lucia always impresses me with her great faith and her determination to follow Christ. She's a woman of prayer, often very inspired, and endowed beyond that with a strong personality. Several years ago, she went through a terrible trial as a mother and grandmother. She was an all too common example of a woman crushed by an unjust family event, which generated within her an ocean of bitterness.

Lucia has 2 sons. The older one, Ricardo, married Simona. A marvelous little boy, Francis, was born from this union. His grandmother, Lucia, often took him to her house, because his parents were caught up in their work and were unable to devote much time to him. Thanks to Lucia, Francis enjoyed that loving feminine presence, that caring sensitivity, those precious hours of tenderness, which every little human being needs so much at an early age. But, very quickly, the couple entered a marital crisis; in short, there was 'water in the gas' (as we say in French), and nothing was working any more.

I will let Lucia tell what happened: "I used to think the love which united Ricardo and Simona, sealed in the Sacrament of Marriage, would endure forever, but, unfortunately, it broke into pieces. At first, the situation was a little more tenable, and I served as a lightning rod to protect my little Francis. He witnessed terrible scenes of the marital strife between his parents. These tore his little heart apart, but he was unable to talk about it or confide in anyone about his suffering. He also had to endure the more and more frequent presence of the respective lovers of his parents, even to the point of cohabitation with them. Shuttled from one house to another, I saw him losing his bearings."

Poor little Francis couldn't find himself anymore, and the wound of the parental division grew worse every day. We know the consequences of drama like this: nightmares, instability at school, depression, agitation, suppressed anger. And, above all, those waves of profound sadness which can make a child lose his taste for life.

She continued, "Ricardo asked for an annulment of their marriage and got it. Simona, in turn, asked for a divorce, but with demands that completely took my breath away: she wanted my son's parental rights removed, his submission to drug and psychological examinations, and enormous child support payments for her and their child. And to top it off … she demanded that the little one be put in the care of a psychologist and a social worker!

I screamed from the pain, from the anger, from the indignation, from the bitterness, shedding tears mixed with the worst name calling that you can imagine. Since I live in the country, I opened wide my windows and yelled with all my being, so the entire universe would be inundated with my anger. I had succumbed to the power of the devil. 'It's not what goes into the mouth that contaminates a man in God's sight." Jesus says. "It's what comes out of the mouth that contaminates the man,' (Matt. 15: 11).

"I no longer slept at night; I had lost my peace. I was going to confession, but that became more of a way to let off steam than to confess my sins, and peace did not return. I regularly placed the entire situation, my son and my grandson, at the feet of Christ during Holy Mass, but instead of letting go of my suffering, I wanted to hang onto it as a tangible demonstration of my submission to a wrong done to me.

"During my daily Mass, I had the habit of exchanging the kiss of peace with those nearby. Then, I would close my eyes and send that peace to my dear ones as well. But I sensed clearly that "His peace" couldn't find its way to me because my heart preferred to accommodate new "occupants": Mrs. Hate, Miss Rebellion, Mrs. Anger, Mr. Desire for Vengeance, I could go on and on. One day, I realized that I had to make peace also with Simona, and only then would I be liberated from my interior demons, which were gnawing away at me to the point of ruining my life. But then, forgiving her was for me totally impossible."

Impossible?

"The words of the angel to Mary at Nazareth came to my mind: 'Nothing is impossible for God.' Surely, there was a way to get there. So, I asked Jesus for His help. I wanted Him to teach me to act as He would have acted with us at the moment of His crucifixion, when He interceded for us. 'Father,' He said. 'Forgive them, for they do know not what they do.' I said that to Him, knowing that on my own, I wasn't capable, but I had good intentions! I remembered then this word from Our Lady in Medjugorje:

'Dear children! Again I call you to prayer with the heart. If you pray with the heart, dear children, the ice of your brothers will melt and every barrier shall disappear. Conversion will be easy for all who desire to accept it. That is the gift which by prayer you must obtain for your neighbor. Thank you for having responded to my call,' (Our Lady's message January 23, 1986).

"It was then that I began a rather bloody battle between the call for mercy from Jesus and my own rebellious nature. Putting aside the violence of my negative emotions and focusing myself instead on the person of Jesus, I made myself say these words silently: 'Simona, I beg your forgiveness for all the harm I've done to you (truthfully, during the whole time, I had not sent her only blessings!). I forgive you as well for all the harm you have done to me, and I give you the peace of Jesus!'

"I succeeded in painfully repeating that sentence at each Mass at the moment of the sign of peace, but curiously, with less and less difficulty: in His great Mercy, the Lord was in the process of healing me! It took Him three months to achieve full victory in my heart.

"Finally, one day during Mass, I felt for the first time that the words of forgiveness addressed to Simona were sincere on my part. My whole being agreed, as though by a miracle. I was astounded! My joy was so great that, when I got back home, I grabbed my phone and invited Simona to have coffee with me. On that day, I think there was a great feast in Heaven! The Angels and Saints must have watched us sip our espressos like two old friends who had found each other again after a long and painful absence. Only God could do such things. May His name be blessed!"

Able to Love as God Loves?

Lucia's testimony sheds great light on the spiritual combat that we must wage on the real forces around us. We are often unaware of the stakes of the battle.

Here, I must give some explanation about the particular faculties of the human being, according to traditional anthropology drawn from St. Thomas Aquinas, St. John of the Cross, and many others. We are made of spirit and flesh, the flesh being composed of the body and the psyche. Both are "created in the image of God and after His likeness," (Gen 1:26). The spirit is inviolable, that is, neither original sin nor the wounds of life can reach it. It is composed of three superior faculties: the interior will (our free ability to adhere to God), the interior intelligence (our ability to penetrate the mysteries of God) and the interior memory (the trace of God in us). While sin may keep the image of God intact in our minds and hearts, we will lose our likeness to God. The body and the psyche, sometimes called together the soul, are marred by wounds and sin. They are made up of affectivity, imagination, and memory (that which permits us to remember the past).

The human being is capable of loving as God loves. It's even a commandment: "Love one another as I have loved you," (John 13: 34). The effect of original sin means that we are sometimes attracted by evil and unaware of our grandeur. The sickness of our human nature, wounded by original sin and by the other sins we've added to it during the course of our lives may make us forget that we have a spirit to which God unites Himself in our innermost being. "The Spirit Himself testifies with our spirit that we are children of God," (Romans 8:16). If only the faithful and the whole world knew that!

The Real Challenge of the Gospel

In the case of Lucia, her entire human nature rebelled against the injustice she felt as a victim, and on behalf of her family as victims. Her affectivity, her maternal instinct told her to rebel and to strike hard. In other words, to return evil with evil. Fortunately, she became aware of this slavery and decided to get out of it. As Saint Peter teaches, "Do not return evil for evil or reviling for reviling; but on the contrary bless, for to this you have been called, that you may obtain a blessing," (1Peter 3: 9).

That is when her beautiful soul, accustomed to being with the Lord in prayer and sacrament, took the high road and achieved an act of free will. With God and His help, she thought, 'I could get to a place of forgiveness.' She opted for the supremacy of grace over her wounded nature; she decided to open herself to a new dimension that her soul was capable of understanding. That permitted the grace of God to fill her up little by little. She made the best choice. Brought down by the hatred of her enemy, she called upon the most noble part of her being, her spirit.

Thus it is, that at the end of this story, we see that grace triumphed over the weaknesses of Lucia's nature. In other words, it triumphed over sin. If, in such circumstances as these, Lucia was able to subdue the tide of her negative sentiments enough to throw them into the abyss of mercy, we are all capable of it.

This is the challenge of the Gospel, which invites us to let die the works of the old man in order to let emerge the New Man, re-created each day by the grace of God.

Candidates for Marriage?

In our world today, what a tragedy it is to see so many marriages fall into shreds, one after the other! As if our society were organized to facilitate the failure of marriage. The case of Ricardo and Simona, and the succession of their crises, betrayals and break-ups, the snowball effect of their hatred, became normal! But why accumulate so many wounds when all of that chaos and pain could have been avoided?

My objective here is not to denounce the civil laws which go against God's plan for men and women, nor do I want to keep listing the innumerable victims of these impious laws. Rather, I propose that we examine together some ways to help a marriage succeed and how to avoid the traps which can threaten it.

Why not look at the example of my own parents. Their love story could have ended in disaster! But their secret was that they began well, anchored on solid principles. That enabled them to get through the storms. What family isn't shaken one day or another by those storms which surge over us with such violence and threaten to shatter the communion of hearts?!

Here's the story of my parents, a story which might offer a key to the security of other couples.

From early childhood, my father felt a great deal of love towards Our Lady; he was barely 4 years old and in nursery school, when a nun revealed to him the depths of the loving heart of Mary. In his way, he fell in love with the Mother of Heaven and, in his childlike simplicity, he was already beginning to say to her: "Mama, take my heart. I give it to you!" So, when he reached the age of marriage, he asked her: "Most Blessed Mother, help me meet the woman God has prepared for me. When I meet her, please make me feel inside that this is the one." His heart was therefore at peace, and my father didn't become preoccupied searching for a wife. He also said a prayer which I have proposed that all young people adopt: he invoked the guardian angel of his future spouse and asked him to protect her, so that she would remain pure, good, amiable, of good health … and pretty!

As a matter of fact, when my parents did meet after World War II, they recognized each other almost immediately. The moment my father saw my mother, he was overcome with a deep conviction and said to himself: "She's the one!" But little did he know what my mother must have revealed to him later … She had also consecrated her future spouse to the Blessed Mother and had asked her: "Please protect him and take good care of him." Moreover, every day, she sent her guardian Angel to this stranger so that he would be protected from danger, because the war was raging at that time.

As it happened, my father endured three years in Nazi concentration camps. He came close to death several times, and each time, an inexplicable event occurred. By way of example, one day he "broke ranks" during a roll call, when the guards counted the prisoners. My father instinctively went to pick up another detainee's cap, which had blown off. An unpardonable offense punishable by death! A terrible sanction was imposed on him: he was locked up for several days afterward in a special cell in which he could neither stand up nor sit down. During the entire day, he went to work without having anything to eat or drink. On the third day, my father sensed that death was coming, and he commended his soul to Our Lady. At that precise moment, the door of his cell opened and an SS guard shouted that he needed my father to replace the camp doctor, because he was ill. For doing this, they gave him food and drink. That is how my father was spared "by a whisker".

I have to admit that my parents had very different personalities! Life was not always rosy between the two of them, far from it! I remain firmly convinced that by choosing to entrust their family to the heart of God and by faithfully practicing daily prayer together, they saved their loved ones from the destructive plans of Satan.[15]

Without going on too much about the story of my family, I want to affirm and reaffirm that, when God is placed at the centre of our lives, when He is loved and venerated, He can accomplish within us His divine and positive plan, that plan of unity and happiness which was asked of Him, using even our greatest difficulties to help us grow. The winds may blow, the waves may crash against the fragile boats of our households, but marriage is anchored on solid foundations, and it remains in good shape. Over the years, human love, although very much based on the tangible, transforms itself little by little until it blossoms into a divine love, a selfless love. God is then the Master on board, and a shipwreck is avoided.

I like to quote these words from one of our friends, who declared, after some years of marriage: "If love makes you blind, marriage brings back your sight!" Over the course of time, the bases of our choices are tested, and it is then that we can congratulate ourselves for having put God first. On the other hand, if we have failed to do that, we begin to cry out to Him in distress, because it is never too late to ask for His mercy!

---

[15] "Today, as never before," said Mary in Medjugorje, "Satan wants to destroy your families. Therefore I invite you to pray as a family and for the family. Family prayer is the remedy to heal the world of today."

14
My Mother's Wink in China

Odile Maillard, mother of the author © Photo Dominique Lefevre

In November 2015, I visited several Chinese villages, because I had good contacts there who wanted me to meet some friends. When leaving Bosnia, I had asked God not to take my little 94-year-old mom, Odile, home to Him during my absence. But, on November 23, three days before my return to Europe, my brother called: "Mom is not doing well at all; she's having lots of respiratory distress. Her passing is imminent." So, I prayed to Father Slavko Barbaric, a Croatian Franciscan saint I had known well, to intercede on my mom's behalf and have her taken to heaven as soon as possible. My mom loved this priest very much, so I knew that he would take care of her. The next day, November 24th, the anniversary of Fr Slavko's birth into Heaven, Mom went off to the Father in peace. She simply stopped breathing in her sleep.

Getting such news when you're on the other side of the world really shakes a person!

The following day, November 25th, I was scheduled to meet two groups of friends in two different cities. In the morning, all went well for the first group, but, because of snow and ice, the highway to the second city was closed. In the region of China where I was, not far from Beijing the capital, it was horribly cold, less than 30°F, without taking the wind chill into account. We were, without a doubt, trapped. Now, this last meeting was very important to me. I just couldn't swallow the news that we might not make it, and I said to myself: "to come this far and get stuck … no, there must be a way!" I didn't want to surrender, even though my little team had already given up on the trip, in the face of the incontrovertible evidence: the roads were blocked by snow! Of course I was thinking a lot about my mother and her going to the Father, and I was praying for her soul.

Then, a luminous thought came to mind. Silently, I spoke to my mother from the heart and said to her: "Mom, if you're already in Heaven, give me a sign! Open up the road! I know I'm asking the impossible, but in Heaven, nothing is impossible for God. Would He, who knows how to calm the most violent storm, be suddenly paralyzed by snow? Would tons of ice be able to render the right hand of God ineffective?"

During the noon meal my Chinese friend, who had invited us, suddenly spoke up: "Come to think of it, I know someone who works for the highway department. I'm going to call him!" Outside, it was snowing heavily, and everyone could see the situation deteriorating more and more, to the point that even my access to the airport the next day was being threatened. On the telephone, the information was confirmed, and the employee of the highway department told us: "Come over here and see for yourselves, there is nothing we can do." We decided to take him up on his offer and go to the entrance ramp of the highway. As a matter of fact, long lines of trucks were stuck in front of the barrier to the highway, their drivers were ready to spend the night in the cold and with no certainty about the next day.

Secretly I continued to talk to my mom: "You can do it! C'mon, open the highway!" Hearing the impossibility confirmed, our car started back to the home of our hosts. But then, out of the blue, our driver declared: "I know a way! We'll try it!" Since everything was spoken in Chinese, I didn't catch it all, but I understood that this man had more than one trick up his sleeve, and that he wanted to make one last try. We soon found ourselves in the middle of nowhere, and in less than ten minutes, in a deserted place, we found a tiny access road, which – oh, miraculously – was open! The driver took this road without any fear or speaking about it, and before long we were making our way down the highway, almost alone, slowly but surely, speechless in the face of this incredible miracle! Then mom even managed to give us another little sign: At that exact moment, when thick clouds were covering the sky, the sun broke out for several minutes between two dark gray masses. I took it as a 'wink' from Mom, who seemed to say to me: "You see? We succeeded!"

Glory be to God, Who allows Himself to be touched through His Divine Providence! It would be futile to try to describe to you the joy flowing from my heart. The immense joy of knowing that my mom was really living with God and capable of answering my somewhat audacious prayer. The joy, also, of being able to meet with this group of friends who were resolutely waiting for me that night. We were definitely not disappointed by that marvelous time together!

My mother was a woman of great prayer. She was a consecrated widow, and for a long time, she had St. Joseph wrapped around her little finger. And dare I say … He and his wife Mary certainly seemed influential in the business of the highway with her, in their own inimitable way!

Why not make a symbolic interpretation of the event? I now have reason to rejoice even more: if one day, I find in my neighbor a block of ice instead of a heart, I will not be discouraged. I know that prayer is capable of melting that ice and opening up an unexpected way into the treasures of tenderness that have, up until now, been hidden inside him.

Let Them Live or Hasten Their Death?

What is this story doing in a book about mercy? My mother was 94 years old when she left us. The last years of her life were difficult because she gradually developed dementia, losing all short-term memory as well as control over her body. She had always been someone who prayed, consecrating her life to God when she became a widow at the age of 50. And yet, she had faults, as we all do. With her strong sense of duty, she would sometimes be a bit legalistic, which would result in judging people, nothing too unkind, but sometimes absolute. It made us laugh as children because she perfected the art of adding something awful to a nice compliment about someone.

For instance, when speaking of a man she knew, she would say something like: "Oh, so-and-so, what a treasure! Ugly as a little monkey, but so nice!" She never missed an opportunity, so we would jump on the occasion to burst out laughing while imitating her in front of her, and then she would be sorry… but five minutes later she would do it again!

My mother suffered from a grueling illness. I am convinced that, in His mercy, the Lord enables some of us to do our purgatory on earth to avoid our having to do it in the next world, because it would be so much more painful there. According to many mystical witnesses given to us in the Church, in purgatory the smallest suffering is more painful than the greatest suffering on earth because it is a suffering of the soul.[16]

---

[16] See Chapter 38 about the souls in Purgatory.

Those Who Have Difficult Circumstances at the End of Life

We sometimes have an understanding of suffering that is too limited and earthly, we see it at face value as an enemy that we must get rid of. Our Lady said to Vicka: "Know that there are very few people who have understood the great value of suffering when it is offered to Jesus." Obviously, it is important to relieve pain as much as possible. But when nothing more can be done… It is up to God alone to decide whether a sick person should or should not go on living. It is a serious mistake, a lack of love and a lack of wisdom to want to artificially shorten a life based on the excuse of avoiding suffering for that person. We cannot "alleviate suffering" by helping a person to die, i.e. allowing the person to starve to death or dehydrate to the point of death when their body is still able to assimilate food. If it is not able to make energy out of food, then by all means, the body cannot handle the nutrition it is offered! If the Lord's plan is to spare people the pain of purgatory by enabling them to purify themselves while still on this earth, who are we to decide otherwise? We would then be doing exactly the opposite of what we wanted for these persons, because we may be adding even more painful suffering in the afterlife. That is the true challenge of euthanasia!

Here is a question for your personal reflection: if, in His providence, God allows someone to be purified on earth during a time of illness to be able to go straight to Heaven, and if someone decides to shorten their life, what happens to people who have been deprived of their time of purification? What happens to the care giver who hastened the patient's death? I don't have the answer, but we can reflect on it! Because this is about misplaced compassion, even if it often stems from a good intention on the part of unbelievers who do not know that after death, there is Eternity. Dying with dignity? Of course! But true dignity is to die having been made worthy to enter into Glory!

15
SERAPHIA'S VEIL

"No, Seraphia, I forbid you to go out today to see this imposter! Don't you see what a mess he's gotten us into? Open your eyes! He's a troublemaker! You can clearly see that his doctrine doesn't stand up! And for himself to believe he is the son of God … Why not God Himself while he's at it?"

Seraphia's heart was bleeding. It was torn to pieces. She withdrew to her room to cry. How much she loved this Jesus, her nephew whom she adored! Already, when he was 12 years old and had remained in Jerusalem after the feast of the Passover without his parents' knowledge, she had gone to the Temple to give him something to eat, while he discussed things with the Doctors of the Law. How proud she was of him, this little guy who impressed even the scholars with his intelligence and his answers!

We should mention that Seraphia was Mary's cousin, barely older than her, tall and rather imposing, according to the revelations of Marthe Robin.[17] She had known Jesus since he was born, and as she watched him grow up, she gradually discovered in him a profundity of goodness and light. Where did this grace come from? No matter, Seraphia happily soaked up every word he said. When Jesus began his mission and was on the road, she kept her eye out for him, so she could go and

[17] The Venerable Marthe Robin, a French mystic, is on the path to beatification. For fifty years, she relived the Passion of Christ in her soul as well as in her body. In her writings, we find an inexhaustible source of information about the protagonists in the Passion.

listen to him speak. But her husband, Sirach, a member of the Temple Council, who held a position of high ranking in Jerusalem, had begun to hate him, undoubtedly influenced by certain Pharisees and High Priests. Frankly, those men did not hide their doubts about the mental health of this rebel, accompanied by his deplorable bunch of grubby, uncultured hippies, who shamelessly violated, as he did, the mitzvot about Shabbat and so many other precepts.[18] Didn't he absolutely cross the line when he declared it necessary to eat his flesh and drink his blood? And he was serious!

"You see, Seraphia," her husband repeated to her. "Your Jesus just takes it too far! I don't understand how you can believe all this nonsense! Just because he's your nephew doesn't mean you have to swallow every word that comes out of his sick mouth!"

But that day, alone in her room, Seraphia heard the ranting of the crowd. From her terrace, she even saw, on the long Via Dolorosa, the sinister procession that was taking Jesus to his death. It was too much! Séraphia couldn't remain there powerless in the midst of this drama; she was freaking out! She had to act, and quickly! In a burst of inspiration, she prepared an excellent, aromatic wine, hoping to get Jesus to drink it for comfort along his painful way. She called out to her daughter, who was barely 10 years old, put her in charge of the flask of wine, and covered her own head with a veil, so she wouldn't be recognized.[19] She took with her a white linen cloth and hurried outside to meet the doleful caravan that surrounded Jesus and Joseph of Arimathea. Her daughter went with her. They both crossed paths with small groups who were headed to the Temple but who kept their distance as soon as they saw Jesus, for fear of defiling themselves before the Passover.

[18] A mitzvah (plural: mitzvoth) is a precept to be observed by religious Jews.

[19] Seraphia had two little boys, but they had their throats cut at the time of the massacre in Bethlehem ordered by Herod. After that, she adopted this little girl.

Some, however showed pity for the Savior who was so cruelly treated by these heartless demonic men determined to make Him suffer.

After passing through the crowd, Seraphia and her daughter still had to pierce the impenetrable wall formed by Caiaphas' agents, soldiers on horseback, and armed guards with lances and chains, all of whom escorted Jesus. At the risk of being arrested and tortured to death, Seraphia threw herself against that barrier without calculating the danger. Nothing stopped her. Love gave her wings; love banished fear! Her little daughter stood resolutely by her side. They were there, now, close to Jesus. The Roman soldiers had no time to react. Seraphia was horrified seeing Jesus who no longer looked human. He had been savagely beaten by the soldiers all night long; his face was swollen. He was covered in blood, spit, and mud. On his head he wore a crown of thorns. He was unrecognizable… And yet, in the very depths of his abandonment, his gaze rested on her. His magnificent gaze! A divine moment between Him and his beloved aunt Seraphia! This singular expression of Jesus possessed the power of infinite love. Seraphia, with all the tenderness she had in her, let her eyes drown in his. Then, ignoring the threats of the soldiers, she took the white cloth and with great gentleness, wiped the face of Jesus, cleaned it of spit, mud, and blood: a gesture of perfect love, utterly inspired by the Holy Spirit. What immense consolation for Jesus! He, Compassion itself, was made the object of compassion! In his abandonment, he had received from this woman a gesture of pure, unadulterated love, a gesture that he himself never stopped lavishing on all his wounded children.

To immortalize this act of love, he accomplished a marvelous miracle: he imprinted his face on the linen veil. From then on, no one could forget what Seraphia had done. Since that moment, we have had the most beautiful icon in the world produced by God Himself. This icon eventually inspired Seraphia to be re-baptized Veronica, *vera icona,* that is, "true icon." A new name which has come down through the ages and by which we venerate her.[20]

The little girl was hiding the flask of wine under her coat. She timidly lifted it up to Jesus' face, but the bowmen and soldiers saw her gesture and, with horrible curses, pushed her away. They took ahold of the flask and drank the aromatic wine that was meant to quench the thirst of Jesus.

The gesture of Seraphia put a halt to the procession interrupting the plan of the soldiers, which provoked the anger of the Pharisees and the soldiers themselves. Furious at the sight of this public homage of Jesus, they beat him and mistreated him even more. Seraphia returned home in haste, totally overwhelmed by what she dared to do and experienced. A woman of great intention, as she would with all of her linens before washing them, Seraphia delicately laid the shroud on a little table. But when she unfolded it, she fell on her knees before the great mystery that was revealed before her eyes.

In reality, what had Séraphia-Veronica done? She extended mercy to the One who is in essence Mercy itself! She did all in her power to console and comfort the Tortured One, thus giving him the most beautiful proof of her love.[21]

2000 years later, Jesus needs our love and mercy more than ever. There are so many ways to answer Him. One of the most powerful means is by adoring Jesus and contemplating Him in his Passion. Veronica teaches us that the more we contemplate him with compassion in his Kenosis – a term that signifies his humble abasement – the more He imprints his image onto our souls and the more He communicates His divinity to us.

---

[20] This veil was carefully preserved by the Church and is now found in St. Peter's Basilica in Rome, under the cupola, found near the right pillar, just under the statue of Saint Veronica. The cloth has darkened with time, but a miracle happened in 1848, when it was exposed to the eyes of the young faithful on Good Friday: although it was no longer possible to discern the features of Jesus on the darkened linen, it lit up for several minutes, and all could admire His face. Then it returned to its dark color.

[21] After the Resurrection of Jesus, Seraphia's husband converted and defended the first Christians.

In turn, we become love. We are transformed into the One we contemplate. What a splendor!

This linen veil of Veronica's is like our heart. It symbolizes the intimate place in our heart where the Divine Operation transforms us when we contemplate Jesus with love.

Jesus taught Sister Faustina: "Know, my daughter, that when you meditate on My sorrowful Passion for only one hour, your soul is enriched with a new level of glory and beauty, identical to what you would acquire if you were scourged for a year."

What power there is in the contemplation of the Passion of Jesus! The power of consolation for Jesus and of transformation for us! When we look at him with love and sincerely desire to join Him in His suffering, He communicates to us in return His beauty, His love, His tenderness, and His divinity … He communicates Himself entirely to us.

We can recognize a trace of that deep look of Jesus in the poor, in the most impoverished people we find around us. But poverty is not reserved for beggars, the sick, or the handicapped: it touches equally those who seem rich and successful, and who might be of high social or professional rank.

We are called to extend our compassion to the rich as well as the poor! How many times have I noticed the secret distress of the rich, which is often greater than that of the poor?! How many of them commit suicide! Sometimes we don't even suspect the inner suffering of those around us.

Let's ask Our Lady to lend us this gaze of Jesus. The gaze of Veronica. The gaze of God the Father, who is able to see the beauty of the soul in the midst of all this misery. Let us desire to meet the soul of Jesus, so we can drink from the fountain of His heart, like Veronica did.

16
The Epitome of Courage: Corrie Ten Boom

Corrie ten Boom, Holland

Like a lot of pilgrims going to pray in Jerusalem, I was well-informed about the Alley of the Just Ones, which leads to *Yad Vashem*, the holocaust museum. Just who are these "just ones?" They are the non-Jewish people who risked their lives to save Jews being tracked down by the Gestapo during the Second World War. Among the 6,000 names, one can find that of Corrie Ten Boom, along with the name of her father,

Caspar, and her sister, Betsie. They were a simple family of very fervent Protestant watchmakers from Harlem, Holland, whose heroic courage defies the imagination. Thanks to them, hundreds of Jews were able to escape certain death.

Corrie was 48 years old in 1940 when German troops invaded Holland. The tranquil life of this watchmaker and his family was about to take a dramatic turn. There's simply no way to quantify the arbitrary arrests of Jews in the middle of the street and the disappearance of so many. Hate and fear gripped Harlem. But a secret prayer took form in the heart of Corrie: "Lord Jesus, I offer myself to You for Your people, in any circumstance, in any place, at any time."

The offer didn't take long to become real. One spring evening in 1942, a veiled woman knocked at the door: "My name is Kleermaker. I'm Jewish. May I come in?" Her anguish was tangible. Casper kept calm: "Of course," he said. "In this house the people of God are always welcome."

Corrie remembered: "And thus began, in an unexpected way, *God's hiding place*, a name which described our clandestine activity. Since we had kept up friendly relations with half of Harlem, soon a dozen Jews came to help us by being messengers, while 80 older women and men offered their various services. We led this double life for almost two years: to the world outside, we were still an old watchmaker and his two unmarried daughters living over their store. But in reality, our old house, lovingly named "BJ", full of nooks and crannies had become the center of a secret organization whose reach extended to all of Holland. Every day, a dozen aides came and went, so that we could manage the contacts and appeals for help. One time, for example, we learned that a hundred babies in a Jewish orphanage in Amsterdam were going to be assassinated. Without hesitation, our agents, disguised as German soldiers, carried away the hundred Jewish babies! Many Jews found refuge at "BJ" before being transferred to safer places."

Every saint has his Judas. For the Ten Boom family, it was Jan Vogel who played that sad role. Although he was Dutch, he had colluded with the Germans from the beginning of the occupation, and he exposed them in February of 1944.

The watchmaker and his two daughters were seized in a raid and put into prison. The head of the Gestapo wanted to send Casper Ten Boom back to his home, because of his old age, but Casper responded in a firm voice: "If I return to the house today, I will begin again tomorrow to open my door to anyone in need. It's an honor for me to give my life for God's chosen people!"

For Corrie and Betsie the nightmare had only begun. The two sisters were sent to a work camp in the south of Holland before being deported to the infamous extermination camp of Ravensbrück in Germany. Before being taken to Germany, the Ten Boom sisters learned the name of the person who had betrayed them. Betsie began to pray for him immediately, but for Corrie it was completely against her gut: "I thought about my father's last hour, about his solitude in a hospital hallway, about his clandestine work so brutally interrupted, and I realized that if Jan Vogel had been in front of me at that moment, I would have killed him. My whole body was suffering because of the violent resentment I felt toward that man, who was the cause of such misery. I couldn't close my eyes at night, and prayer had become impossible for me. In the space of one week, I fell physically and psychologically ill. Finally, I asked Betsie, who never seemed to experience hate towards him: 'Are you completely indifferent about Jan Vogel? Aren't you tormented when you think about him?' She answered: 'Oh, yes, Corrie. Ever since I learned his name, I have constantly been distressed for him! What suffering he must be enduring!' Was she leading me to believe, although indirectly and with gentleness, that I was as guilty as Jan Vogel? Hadn't I assassinated him in my heart and through my words? Finally, I was capable of praying: 'Lord Jesus, I forgive Jan, as I ask You to forgive me. I would have done him harm. Bless him and his family as well this very minute.' That night, I was able to sleep soundly for the first time."

It was after this extraordinary declaration, in the horror of

Ravensbrück that Betsie inevitably succumbed to inhumane treatment by her torturers, in the eyes of her sister.

Thanks to an administrative error, Corrie was freed from Ravensbrück on January 1, 1945. It happened just in time, because one week later, all the detainees of her age as well as all the older prisoners were executed.

Back in Holland, Corrie never stopped thinking about Betsie's last words: "We have to tell the world what we have learned here… We have to tell them that He (God) will always be able to bring us out of the abyss, no matter how deep it may be. People will listen to us, Corrie, because of what we have experienced here. I pray every day that we will be able to show, even to our persecutors, that love is greater than anything else." As a testimony of faith, who could say it better?

When the war ended Corrie was 53 years old. In the spring, near Harlem, Corrie opened a rehabilitation center called "Bloemendaal" to welcome the survivors of the Holocaust. She recounted that: "Soon there arrived the first of hundreds of people who eventually followed, persons who were traumatized, made mute, or who kept speaking without ceasing of the losses they had endured; people who were resolutely aggressive or withdrawn into themselves. Wounded in body and soul, they had only one means of healing: forgiveness. Surprisingly, it was not the Germans who were the most difficult for them to forgive, but their own Dutch compatriots who had collaborated with the enemy. The situation of those old accomplices of the Nazis was unenviable: they were despised, chased from their apartments, out of work. Because they were hated, I opened wide to them the doors of 'BJ', my home."

But that's not all. In 1949 someone proposed to Corrie that she utilize the old concentration camp, Darmstadt, for her reconciliation work.

Strangely, her sister, Betsie, on her miserable deathbed, had hoped for the possibility of transforming a concentration camp: "A concentration camp in Germany, Corrie," she would say, "but without barbed wire, where people destroyed by hate and violence could come freely to learn to love again... We would paint the gruesome barracks bright green, and, in front of the windows, we would put boxes of blooming flowers."

Corrie rented the old concentration camp, which very quickly became a warm, welcoming center for 160 German refugees. 160 refugees? But there were some 9 million in the ruins of post-war Germany, executioners and victims all mixed together! Yes, she knew that the merciful love of Jesus was always near to the victims as well as the guilty, to the sufferers as well as to the authors of their suffering.

The Case Bounces Up

Towards the end of the war, after learning that her betrayer had been condemned to death, Corrie decided to write to him: "Your betrayal led to the death, after ten days of detention, of my father, aged 84, and that of my sister, after ten months of atrocious suffering in a concentration camp. My brother Willem was on the brink of death when he got out of prison; his son Kik never returned from the Bergen-Bergen concentration camp. As for me, I lived through the indescribable nightmare; but I have forgiven you. It is Jesus who has given me the strength, He who said, 'Love your enemies!'" She had underlined that sentence in the New Testament she sent to Jan Vogel. The man responded: "Your forgiveness is such a great miracle that I have dared to say, 'Jesus, if You have put into the heart of your disciples a love as great as that, then there must be hope for me!' After reading in the Bible you sent me that Jesus died on the cross for the sins of the world, I surrendered into His hands my abominable sins, and I know that He has pardoned me, because your forgiveness has convinced me of the reality of the forgiveness of Jesus." A few days later, Jan Vogel gave his soul back to God.

But we must go even further. Corrie wrote to two other Dutch traitors who were also condemned to death, Willemsen and Kapteyn. These collaborators of the Gestapo had beaten Betsie and Corrie until they were covered in blood, then left them unconscious. In prison, each man received a letter from Corrie. She assured them of the forgiveness of her family and of her own prayer that they, in turn, would accept the pardon of Jesus. Two answers reached her. In the first, she read, "I know what harm I've done to your family. The fact that you have been able to pardon me is tangible proof that Jesus can pardon me. I have confessed to Him all my sins." But the second response made her tremble: "I am not only responsible for the death of your loved ones, but for the extermination of thousands of Jews. I only regret one thing: not having been able to kill more of them, as well as people like you."

Near the Pinnacle of Mercy

For 32 years, up until the age of 85, Corrie practiced this apostolate of mercy. With what conviction and what ardor she testified to the experiences she lived through in the concentration camp of Ravensbruck and to the power of forgiveness! She toured the world several times announcing this Christian message and touching thousands of hearts. She traveled across all the continents; she was seen in more than 60 countries; she spoke on the radio and on television and caused countless tears to flow. Who among us doesn't have some forgiveness too difficult to give? During one of her conferences, Jesus was waiting for her – to render a truly heroic act. I will let Corrie tell it:

"It was 1947 in a Church in Munich. I had left Holland for Germany shortly before, for the purpose of testifying to the forgiveness of God for every person. It was exactly the message that this country: conquered, desolate, devastated by bombs, needed to hear most. And it was there that I saw him! He was thin, wrapped in a grey overcoat, clearing a path through the crowd. The memory shot through me like a bolt of lightning: the enormous room filled with mocking men … In the middle, the miserable pile of clothing and shoes, and then the humiliation of having to walk nude in front of the SS every Friday. The silhouette of my emaciated sister passed before my eyes, and here was this man standing before me, beaming, his hand extended – one of the cruelest guards of the concentration camp: 'A marvelous message, Ma'am,' he said. 'How wonderful it is to hear, as you said, that He has washed away all of our sins.' I, who had just spoken so eloquently about forgiveness, was pretending to search through my notes, so I wouldn't have to shake his hand. It was the first time since my liberation that I had found myself face-to-face with one of my torturers. 'In your lecture, you brought up Ravensbrück,' he said. 'I was actually a guard there. But that's all in the past. At Christmas time, I became a Christian, and I know that God has pardoned me for the atrocities I committed then. However, I begged Him to give me an opportunity to ask for forgiveness personally from one of the victims! That's why I'm asking you: 'Can you forgive me?' Again he offered me his hand, at the same moment that a bitter desire for vengeance was mounting inside me. Could he simply erase the slow and horrible death of my sister Betsie merely by asking for pardon? Nevertheless, Jesus died for this man. What more did I want? 'Lord Jesus,' I prayed, 'forgive me and help me to forgive him!' This whole thing lasted for no more than a few seconds, but it felt like hours to me, given the difficulty of the battle I was fighting, the most difficult I had ever been asked to fight. I attempted to smile, while forcing myself desperately to put out my hand, in vain. I felt nothing, not the least spark of affection, not the least bit of mercy, but, regardless, I had to do it, because Jesus said, 'If you do not forgive others for their trespasses, your heavenly Father will not forgive you in return.'

At Boemendaal, I had so often spoken on this theme, and I had been able to point out that only those who had pardoned their former enemies were capable of returning to the world and re-building their lives, regardless of the state of their health.

And I stood there with an icy heart! 'Forgiveness is not a feeling,' I told myself. 'Pardon is an act of will, and the will can act outside of our feelings. Jesus, come to my aid! I can't forgive him. Give me Your forgiveness,' I said all in one breath.

When I lifted my hand stiffly, mechanically, to put it into his, something unbelievable happened: a current seemed to pass from me to him, going from my shoulder to my arm, then to my hand, while waves of benevolent warmth flooded over me. My heart was aflame with such a love for this stranger that I was completely overwhelmed. I told him without holding back my tears, 'Brother, I forgive you with all my heart!'

For several minutes we remained that way, hand in hand: the former guard and the former prisoner. Never before had I felt with such intensity the love of our gracious God. At that moment, I discovered that the healing of the world depended neither on our forgiveness nor on our goodness but solely on the forgiveness and goodness of God. When He tells us that we should love our enemies, He is giving us, along with His commandment, the love necessary to live it."

17
Jakov and the Irresistable Moped

Jakov Colo at 11 years old, © Photo Btruchet 1982

When the apparitions first began in Medjugorje, young Jakov Colo was just 10 years old. He no longer had a father, he had no brothers or sisters, and his mother was already growing old. The year after the apparitions started, he lost his mother. The Blessed Mother then asked his cousin, Vicka Ivankovic, seven years older, to be a second mom for him.

Vicka took this role very seriously.

In France, people might have referred to the Jakovs of that era as "nice little children of the street." He had grown like a weed with no restraint, deprived of the solid structure a true family gives, in a village where Communist oppression allowed him little freedom.

In spite of it all, he had held onto his innocence of heart. One little anecdote: Father Jozo Zovko, the Parish Priest of Medjugorje at that time, who, during the first days of the apparitions, didn't believe them to be real, wanted to test the sincerity of each of the visionaries. He took them aside, one by one, so he could bombard them with questions, certain that they were going to contradict one another and thus demonstrate that the entire affair was pure fiction directed by the Communists to ridicule the Church. I was able to listen to the tape recordings of the interviews, and the frankness of Jakov's responses to his Priest, Father Jozo Zovko, enchanted me. Father asked:

"Jakov, when was the last time you went to confession?"

"Um, last year at school, when you made us all go!"

"And you haven't been since?"

"No… But… you know, now that I have seen the Gospa, I won't be committing any more sins!"

Next, Father Jozo asked him:

"And how did she speak, this Blessed Lady?"

"She didn't speak. Her voice was kind of like music."

"What's that? Music? Can't she speak like everyone else?"

"Listen, Jozo, I'm just telling you what I heard. That's the way it was! When she spoke, it was like music. That's it."

Another remark of Jakov's: "Now that I have seen the Gospa, I'm not afraid to die anymore."

One summer day, when the temptation was very strong,

Jakov sneaked over to his neighbor's house, and, without his permission, borrowed the brand-new motorbike he had dreamed of trying out. (It was certainly not today's latest model!) Obviously, this was totally forbidden to him, because he was too young to ride it. But, thanks to a quiet moment and no sight of anyone on the horizon, he jumped onto the machine and drove it along the pebbled, dusty path which wound around near the foot of Apparition Hill. Right from the start, the speed of the bike surprised him, and he soon lost control. At the first turn, he was thrown off after hitting a pothole, and he landed in one of the many clumps of thorny bushes which lined the road. The moped was damaged, and Jakov himself was wounded, not seriously, but one side of his body was very bloody. He began to cry. He was afraid of the reaction of his neighbors, knowing that he was at fault for having taken their motorbike. He went and hid behind a shrub. In tears, hurting from his injuries and upset about the damaged motorbike, he was ashamed of his disobedience. Vicka heard him crying and compassionately ran to see what happened.

While she was trying to console him the hour of the apparition of the Blessed Mother came. So, right in the middle of that delicate and unexpected situation, without seeming to be the least bit concerned about the thorns, Our Lady appeared to both of them. It was 6:40 PM. In her maternal love she did two things consecutively: first, she pulled Jakov tenderly onto her lap and consoled him over his pain, while at the same time cradling and caressing him – as any mother would do for her child who hurt himself in a fall. Then, after comforting him so kindly, she told him firmly that he should go to his neighbors' home to ask for their forgiveness in having damaged their motorbike, and that he had to confess this sin.

Now there's a truly good mother; there's true mercy in action!

18
I Will Never Forget the Gaze of Jesus

The visionary Vicka Ivankovic speaking to pilgrims
© Photo Bernard Gallagher

Some time ago, Vicka told me that during the apparition on Good Friday 1982, Our Lady appeared to her with Jesus. However, it was not the way she comes every year at Christmas, when she is radiant with joy, holding her newborn Child. On that day, Jesus appeared as an adult. He was suffering His Passion and wearing his Crown of thorns. Vicka Ivankovic recounted to me, with a great deal of emotion, the story of that apparition, which revealed to her the depth of Christ's mercy. His blood was flowing down his forehead, his cheeks, and his beard. His face was covered in spittle and mud, swollen from the blows he had received during the night in Caiaphas' prison, and from the cruel abuse Pilate's soldiers had inflicted on him. He was wearing a red cloak, which was torn and stained with blood. It was quite a shock for her, to say the least!

"Dear Children," the Gospa told her, "today I have come with my Son Jesus in the midst of his Passion, so that you can see how much he suffered for you, and just how much he loves you."

I asked Vicka: "Did Jesus also speak to you?"

"No," she answered me. "Jesus remained silent. He didn't say anything. But I looked into his eyes, and I saw such tenderness there, such love, such humility, that for me, it was more powerful than all the words he could have said. I saw how much he suffered and at the very same time, how much he loved us! You know I will never forget Jesus' gaze in the midst of his Passion!

It goes without saying that this vision increased ten-fold the love Vicka has for Jesus!

The visionary Marija Pavlovic, who was also present that day, told the story of that apparition of Christ in an interview on Radio Maria, in Italy, on February 25, 2016. She explained the context in which this apparition took place and the lessons the visionaries were able to glean from it for their own lives: it was precious assistance for the suffering they endured at that time and certainly a help for them today.

"At that time," Marija said: "We were being persecuted by the Communists. They took us to the mental hospital which was filled with people who had mental disabilities. We suffered greatly because they told us that we would end up like that. We were children, sixteen years old, and we were afraid. When the Blessed Mother appeared to us, we began to cry, and we told her that we didn't have the strength to continue. We were too exhausted.

"Earlier, the Gospa had warned us that we should not eat or drink anything the Communists gave us. We should accept nothing from them. We learned later, from one of those men, that they had tried to drug us. They had their plan: they were going to say on television that we were drug addicts, and they wanted the viewers to see it. Fortunately, Our Lady warned us ahead of time of the danger. Later, they took us to the village church, and, that night we went home, exhausted.

"That was when the Blessed Mother appeared to us. We told her that we couldn't take it anymore, and that we didn't deserve what they were doing to us. To scare us, for example, they would tell us, that Vicka's father, who was working in Germany, would be arrested and put into prison when he came home; that he wouldn't be able to earn money to support his family, and that Vicka's family would die of hunger.

"We told Our Lady everything that they had done to us, how they had arrested us and brought us to the mental hospital, and how they threatened to leave us there forever, and also how they told us we would become insane. It was at that point that she showed us Jesus, crowned with thorns, covered with wounds, and bathed in blood; then she said to us: 'Just as he did that out of love for you and for humanity, go and do likewise for Him.'

"Jesus Himself said nothing," added Marija. "He simply gazed at us. That night I was unable to sleep, it had left a very deep impression on me. I will never forget it!"

The same goes for all of us, who endure, at one point in time or another, those difficult moments which can sometimes seem insurmountable. The words expressed by Mary at the side of her suffering Son gives us keys of enlightenment for getting through these challenges in a new and different way. We simply place ourselves under the gaze of the merciful Jesus. In such circumstances how can we not be united with Him? Because of this union with the agonizing Jesus, our own suffering is transfigured. It takes on a whole new meaning and even becomes the source of fruitfulness.

Wings for Our Hearts?

A source of fruitfulness: that's what Our Lady dreams of for us! She wants us to be saints, and she knows how to help us along the way! She knows very well the path to sainthood, and she ardently desires to help us discover it, to help us follow it and to accompany us along the way. She invites us to take her hand and to abandon ourselves with confidence along this path which leads directly to Heaven. As the first and humble disciple of Jesus, didn't she herself take this majestic path? She knows that there are no glorious mysteries without the obligatory passage through the sorrowful mysteries. With the gentleness and compassion which characterize her, she reassures us along this road full of potholes. What do we have to be afraid of, if the one who guides us is also the one who crushed the head of Satan? Far from removing the obstacles along the way, she helps us discern them and bypass them. She does most of the work, but she leaves us one task. She does not steal our crosses! Indeed, she knows better than to deprive us of these providential opportunities to grow and fortify ourselves for battle. By walking with her, in the embrace she always offers from her motherly heart, we can march from victory to victory. As she does!

The saintly Curé of Ars, an expert in matters of the cross, identified himself so completely with Christ in his extreme love for Him that he dared to say these astonishing words: "If we could see the beauty and grandeur of our crosses, we would steal them from one another!"

These words from Marthe Robin express the same thing in a different way. Like the Blessed Mother, Marthe never sought to tone down the evangelical message, but, on the contrary, to give it all her strength, all the power so often hidden from our eyes. She said: "The beautiful mission of Mary is to bring to Jesus all those who come to her. Let's make ourselves small in the arms of our beloved mother. Let's put ourselves near her. She will tell us that our whole duty as a Christian is to resemble Jesus and that there is only one way, always and every time, to resemble him: to renounce ourselves, take up our crosses, and follow Him.

"But she will also tell us what she knows from experience: with Jesus, to renounce oneself, to take up your cross, and to follow Him by carrying it, is not to put millstones around your feet but wings on your heart, to put joy, happiness, and Heaven in your life… It is to ascend, to approach God, step by step. She will tell us that the cross is made lighter day by day and cherished more, when you carry it by allowing yourself to be sanctified by Christ.

"When you suffer, when you cry, when you are alone and sad, it's not difficult to make yourself childlike; you have such a need for help, such a need for a mother at your side. And who doesn't suffer? Who doesn't need to be consoled and pardoned, to be loved and healed?"

What a grace it is for us to have Our Lady appear today as she does in Medjugorje, and to be able to hear directly from the witnesses she has chosen for herself! What a grace it is to rediscover like this, in every circumstance, the magnificent meaning of our lives!

19
MARILYN MEETS THERESE OF LISIEUX

Marilyn Monroe in 1953

I cannot write this book without citing extensively the prayer of St. Therese of the Child Jesus, a prayer which offers the Holy Face of Jesus to God in order to draw down His mercy.

This prayer, which emanated from the heart of a young girl barely 22 years old, is, for these modern times, a kind of pinnacle, a striking example of merciful love. The masterpiece could have remained hidden in the back of a dusty drawer in a cloistered Carmelite convent; but for God, it was urgent to reveal the profound depths of His love. He found Therese and permitted her manuscript to be circulated throughout the world. He needed this childlike soul to show people the path to His heart and to offer them the treasures of His mercy.

This offering, of God to humanity, is the secret to the fruitfulness of Therese. Because of it, the one who became the greatest saint of modern times (as St. Pius X noted), was able to keep her promise to spend her heaven doing good on earth and to bestow her well known shower of roses on so many souls ravaged by suffering and adrift from God. One such soul was, surprisingly, the famous Marilyn Monroe. May this prayer also find an echo in our own hearts!

> "O My God! Most Blessed Trinity, I desire to Love You and make You Loved, to work for the glory of Holy Church by saving souls on earth and liberating those suffering in purgatory. I desire to accomplish Your will perfectly and to reach the degree of glory You have prepared for me in Your Kingdom. I desire, in a word, to be a saint, but I feel my helplessness and I beg You, O my God to be Yourself my Sanctity!
>
> "Since You loved me so much as to give me Your only Son as my Savior and my Spouse, the infinite treasures of His merits are mine. I offer them to You with gladness, begging You to look upon me only in the Face of Jesus and in His heart burning with Love.
>
> "I offer You, too, all the merits of the saints (in heaven and on earth), their acts of Love, and those of the holy angels. Finally, I offer You, O Blessed Trinity! the Love and merits of the Blessed Virgin, my dear Mother. It is to her I abandon my offering, begging her to present it to You.
>
> "Her Divine Son, my Beloved Spouse, told us in the days of His mortal life: 'Whatsoever you ask the Father in my name he will give it to you!' I am certain, then, that You will grant my desires;

I know, O my God! that the more You want to give, the more You make us desire. I feel in my heart immense desires and it is with confidence I ask You to come and take possession of my soul. Ah! I cannot receive Holy Communion as often as I desire, but, Lord, are You not all-powerful? … Remain in me as in a tabernacle and never separate Yourself from Your little victim…

"I want to console You for the ingratitude of the wicked, and I beg of You to take away my freedom to displease You. If through weakness I sometimes fall, may Your Divine Glance cleanse my soul immediately, consuming all my imperfections like the fire that transforms everything into itself.

"I thank You, O my God, for all the graces You have granted me, especially the grace of making me pass through the crucible of suffering. It is with joy I shall contemplate You on the Last Day carrying the scepter of Your Cross. Since You deigned to give me a share in this very precious Cross, I hope in heaven to resemble You and to see shining in my glorified body the sacred stigmata of Your Passion.

"After earth's Exile, I hope to go and enjoy You in the Fatherland, but I do not want to lay up merits for heaven. I want to work for Your Love alone with the one purpose of pleasing You, consoling Your Sacred Heart, and saving souls who will love You eternally.

"In the evening of this life, I shall appear before You with empty hands, for I do not ask You, Lord, to count my works. All our justice is stained in Your eyes. I wish, then, to be clothed in Your own Justice and to receive from Your Love the eternal possession of Yourself. I want no other Throne, no other Crown but You, my Beloved!

"Time is nothing in Your eyes, and a single day is like a thousand years. You can, then, in one instant prepare me to appear before You...

"In order to live in one single act of perfect Love, I OFFER MYSELF AS A VICTIM OF HOLOCAUST TO YOUR MERCIFUL LOVE, asking You to consume me incessantly, allowing the waves of infinite tenderness shut up within You to overflow into my soul, and that thus I may become a martyr of Your Love, O my God!

"May this martyrdom, after having prepared me to appear before You, finally cause me to die and may my soul take its flight without any delay into the eternal embrace of Your Merciful Love.

"I want, O my Beloved, at each beat of my heart to renew this offering to You an infinite number of times, until the shadows having disappeared I may be able to tell You of my Love in an Eternal Face to Face!...

Marie-Francoise, Therese of the Child Jesus and the Holy Face,
Carmelite religious
This 9th day of June,
Feast of the Most Holy Trinity,
In the year of grace, 1895.

(Extract from the *Autobiographical Manuscripts of Saint Therese of the Child Jesus*, chapter entitled 'Act of Oblation to Merciful Love'. Carmel of Lisieux edition, 1957.)

A Vibrant Quest for Love

If we were looking for the polar opposite of "little" Therese, we might recall the "great" Marilyn Monroe, the famous Hollywood actress and model. And we might contrast the offertory prayer of Love from Therese, which is so complete, with the equally total passionate investment of Marilyn in her vain quest for love and recognition. Of course, any comparison between people has its own limits because only God searches man's heart and tests his mind, (Jer. 17:10).

But, in your opinion, what would have happened if little Therese had been born in the environment of Metro Goldwyn Mayer in Hollywood to a young mother who was somewhat mentally unstable; and if the little Norma Jean – who was to become Marilyn Monroe – was born in the loving and very Catholic household of the Martin family, in a peaceful town in Normandy? In your view, in which girl would the seeds of sainthood have taken hold?

The answer isn't obvious because Marilyn and Therese both had the same fundamental vocation. As a matter of fact, it's actually been proven. Both pushed to the extreme their quest for unbridled love; in it, they invested all their strength, their energy, and even their own lives, all the way to the point of dying for it. They both staked everything on it and burned to "succeed in love." This vocation which they had in common, this total determination which animated them, went far beyond their familial and social differences. The Lord is capable of planting the seed of sainthood wherever he wants, sometimes in surprising situations, as has often been demonstrated.

And if Marilyn hadn't known the true face of Jesus until the moment of her death, that very particular instant between the lethal effect of the sleeping pills and her final entry into eternity, how can we not imagine that before such a face she didn't cry out: "Jesus, save me, save me!" We can't forget that the principle job of Jesus is to be our Redeemer. So, the more His child emits signals of distress, the faster He hurries to her side – it's normal, as we shall see later on.

Right from birth, the cruelty of life was waiting for Marilyn. No father, and the mother, in the throes of great psychological imbalance, had multiple lovers and was conspicuously absent. She was placed very early into a mental health hospital. Marilyn received very little affection from her and would become a child of the state, shuttled from foster home to foster home. Unfortunately, the cloud of insanity prevented any real communication between her and her mother. One detail stands out though. In between two hospitalizations, her mother worked as a film editor both for Metro Goldwyn Mayer and for Paramount. So Marilyn had the best seats for all the latest films.

Thus, little Norma Jean had an unhappy childhood and these wounds affected her until her death, "As a child," she said. "I had no kiss in my life, no caresses, no love, nothing." She also said, "When I was surrounded with all of these people who were interested in me because I was a star, I remembered little Norma Jean in whom no one had any interest and I felt desperate."

At first, Marilyn's mother entrusted her to neighbors, who would babysit her for several dollars a week. These neighbors were poor and austere, very pious, and actually very good people. Marilyn stayed with them until the age of 7. At their home, she began to pray, to sing hymns, and to listen to Scripture every day. She also went to Sunday school and entertained herself by singing her favorite hymn at the top of her voice: "Jesus loves me, this I know."

At the age of 7, Marilyn moved to the home of an English couple, actors, who quickly plunged her into a very different world, more artistic and bohemian, where even the idea of God was absent. In this house, she would say later, she was the victim of sexual abuse.

When Marilyn reached the age of reason, she began to search for her identity. Her conscience, still completely naïve and pure, had already been put at risk with a total displacement of values. In addition to her emotional emptiness and the violence inflicted on her, she felt lost. In her first family, going to the movies and drinking alcohol were considered sins. Whereas now, she saw two movies a day and no one seemed to worry about it. What was the truth? What was truly good or truly bad? There was no one to take her aside and answer her questions in a gentle way. On a psychological level, she was developing a sense of insecurity and a fear of facing the outside world. It was also during this time that Marilyn's mother, after an explosion of delirium (a schizophrenic crisis), was forcibly taken to a psychiatric hospital. It was the very same hospital where her grandparents had died; both suffering from dementia. Thankfully, Marilyn did not learn that fact until adulthood, a delay which certainly preserved her from much anguish.

She was 7 years old and couldn't call anyone "mom" in person, just like Therese! And, curiously, she seemed to endure the trials and lack of an adult around better than Therese, who still had her father. Marilyn familiarized herself with her new territory, one that was completely atheistic, if not totally debauched. It was during this time, within this new family, that Marilyn began to sink into a feeling of inner emptiness. She completely lost her bearings, gone was that equilibrium so indispensable to children, that she never fully recovered. This is where the story of a slow erosion of her natural enthusiasm, her capacity to marvel and wonder about life and to be excited about life began.

Her mother never came out of the hospital; the old English couple who taught her the ways of the Lord ended up going home to England, and she was entrusted once more to neighbors who, this time, were practically strangers. There she stayed until the day she found her suitcases behind the front door. The label read: "Los Angeles Orphanage." At that moment, she fell apart. She began to scream that she wasn't an orphan, that she wouldn't go there, that her mother was alive. The poor thing! They dragged her by force to the orphanage.

Imagine those years spent in an institution and the trauma it meant for her. I want to cry for all those adolescents who are offered no inspiring perspective and who self-destruct or wander without purpose. Those adolescents to whom you can't talk about love without discussing condoms or abortifacients. To whom you can't talk about life without adding unemployment statistics. To whom you cannot talk, above all, about God, because, for all intents and purposes, He is dead, and people seem to have found something much better, thanks to the pop psychology of New Age thinking and so much else of that false genre.

Marilyn had, in spite of everything, a tiny corner of escape from her unhappiness: that was the movies on Saturday afternoons. She adored the cinema. One of her biographers said that she loved the movies as passionately as a patient hanging onto life in the hope of remission. That was it exactly: she compensated for all that was missing in her life by dreaming alongside the big stars of Hollywood. We can easily imagine the fascination she had for that sparkling universe in the American films of that era. It was the Golden Age of Hollywood when dreams were churned out hand over fist, and Marilyn, more than others, nourished herself heart and soul with the dreams spun on Saturday afternoons.

It was from the movies that Marilyn drew her perception of love, the love that she had yet to experience personally. And it was from the movies that she conceived her mental scheme for how to obtain love, namely through seduction: the super-seduction of the movie stars. For her, that's how love was won, through seduction. And since love alone rendered happiness, she concluded that to be happy in life, you had to be very, very seductive.

During this time of full adolescence, Marilyn experienced something that would dramatically change her existence, something that would reach her very core. The anecdote is so simple and banal that it might have gone unnoticed, but you're going to see what a profound resonance it had in the very fiber of Marilyn's being.

One day, when it was raining and she felt depressed, Marilyn ran away from the orphanage. She was brought back by a policeman and then sent to the office of a woman at the orphanage whom she had never seen before. Naturally, she expected to be scolded, maybe even beaten. But, to her great surprise, the woman approached her with a great deal of love and gave her some dry clothes to replace the rain-soaked ones. The woman took her into her arms and told her she was pretty and had beautiful skin. She called her "my child" and took out her own powder to dab make-up on her. For Marilyn, this was the highlight of her life. She would later write: "It was the first time in my life that I felt loved. No one before had ever noticed my face or my hair or my own self as an individual."

At that point, her whole life changed dramatically, because, for the first time, she had tasted human tenderness! For her, it was a true miracle. And at that point, also, she began an association of ideas which would take her far: if I am loved, it's because I'm pretty and have lovely skin. So, a path was chosen. Marilyn would invest herself completely in her body. If the beauty of her body could unleash such tenderness, she had to gamble everything on it. Because of her beauty, she would finally have access to what she wanted most in the world: to be loved. And for her, to be loved was a matter of life and death.

Without her slightest perception, a spirit of idolatry took form in Marilyn, in that terrain so profoundly wounded by life. How can the absence of God, the absence of any relationship with God, cause such a heart so thirsty for love to fall into idolatry? When the lack of human love is at work burrowing through the heart, a person is ready to do anything to obtain that love. In Marilyn's case, this quest for love would drive her to rush into interminable sittings for make-up and to spend hours posing in front of the mirror studying just what fashions were most seductive, and exactly how to get noticed. Eventually those hours won her the marvel of all the photographers, because no one knew how to work the camera like she did. She had the reputation of being almost magical in that area.

The young girl would be easy prey for the Hollywood industry. She was to become the first woman enjoying the status of a "sex symbol" and she would contribute to that reputation in spite of herself to allow the image of a "femme fatale" and of being easy who would deeply change the mentality of men and be forever in their minds. We know too well the disastrous consequences of this for our society.

Compare her now with little Therese, who went through something similar. At the age of 11, she, too, would experience a determining event: her First Communion. On that day, she said simply, "Oh, how sweet this is, this first kiss from Jesus on my soul!" With one simple anointing, with one simple moment of sweetness, Therese's life was forever changed. She added, "It was a kiss of love. I felt loved, and I responded: 'I love You, and I give myself to You now and always.'"

She may not have been very grown up at that age, but she had already understood everything. After that first kiss, as she wrote, she rushed headlong into what had been revealed to her as the most beautiful of treasures: to be Jesus' beloved and to do nothing other than to be one with Him.

As for Marilyn, after that experience of the "happiness" won by love, she would do as Therese did: she would sacrifice everything to obtain that love in a permanent way and be able, finally, to be satisfied. We will see that, even though the goals were really the same for both women, their paths were different, and it is here that we arrive at the real drama of our story: all paths do not lead you to where you would like to be!

In contrast to Marilyn, Therese was born into a true family, where relationships among its members were marked with great tenderness, profound respect, and high standards. All eyes were fixed on the prizes afforded by the essential values of life. Certainly, Therese had absorbed the knowledge of God and His love right from the cradle. She as far as to say that from the age of three, she never refused God anything. Of course, that was a grace that came from on high, but the terrain below had to have been well prepared for her to welcome that grace.[22]

The Lord was very present in her home. She was asked at the start of each morning, "Have you given your heart to Jesus?" But then, at the age of 4, her paradise came to an end

[22] Theresa's parents Zélie and Louis Martin were canonized on October 18, 2015 by Pope Francis

because her mother, Zélie Martin, died. The wound from this shock was so profound that the happy character of Therese began to change completely. She became timid and afraid of people. Hypersensitive already, she would cry about nothing. Fortunately, her sisters and her father surrounded her with great affection. Despite her age, Therese already had great natural wisdom: she understood that life on earth was nothing but a short journey; that the essential was elsewhere. In addition to her mother's death, Therese also experienced the effects of having three brothers who also died.

At the age of nine, following the departure of her sister Pauline, her second mother, she was overwhelmed by nervous trembling and hallucinations. She experienced terrible fears, which were totally inexplicable. She stayed in her bed, nearly catatonic, and no one really knew what had come over her. She no longer slept, and more importantly, no longer spoke. Her eyes remained fixed in a stare, and that lasted for many months. One day, she managed to cry, "Mama! Mama!" She turned towards the statue of the Virgin, which sat in a place of honor facing the bed. Amazingly, the Mother of God, turned her face towards Therese and smiled at her. "A ravishing smile," Therese would say. "The Holy Virgin looked so beautiful to me, so beautiful. I had never seen anything so beautiful." And with that smile, Therese was instantly cured. The tenderness of the Blessed Mother had penetrated the depth of her soul and delivered her of her terrible malady.

I think the driving force of Therese's life, that inner dynamism which was truly rock solid, was to comprehend very early the ultimate purpose of her existence: to understand the 'why' of life and to marvel over it. Why did she enter the Carmelites; why did she embrace so courageously this monotonous life full of hidden sacrifices? It's because at an early age she experienced the giddy heights of being loved, loved by Love itself! For her, the Carmelite existence was the means of not letting Him out of her sight. It was the supreme adventure of constant heart-to-heart communication, intimate conversations hidden from the eyes of the world.

Now, we are getting to the heart of our topic, which is true adoration, adoration in mind and in truth, so very much linked to that abyss recalled by Therese. To adore, meaning to pour all one's being toward, to focus one's life on, to pray for… You cannot love without having had the experience of the abyss which exists in all of us. To love is to cast our own abyss into the abyss of God. The abyss calling the abyss, as the psalm says. That's the reason that love is at the very doorstep of everyone as the simplest mystical experience of all. I would even say that the need for love is the most visceral need of mankind. Who among us can say that he has never recognized in himself the existential hunger for love and for life? Who has never felt the pain of a hollow heart? To love is simply to throw that abysmal emptiness that we carry around into the even greater depths of God's heart. To quench our thirst in Him who is the wellspring, the only and unique source capable of truly quenching it. I really like these words of Therese, which explain this sentiment so well: "You alone, oh Jesus, can satisfy my soul, because I need to love to the infinity." It is the infinity of our desire which meets the plenitude of His gift.

Marilyn might very well have experienced the second part of that sentence: "I need to love to the infinity." All her adult behavior proved it. But from whom was she expecting this infinity of love? She tried to satisfy her yearning with many around her. And what a drama it was for her to search so far and wide in this quest for love. It was to the point of exhausting all her hope, to the point of despair and suicide. Yes, "You alone can satisfy my soul!" The grace of Therese was to have known very early "the email address and telephone number of Jesus", if I may dare put it that way, of He who could satisfy her soul, and to have been able to pour herself, heart and soul, into the adventure with Him. This grace spared her much wandering and treachery. She herself said it clearly: "With a heart like mine, I ought to be captured and have my wings clipped." And, above all, the mark of genius that the Holy Spirit inspired in her was that of understanding that her littleness, her weakness, her total impotence to do great things by herself was what attracted the love of God the most on her.

We should emphasize that there is a giant chasm between this particular revelation of the Holy Spirit and the murmuring of the spirit of the world, the spirit of the world condemned by Jesus, because it leads to destruction and death. The world tells us at length sometimes that if you want to be successful and be loved, you must be rich. You must be beautiful, intelligent, young and dynamic, profit-making, efficient, in good health if possible; in short, the expectations and norms are excessively harsh and severe. If anyone loses these qualities, he or she is thrown away, abandoned. People aren't interested in that person anymore. Advertising and the whole economic system are entirely founded on this idea. From it comes the terrible anguish of losing in love, losing one's health, losing one's beauty, losing one's youth. And from it comes the obsessive fear of growing old that most of our contemporaries have. The fear of growing weak in any area. The world is cruel beyond measure. Hospital psychiatric wards are full of depressed people who are really just victims of this inhumane mentality.

So, what a breath of fresh air it is to read Therese's work! What a splendid God she reveals to us! What liberation! Are you poor? Then, you are the most cherished. You don't have many gifts? Then all that is Mine is yours; I give it all to you. You're wounded? Then you are, more than others, capable of understanding My mysteries and becoming one with Me. Are you too weak to go up the stairs alone? Well, then, hop into my arms and I will carry you to the top. Here is the true face of love which Therese unveils to us. And I say to her thank you, thank you for having breathed upon the world the breath of the Beatitudes and mercy.

Marilyn was the victim of a confusion which would cost her dearly, since it would eventually take her life. She wanted to become rich in order to acquire love, since in her mind it was beauty which attracted love. She destroyed herself by thinking that beauty was her only asset.

Marilyn became a symbol for our society, and not just a sex-symbol. In her adolescence, when she discovered the impact of her beauty on those around her, she conceived, little by little, a large project. She began to dream of becoming a big star one day. Imagine the atmosphere that she was living in: on the one side, the dreary, banal life in a boarding school, and on the other, a whole new world sparkling with light, full of the captivating adventures and romantic stories delivered by Hollywood movies. Since it's normal for an adolescent to identify with someone he or she admires, Marilyn began to imitate these big stars and to become centered on herself, watching herself live, keeping an eye on the effect that she produced, etc. After her first marriage failed (basically, she married to escape having to stay again at the orphanage), she showed exceptional skills as a beauty model. While at the agency, she became even more fanatical at molding her own image. She relentlessly got caught up in that trap of cupidity. She believed, with an iron-clad will, that by this means everyone would love her, every man would desire her, and that, finally, she would be the queen. She would be the star of stars.

What struck me about Marilyn's logic in her early years, as well as Therese's at the same age, was that both of them had their sights set on the same thing: unconditional love and glory. They each searched furiously for glory and they were right to do so. They were both made for glory, as every one of us is, because God created us for His glory.

Therese had a passion for tales of chivalry and the stories of great heroines, like Joan of Arc: "The good Lord has helped me understand that true glory is the kind that lasts forever!" She wanted that glory! Actually, she just wanted the best. "I used to think that I was born for glory," she wrote, "and while I was searching for the best way to obtain it, the good Lord made me realize that it wasn't necessary to do outstanding works, but to remain hidden and practice virtue. The good Lord made me understand as well that my personal glory would not be evident to mortal eyes, but that it would consist in becoming a great saint."

That's it! Nothing less! When the adolescent Therese crossed through the gates of the Carmelite monastery, she aimed for glory, the kind that Jesus had shown her, the kind, above all, that would come from Him and not from her, the kind that He would pour in to her Himself, drop by drop, into the hidden embrace of His love. He would give His glory to her, for He would make her a queen. Didn't Jesus say in Scripture, "I have given them the glory that You gave to me so that they are one, just as You, Father, are in me and I in You," (John 17). And Therese would be a great saint, she was sure of that, because she knew that God, in His great mercy, never puts a desire in our hearts without the means to achieve it.

The Lord splendidly confirmed all her inspirations! Therese not only became a great saint in Heaven, but her autobiography became known throughout the world. It was a thundering success, an extraordinary best-seller! What a journey she had, this petite, obscure Carmelite, barely out of her adolescence, with no diploma, and sick from tuberculosis! Now, tens of thousands of Christians and non-Christians have begun to devour her book, *The Story of a Soul*, and to live out her spirituality! And now her glory is apparent in the eyes of the world.

It is also the result of a great deal of suffering. The Lord revealed to Therese, a little before her death, the stunning success she would be, and He let her know that the whole world would love her. It is important to remember that this was a glory totally tied to love, as true glory always is, the kind that comes from God. The glory that comes from people engenders divisions and jealousies and eventually fades away forever. We understand now that it was precisely that kind of glory that led Marilyn astray. She found herself in a 'cul de sac'.

Like Therese, Marilyn touched me with her desire to go far, her insane desire to be loved and her ambition to outdo everyone. She was as convinced of all that as Therese was about becoming a saint. Her intuition was basically good: she wanted unconditional love. Her mistake was in not knowing the true and sole source of love. She expected it from people. She expected the glory that comes from man. That glory is simply called vainglory. So, actually, instead of plucking the good fruit of love, and after having enjoyed being the center of the world for a rather short time, she embraced emptiness.

It is certainly difficult to say exactly what God's design was for Marilyn and for her life. Her obsession was truly just beauty – to unleash emotions within others using her beauty. But, instead of connecting herself to the true source of that beauty, she stayed focused on herself, on her own "Ego." She began to slide down that slippery slope that has ruined so many good artists; she allowed herself to be fascinated by her own gifts. You might even say she began to adore her own image. Obviously, she expected others to adore her. Here we touch the core of idolatry. Idolatry means "the adoring of an image." What drama! She bore within her this overwhelming desire to adore, this desire to plunge herself into an abyss of love, which was so noble. And that is how she turned away, no doubt unconsciously, the amazing potential for love in order to embrace her own image. It was at that moment, without even being aware, that she destined herself for despair. As we might say today, she bought her ticket to despair. And, since she always took things to the extreme, she quite literally condemned herself to death. As for the path she chose, whose fault was it considering her childhood?

While Therese was faithfully and lovingly accompanied on the spiritual level from her very infancy, Marilyn instead never had anyone to confide in. She was constantly left to her own fantasies; no one would show her any direction in life. No one helped her to attach her desire to the One who could fulfill it magnificently. Moreover, she was the victim at that time, of a sect that we see multiplying in the United States where her best friend would sometimes bring her. It was a rather esoteric sect in which the triumph of the individual ego prevailed over all, and in which the voice of instinct was a manifestation of the divine spirit.

Marilyn quickly climbed up the steps that led to her celebrity status. She created quite a furor on the big screen. She earned millions of dollars for her producers. Everyone wanted her. Her image was all over publicity posters as well as on the walls of private homes. Every woman wanted to look like her, and some even had their faces redone in order to have her nose, her mouth, and everything else. Men dreamed of holding her in their arms (to put it mildly). In short, she had become a true LA star in the fullest sense of the term. She still incarnates today the feminine object, the woman born to seduce, but from whom no one can demand anything else.

At first, Marilyn totally integrated this personality within her; but one day, she arrived at a crisis: she had had enough of this futile image of herself. She was less and less willing to accept the artificial exaltation of her personality and her identity. And so, there began to grow, little by little, a terrible chasm between her public image – what everyone expected of her – and her genuine poverty, real and piercing, her difficulty in finding happiness, her interior solitude, her chronic insomnia, and, perhaps, the specter of the insanity which might come from her mother and her grandparents. Anxiety gradually took over. She saw a psychiatrist every day, and assuaged herself with medication. It appears as though, at that moment, she would have loved to cry out that she was not only a desirable body, but that she had a heart as well and, especially, a soul; that she had more to give than her legendary sensuality; that she refused to be imprisoned in this person limited to its curves and vampy smile.

In the biographies of Marilyn, I searched a long time for any truly spiritual words that might have come from her mouth. I admit that I had some trouble doing this, but I finally found one sentence. At the height of her fame, she repeated often to those near her these words of Jesus: "Of what profit is it for a man to gain the whole world if he loses his own soul?" (Mark 8:36) What lucidity! She had an intimate awareness, while she was in the process of losing herself.

As for me, I don't believe at all in fate. Marilyn could have very well become a great saint simply by remaining faithful to the inspirations that the Lord was sending her, instead of conforming to the world, which was contemptuous of God.

As for Therese, she could have very well become an unbearable, spoiled little girl, a conventional child, satisfied with herself, who spent her time taking advantage of those around her, and taking everything for granted. One thing is certain, and that is that Marilyn did not receive any less grace than Therese.

The history of the Church demonstrates that people far more depraved than Marilyn reach a very high degree of sanctity. When, in the last years of her life, Marilyn saw that her existence was basically nothing but emptiness, solitude and desolation, she could have cried out, "Jesus, save me! I am not worthy, but take me into your arms and forgive me!" Yes, she could have said that. Who knows what was going on inside her conscience – perhaps only God. But she didn't believe that God's mercy was for her. Did she think that the ultimate door of salvation was closed to her, and did she die in that thought?

It was ruled that her death was a "probable suicide" that took place in her apartment in Los Angeles with the help of sleeping pills. However, this death came about at a moment when Marilyn decided not to follow the path designed for her, that of a seductress. At the time of Marilyn's death many voices hypothesized that she was assassinated. Recently, in April 2015, on his deathbed, Norman Hodges, a CIA agent, declared that he had killed Marilyn Monroe with his own hands and then made her death look like a suicide. She was 36 years old, it was August 5, 1962, the Vigil of the Transfiguration.

At the Carmelite monastery of Lisieux, nearly 70 years earlier, an event took place which is strongly connected to the life of Marilyn and which certainly changes the issue. On that day, an image came to the eyes of Little Therese. It was Jesus on the cross, and Therese only noticed one detail: His pierced hands were streaming blood; this blood fell onto the ground, and there was no one to collect it. It was lost in the ground. Therese was struck to the depths of her soul. She understood in a flash both the drama of God and the drama of mankind. Two thirsts which were not united. God was lacking man, who was not coming to quench his thirst at the source, and man was desperately lacking God, because his soul was made for Him. Man was basically dying of thirst right next to the spring! Marilyn died of thirst beside the spring, and the spring was tortured, because it couldn't give its water to her. God is tortured like a lover whose love is rejected and despised.

Therese, who could not endure such a situation, offered herself as an intermediary between these two thirsts of love. That way, they could quench each other, cure each other. Now, who better than Therese could understand the gaping wound of a damaged heart unable to embrace the object of its love? At the age of 4, after the death of her mother, she fell ill, and gravely so! For years, she was haunted by the suffering of those who didn't know that they were loved by God, loved by Love Itself; she knew that there was no infirmity greater than that in the life of man. However, she had never before this day understood with such acuity that Jesus was the poorest, the most bereft of those who begged for love. He comes, hat in hand, to beg for our Yes, like a child who has no way to force our response. Jesus respects us far too much. So, in order that Jesus finally be loved, that people finally be able to throw themselves into His arms (especially the greatest sinners), Therese had an idea, or rather a brilliant inspiration: she would offer herself to the Merciful Love.

What does that mean? Of course, she still followed her well known little way, which is to seize each opportunity, each event of daily life and make it an act of love. But, in a way, this new offering gave God complete permission to use her as fertile terrain onto which His mercy could fall and spread into the hearts of mankind. A terrain where, even in bloody combat, the mercy which is offered faces the indifference of man. The Divine Mercy and its refusal by mankind.

In making this offering of herself, Therese was prepared to suffer from the combat, of course. But the stakes were too great, too important: she was going to be able to bring back to God thousands and thousands of sinners; she was going to break down the bars of her convent to join them wherever they were. She said that her offering would extend "everywhere in the world and to the end of time." How can anyone resist such inner force? It was stronger than her! The immense compassion for souls that the Lord put in her heart burned within her. She would say, "All at once I was overcome with such a violent love of the Good Lord that I can't explain it, except by saying that it was as if I had been suddenly plunged wholly into a fire. Oh, what a fire and what gentleness at the same time! I was burning with love, and I felt that one minute, one second longer and I couldn't endure this ardor without dying."

So now she was ready for her martyrdom of love! She was going to carry this extraordinary fire of love to the most distant of souls, the most depraved, the most separated from God, even to those who consciously said No to His love and to His forgiveness. Sometime later, Therese came to "sit at the table of sinners" as Jesus did 2000 years ago, not as a rich guest or as a star, certainly not! She had said Yes to spiritual combat, and there she was, plunged into full battle, that murderous battle between light and darkness, between passionate love and the obstinate refusal of that love.

After her pledge, she was invaded by the sentiments and thoughts even of those who did not know God, and she was tortured interiorly by their own torture. She ate the bread of their despair and their bitterness, and her usual consolations disappeared. This was the vertiginous experience of the dark and endless night of people who walked in the shadows; it was like a descent into hell, undoubtedly similar to Marilyn's. Therese then said: "Never did I believe that it was possible to suffer so much, never, never! I can't explain myself except by the ardent desire I had to save souls." It makes sense. She had buried herself in the very heart of God, so why is it astonishing that the darkness of sin made her suffer so much?

She had so often tasted the atrocious suffering of despair that she thought of committing suicide. "If I hadn't had faith, I would have taken my own life without hesitation," she wrote. Ah, yes, like Marilyn! At the point where she should have seen Heaven, she saw only a wall, a wall which stretched all the way to the sky. With the permission of God, Satan tried to make Therese believe that Heaven did not exist. But even though she experienced with great intensity the secret drama of sinners and non-believers, she didn't try to stop her own suffering; she continued to offer everything up and to believe, despite the darkness. She even said that, with her entourage, she was as "cheerful as a lark."

She could well have floundered and completely sunk under the hostile and demonic forces which had elected to live with her. But no, love was stronger than all of them. Therese went from victory to victory. And because she had gone through these three years of cruel trials with faith and love, she reached the hardest of hearts and poured love into them. That's how she became the mother of a multitude of souls, who, thanks to her, found the light. She won! All these big and small "Yeses" in the midst of suffering annihilated all the big and small "Nos" of those who refused God.

As she had so often prophesied, her victories would extend to the end of the centuries. Do you know anyone who does not believe, anyone who wanders aimlessly or who suffers? Pray to Therese! You'll see! She has carved out for herself a solid reputation, and not only in the Church.

Even in the field of show business, Therese was active and super-efficacious! Let's take, for example, the famous French singer Edith Piaf: as a child, she was almost blind, and it was thanks to Saint Therese the Little Flower that she was cured. So each day, and especially before her shows, Edith Piaf prayed to her on her knees. Therese had become her intimate friend and consoled her. She accompanied her right up to her last breath.

I am sure that invisibly Therese was standing at Marilyn's bedside during those long, long nights when Marilyn was planning her own destruction as the only possible solution, even if that solution terrified her. Yes, I dare say that Therese was there, near Marilyn, that infamous last night when the massive dose of sleeping pills plunged her into her ultimate agony because Therese, since offering herself to the merciful God, was inseparable from the destiny of sinners.

Imagine this: That night, when Marilyn presented herself to her Creator and Savior, Therese put in a good word and told her: "Don't worry, Marilyn, I have a passport for you. You and my family have experienced the same things, both of us. I'm familiar with your hell: I spent years there. You have only to tell Jesus that you are me, and I am you. And then, embrace humbly, very humbly, His heart, which gives us the true Fire, and which has always called you by name. You have come home, Marilyn. Here He is at last, the One you were looking for!"

Lumping together these sketches of Marilyn and Therese will demonstrate that there is no misery without a response of mercy! It will also demonstrate that those who love and adore God with all their hearts and with all their strength on this earth will act as escorts on the way to Heaven for those who have invested everything in vanities or vain idols. The true believers are "God's delivery men," and they bear on their shoulders all lost children and bring them to the Father; they stick right with them! And we can imagine what Marilyn and Therese would say to one another when meeting in Heaven. I picture Marilyn talking with Therese and saying to her:

"Therese, when I see your life … It's incredible! As for me, if I had possessed only a quarter of the love you had for Jesus, I would have performed all my life for Him and only for Him! I would have incarnated all the women of Scripture, even the Virgin Mary. I would have done tremendous media hype for Him. You would have seen the scoops! His image would have flashed on all the screens of Hollywood! All of America would have been converted!"

"Marilyn, when I see your life, I cry! I would never have been able to endure what you endured. Knowing myself, I would not have been able to wait 36 years to commit suicide; I don't know how you got up in the morning without being able to tell yourself that your suffering had meaning, without resting your head on a true heart who would never abandon you. I don't know how you lasted so long in despair, in a life which was shattered to pieces... But you see, Marilyn, deep down, I thank you, because it's because of you that I entered the Carmelites, thirty years before you were born, even without knowing you! It was your distress which compelled me to enclose myself in that voluntary prison. It was your cry that haunted me day and night and which broke my heart! It was because of that cry that I had the courage to give up my life little by little and to descend into the arena of hell to bring you to Jesus. It was because of you, Marilyn, and because of all the Marilyns of the world that I was driven to love, yes, to love right to the end, even so far as to die for love! Because you see, Marilyn, I'm going to tell my secret to you, to you who have always wanted to be the queen of love. The summit of love is Jesus, who taught me this. Here it is: "There is no greater love than this: to lay down one's life for those you love," (John 15:13).

20
Be Me!

Thailand 1992. Parish of Our Lady of Fatima in Prachuab.

Cruising along in his minibus, Father John Tamayot felt satisfied. For many years, he never stopped serving his community of the Salesians, and he was proud of having constructed some magnificent buildings to meet the needs of the children they sheltered. He had come up with the ideas, discussed them with the architects, transported the materials, overseen the construction; in short, he worked very hard for its success. At the age of 50, his efficiency was unquestioned by anyone.

While in the minibus, the children were horsing around behind him. All of a sudden an unhappy angst came over him. He couldn't breathe. Nothing seemed right. In front of him, everything went dark. It was a total blackout! Somehow he managed to stop the vehicle. After he was taken by ambulance to the hospital, the doctors diagnosed the incident as a minor cerebral accident due to an anomaly in his neck. "We're going to stretch your neck to relieve it," said a doctor. Basically, after carrying heavy loads for the construction work in his missions – cement, wood, sand – he had tremendously damaged his neck and it had become calcified.

When they began to stretch his neck, he lost all feeling in his right arm! He cried out, "Stop!" But the doctor had just committed a serious medical error. The entire right side of Father John's body became paralyzed. After that he endured long sessions of physical therapy to bring the feeling back, Father John found himself among the invalids in Wing 7 of the hospital.

"How can I stand the rest of my life as an invalid in this wing?" he asked himself. A terrible heaviness came over him. The seeds of depression were planted. Night after night Father John felt increasingly distressed, and feelings of despair took hold of him. There he was, confined to his bed with nothing to do, with no hope of getting better. It was he, the tireless and active worker par excellence. What a contrast with his former life of activity and meeting acquaintances! Struggling with his solitude, and with a terrible feeling of powerlessness, he cried out to the Lord every day: "Help! Help!"

Three months later, in the chapel of the hospital, where Father John was transported every day from his room, he cried out to the Lord the same plea of distress, but this time he added: "This is too much, I can't take it anymore! Take me away from it, I beg You! I want to die!"

Suddenly, he heard the voice of Christ, who asked him:

"My son, how old am I?"

Father John replied, "Lord, You're 33 years old!"

"And you?"

"I'm 50."

"Why haven't you ever thanked Me? I gave you 18 more years to live. At 33 I had already died."

"Yes, Lord. I'm sorry. Forgive me for never having appreciated these extra 18 years of life You gave me."

"You have spoken well about me John, but you do not know me. *Taste Me*." (Father John reported that Jesus stressed the words 'Taste Me'.)

"Lord, what do You mean by telling me this?"

"My son, I didn't consecrate you to be a worker. I didn't consecrate you to be an administrator. I consecrated you to be ME. *Be Me*!

Father John was dumbfounded when he heard the way Jesus said "Be Me!" Jesus added: "While I was suffering, I felt abandoned, rejected, condemned, and nailed. It was a very painful situation. Now, you know."

Father John's being was turned completely inside out. Beginning to comprehend the deep significance of the words of Jesus, he said: "Yes, Lord, thank you for giving me the opportunity to truly re-live Your pain and suffering. Thank you for reminding me that you have consecrated me to *be You*."

From that day on, a great peace came over him, and Father John remained always calm.

Jesus was simply waiting for that moment to pursue His plan of mercy for Father John. A little while after this incredible dialogue, *His* priest began to move the fingers on his right hand. Day by day, Father's legs found their old mobility. Thanks to prayer and re-education, things improved, to the point that all the patients in Wing 7 asked him: "What medication are you on? Where can we buy it?" He told them, "It's the Lord Jesus, only the Lord! Believe in God!"

In light of his unexpected progress, the medical team decided to do an MRI on Father John. The examination showed that his neck was still calcified. They were going to have to operate. But the surgery had only a 50% chance of success. It was all or nothing! Father John put himself in God's hands: "Lord," he said. "I'm depending entirely on You. I give You my life. Take care of me!"

The operation lasted 10 hours. Father John's neck was strengthened with 36 screws and 3 large plates. The success of the operation was quickly realized. He was able to move his fingers, arms, and legs!

It was during my mission in Bangkok, that I met Father John. His face glowed when sharing with me the secret of his happiness: "Now, I have complete trust in the Lord. He consecrated me to *BE HIM*, so I leave everything up to Him. I see my ministry as being a priest for HIM, because I know that it is really HE who lives in me and that He accomplishes through me His work of preaching, healing, and liberating. So let's praise and thank the Lord. May my experience be for His greater glory!"

Father John understood a reality that concerns all of us. Before, he was performing one thousand and one works for God, where prayer was dangerously missing. Through his dereliction of a handicapped person, the Lord made him understand that He was expecting from His priest that he would perform the works OF God, rather than FOR God. That is to say, the works that God Himself had prepared for him to realize according to his Divine design. Father John's generosity was indeed beautiful and worthy to be praised, but Jesus expected more from him. He wanted to teach Fr. John to abandon himself so that he could cooperate in the Divine work of the Lord. From then on Fr. John has been so much more fruitful as a worker for God, and as a priest, he is and will be "another Christ".

21
A Successful Abortionist's Transformation

Dr. Stojan Adasevic, Serbia

Stojan couldn't sleep. Here he was, the renowned gynecologist of Belgrade, the man everyone flocked to because of his well-known dexterity, reduced to seeking counsel from a psychiatrist to solve his problem. How could a big shot like Stojan have to see a shrink? It made the whole world seem upside down!

Frankly, he was terror-stricken. For months, every night, he had the same dream and wondered if he was going crazy. He tried everything to alleviate the dreams: herbal teas, medicines, but nothing worked.

Night after night, week after week, month after month, his dream carried him off to a huge meadow bathed in sunlight, covered in magnificent flowers in dazzling hues. The air was warm and pleasant, and multi-colored butterflies flitted here and there.

In the middle of this paradise of beauty, Stojan's anguish overwhelmed him, and it was impossible to break away from the bizarre heaviness that accompanied such a beautiful dream, with no apparent cause. It completely baffled him.

Who is Doctor Stojan Adasevic?[23]

Even as a medical student, he exhibited the promise of a brilliant career. In Communist Belgrade of the 1960s, he decided to be a gynecologist.

In such an atheistic environment, he was convinced that abortion, as it was taught in the faculties of Medicine, was a simple surgical procedure, similar to an appendectomy. The only difference being the organ to be removed: part of the intestine in one case, and embryonic tissue in the other.

However, throughout his career he was given every oppor-

---

[23] In order to support his point of view, Stojan Adasevic revealed the current practice in Serbia: "Since our laws only protect the life of the child from the moment he takes his first breath, the moment he begins to cry, abortions are legal up to the 7th, 8th, and 9th month of pregnancy." But it gets worse. Stojan spoke about a bucket of water. What's a bucket of water doing beside a woman about to give birth? Before the child has a chance to utter a cry, the abortionist plugs his mouth to prevent him from crying and plunges him into the water. Officially, since the child never cried, he wasn't truly born, and that makes the murder perfectly legal under the term abortion.

At his conferences, Dr. Adasevic quotes Mother Teresa of Calcutta, canonized on September 4, 2016: "If a mother can kill her own child, what can prevent us, you and me, from killing another?" Doctor Adasevic discussed this with the monks on Mount Athos. They made the distinction between methods of contraception and the method of abortion. Abortive methods kill a baby that has already been conceived. That's precisely what the IUD pill and RU486 do. The IUD device, according to the monks, act like a sword that separates the tiny human being from its source of alimentation in the uterus.

Stojan continued: "This is a real war, declared by those who are born against those who are not yet born. In this war, I have found myself on the front lines in different roles: first as the fetus condemned to death, then as an abortion doctor myself, and now as an apostle for the defense of life. It took time for me to grasp that the child in the womb of its mother is a living person well before his birth and his first breath. Contrary to what the Communist professors taught us, the child is living from the instant that the embryo is formed; that is, from the moment the sperm meets the egg."

tunity to see things very differently. Let's go back to a significant episode he experienced during his studies. One day he was in the waiting room at the medical office of the university putting some patient files in order, when a group of gynecologists entered the room. Without paying the slightest bit of attention to this student, hunkered down behind his pile of papers, the doctors began to freely exchange stories about their medical practices. Dr. Rado Ignatovic brought up the painful memory of a woman who came to him to inquire about an abortion. He recalled how he had proceeded with the intervention, but that it had completely failed, and the child was born alive. Then he recounted the woman's entire life story, dropping as an aside that she was a dentist who practiced in a clinic not far away.

Stojan took in every detail of the story until, suddenly he froze, stupefied. He came to the realization that this woman was none other than his own mother!

"She's dead now," one of the gynecologists happened to mention. "I wonder what became of the unwanted child?"

The force was stronger than he was. Stojan could not resist. He got up and exclaimed loudly to all of them: "I am that child!"

A deathly silence fell over those in the room, and, in the seconds that followed, one by one the doctors excused themselves from the room with their heads hanging low.

Years went by, and Dr. Stojan Adasevic never forgot that he owed his life to a failed abortion. It was out of the question for him to do such a stupid thing! Very quickly, he surpassed his professor both in dexterity and fame. "The secret lies in training, in practice, and in the position of the hand," he would say. Faithful to that maxim, he carried out 20 to 30 abortions per day, and at one time he estimated that he performed around 50,000 abortions over the twenty-six years of his practice.

One day in the 1980's, a certain doubt began to enter his mind. New techniques using ultrasound arrived in Yugoslavia. For the first time, Stojan saw on a monitor a reality that, until then, had been hidden from his eyes: the inside of a uterus carrying a living baby, sucking its thumb and moving its arms and legs. Now, one time out of every two, during the course of an abortion, he used to casually lay on the table beside him the fragments of the baby's limbs. But this discovery was still not enough to help him comprehend what he was doing.

Just at that time, his recurrent dream started to become a nightmare. In the beginning, during the first few weeks of his dream, he was only a passing character, who was happy to look around him. But then the beautiful meadow in which he was walking filled up with children who ran, laughed, and played ball games. They seemed to range from three to twenty years old. Stojan was struck by their immense beauty.

In particular, he noticed one boy and two girls whose faces looked strangely familiar, and he asked himself where he might have seen them before. He decided to talk to them. But he had scarcely begun to approach them, when they took off running and screaming from him in fear. Stojan then noticed the presence of a man who was silent and dressed in a black cape. He was looking at the scene attentively. Was this the guardian of the children? The dream woke Stojan up in the middle of the night, and he remained awake until morning, unable to get back to sleep.

One night, in his dream, seized with an unexplainable anxiety, he began to follow the children who were fleeing from him. He succeeded in capturing one, but the petrified child cried out, "Help, help, murderer! Save me from the hands of this killer!" At that moment, the man dressed in black, transformed himself into an eagle, flew towards him and snatched the child from his hands. Stojan woke up with a jolt, terrified. His heart was beating frantically. His room in Belgrade that winter had been cold, but now he was dripping with sweat.

That morning, he decided to call a psychiatrist to make an appointment.

The nightmare inexorably continued. So, Stojan decided to speak to the mysterious man dressed in black and ask him who he was. The stranger answered: "Even if I told you, my name would mean nothing to you." But Stojan, determined not to be deterred from his question, persisted. Finally, the man responded: "My name is Thomas Aquinas." Truthfully, that name didn't ring a bell with Stojan. Never heard of him! But the man in black continued: "Why didn't you ask me, instead, who the children are? Don't you recognize them?" The doctor answered in the negative. The man went on: "That's not true, you know them very well! Those are the children you killed when you performed abortions."

Stojan couldn't accept it. "How is that possible?" He retorted. "Those children are big. I've never killed any children who were already born." Thomas answered: "Don't you know that here, in the great beyond, in the other world, children continue to grow?"

The doctor didn't give up: "But I never killed a 20-year-old young man."

"You killed him twenty years ago in his mother's womb," Thomas answered, "when he was three months along."

At that point Stojan had to surrender to the evidence. He had to admit that he did recognize the faces of the twenty-year-old and the two little girls. Then he realized that he could have easily mistaken them for people he knew well, people who had asked him to perform an abortion in the past. The young man actually resembled one of his friends. Stojan had performed an abortion on his wife twenty years earlier. As for the young girls, the doctor recognized in them, their mothers, especially one of them who was his own cousin. From the moment of that revelation, he promised himself he would never perform an abortion again in his life.

That morning, when he arrived at the hospital, Stojan found another one of his cousins waiting for her boyfriend. They had made an appointment to have an abortion. She was four months pregnant and wanted to get rid of the child. This would be her ninth abortion. At first, Stojan refused, but faced with the insistence of his cousin, he ended up giving in. "Okay," he said, "but this is the very last time."

What followed was unexpected, to say the least. On the ultrasound monitor he clearly saw that the child was sucking his thumb. What happened next is best explained by Stojan himself:

"I opened the uterus and tore the placenta, after which the sac of water broke, and I could work well with my forceps. I latched onto something that I broke, extracted, and tossed onto a towel. I looked and I saw a hand … a rather large hand. The baby was four months along, he was entirely formed at this stage, including his fingers and toes, and all his organs were there.

"Someone spilled iodine on the table and the hand had fallen on that spot, so that the nerve endings came into contact with the liquid. What happened? I looked and said to myself: 'My God, the hand moved by itself.'

Stojan's whole body was trembling, but he continued with the abortion.

"I continued with my forceps, in spite of everything," he said. "I caught upon something else, which I broke and extracted. 'I hope it's not a leg,' I said to myself. I pulled it out and looked: a leg! I wanted to put the leg on the table gently, so it wouldn't be next to the moving hand. My arm was reaching down to lay it there, but at that instant, a nurse dropped a tray of surgical instruments behind me. Surprised by the noise, I jumped and loosened my grip on the forceps. Immediately, the leg fell and landed near the hand. I looked. The hand and the leg were moving by themselves.

"My team and I had never seen anything like it: human limbs were contracting in rapid tremors on the table. I continued, all the same, directing my instrument into the uterus, and I began to break everything inside it. I told myself that, to finish the job, I only had to find the heart. I continued to crush, to crush, and to crush enough to be certain that I had reduced to a pulp everything that remained inside, and I took out my forceps again. I extracted this pulp, telling myself that it had to be made up of bone fragments, and I put it on the towel. I looked and saw a human heart, which was contracting, which was losing momentum but was beating, beating. I thought I was going crazy. I saw the beatings of the heart slow down, more slowly, ever more slowly, until finally they stopped altogether. No one could have seen what I saw with my own eyes and been more convinced than I of what I had just done: I had killed a human being."

His own heart was beating wildly, and everything went dark around him. How long that lasted, he couldn't say. But the terrified voice of a nurse shook him out of his inertia: "Doctor Adasevic, Doctor Adasevic!" she cried. "The patient is bleeding out!" For the first time since his childhood, he began to pray with sincerity: "Lord! Don't save me, but save this woman!"

Stojan saved the woman's life and finished his work. When he took off his gloves, he knew that he had performed his last abortion.

As he might have expected, because he refused to perform any more abortions, strong condemnations were unleashed against him. Never, until then, in any Belgrade hospital, had anyone seen a gynecologist refuse to do abortions. In addition to the pressure exerted on him, his salary was diminished. His daughter was fired, and his son strangely failed his entrance exams to the university. People were saying that the Socialist State had permitted him to study so that he could perform abortions, and now, by not performing them, he was trying to sabotage the State.

At the end of two years under such persecution, Stojan found himself nearly burned out, to the point that he thought about performing abortions again. But the man in black, his heavenly friend, appeared to him in a dream. He told him, while patting him on the shoulder: "You are my friend, my good friend. Keep fighting!" Stojan decided to continue the struggle.

Stojan Adasevic Today

Stojan Adasevic wasted no time joining the pro-life movement. He traveled all over Serbia, giving conferences and lectures on abortion. Twice, on Dr. Bernard Nathanson's program, which aired on Yugoslav state television, he even succeeded to put in a good word for the unforgettable film, *The Silent Scream.*[24]

Thanks to the struggle of Stojan Adasevic, the Yugoslav Parliament passed a measure in the beginning of the 1990's to protect the rights of unborn children. The measure went to the President, Slobodan Milosevic, of sinister character, who refused to sign it. Then, the war of the Balkans broke out and the measure fell into oblivion.

During that war, Stojan tells that he asked himself: 'to what else can we attribute the massacre that is taking place here in the Balkans, if not to our estrangement from God and our lack of respect for human life?'

[24] This film, on the big screen, reveals the behavior of a baby who is happily basking in the uterus of its mother, but who, on seeing the probe of the abortionist coming at him, is seized with fear and tries to take refuge in another part of the uterus. But unable to find a safe space he is quickly aspirated by the instrument of death that had been coming after him.

22
They Crack Me Up!

Children in Kota Kinabalu, Malaysia. © Photo Foo 2016

Children's innocence allows them to have very sensitive connections with the Angels and to the celestial world in general. Their little hearts are marvelous captors of the light of God, because only recently have they emerged from the hands of the Creator. Here are some quotations from children. They confirm that these little ones are often placed in our midst to be our mystical teachers.

The Little Red Hen

My friend Cathy cuddled up with her five-year-old daughter Marie before bed. Together they planned to embark on a journey reading *The Little Red Hen*. You'll remember that in this tale for children, a little red hen finds a grain of wheat. She asks the other animals on the farm – the pig, the cat, and the frog – to help her plant it, but none of them are willing to help.

At harvest time, she asks the other animals to help her gather in the wheat, but each of them finds an excuse, and the little red hen finds herself harvesting all alone. Then comes threshing time, and no one comes to help her. The same thing happens when the time comes to grind the wheat and bake the bread: the little hen asks for help from the other animals, but once again, each of them finds an excuse to run away.

Once her work is done, the little red hen asks, with a smile on her beak, who wants to help eat the bread. This time, all those who hadn't wanted to help her make the bread are eager to eat it. But the little red hen looks them right in the eyes and says: "You have always refused to help me in the work of preparation. You left me alone every time I needed you. Now I'm going to eat my bread alone with my little chicks. So there!"

So, the little red hen ate the bread with her chicks and left not a morsel for the other animals, who had displayed such laziness. The moral of the story: those who do not want to work do not deserve to profit from the fruit of the work of others.

After closing the book, Cathy looked down at her daughter to check her reaction to the story. Little Marie gazed into her mother's eyes, obviously disappointed, and with a very sad expression on her face said: "But, if the little red hen had been Jesus, she would have shared her bread with the others anyway!"

He Adored Love!

At three and a half, Lou was a very precocious little boy with an innate sense of God, and an unbelievable intelligence about His mysteries. One day, while he and his mother were standing in front of a church, Lou's mother began to recall how Lou had been baptized in this very church at the age of one. After hearing his mother tell the story, Lou became very serious and affirmed her saying: "Yes, I remember! It was here that they plunged me into the blood of Christ!"

Around the age of four, Lou asked his mother an astonishing question: "Tell me, Mama, aren't you worried about Jesus?" "No, why?" she answered him. Lou said: "I've seen him on the Cross, and he had his mouth open. It looks like he was having a lot of trouble breathing." Lou had never learned that on the Cross Jesus stopped breathing; he died asphyxiated.

One day they found Lou dressed in a sheet. The sheet had a hole in it and the little one had slipped his head through it. When asked what he was playing, he explained: "Well, this is my priest robe!" So, his mother, astonished, asked him why he wanted to be a priest. He answered in a completely factual tone: "Because I adore Love!"

Another story of the wonders of children's knowledge of God came to me from a friend of mine, Grazia Leotta. She told the following story about her nephew. "One day, when leaving school to go home, my six-and-a-half year-old nephew, David, told me in all seriousness: "Today Jesus told me that the more I count on Him, the more I bring back a victory over Satan!" Who knows what children receive from the heart of God in their daily lives!

It reminds me of a story from another friend of mine, Laurence, who is now 49. One day we were telling these stories of children over coffee and she said: "When I was young, around the age of seven, a sentence from Scripture particularly affected me. It was, "The Son of Man has nowhere to lay his head." That's really upsetting! Poor Jesus didn't even have a place to sleep? Terrible! I racked my brain trying to figure out what I could do? In my childlike heart, I found a very simple solution: every night, I pressed myself against the wall, so I could leave him as much space as possible in my bed."

Sometimes, children receive surprising inner enlightenment and their solutions to practical questions are wonderful! Their souls are so transparent!

At dawn one morning, little Bénédicte, all of eleven years old, was still upset and overwhelmed by a very real dream that had invaded her sleep. To her it did not seem like a dream at all, but rather real life. It felt so true that it really scared her. In her dream, two sinister men had been following her. Their intention was clear: they wanted to kill her. She began to run, but inevitably they were gaining on her. It was only a matter of seconds and she would be lost, and she would die. Her heart beat one hundred miles an hour. Suddenly, someone appeared. Despite her surprise, she recognized him immediately. He was wearing the same cassock she had seen him in on television. More than that, it was that same smile and look, full of goodness that convinced her of his identity. It was Paul VI, the Pope she held so dear. He squared himself between the two men and little Bénédicte, and assured her with great gentleness that he was going to protect her. He asked her to go up higher to hide. The little girl protested: "No, Holy Father, it's too dangerous. They're going to take you and hurt you. You have to run away!" But the good pope answered that he was risking nothing and that no one could do him any harm at all. "For me, they are too late," he assured her. "Hide yourself, my little one!"

To her, in her dream, it was clear that the pope had just saved her life by sacrificing his own. When Bénédicte woke up a short time later, very moved by this strange and powerful dream, she went into the kitchen and was met with a shock. It was August 7, 1978. The radio was just then announcing terrible news that gave her dream an unbelievable dimension: Pope Paul VI had died the previous night between the 6th and 7th of August.

Before entering whole-heartedly into the Love of the Father, had he perhaps been given time to take care of a little girl in danger? These are the wonderful mysteries of the faith revealed to the little ones.

To those who are Innocent, Riches are Given!

A lot of families don't think about encouraging their children to pray: what a shame, what a loss! Early childhood is a unique and privileged time when the soul is still completely pure, and that time will never return. Thanks to their profoundly sensitive spiritual antennae, these little ones draw from prayer great riches for their souls, which will later be wonderful points of reference in a world so anxious to corrupt them. Depriving children of the opportunity to pray and experience God's revelation is a great injustice. Quite simply it retards them, even disables them. And to what gain? The innocent hearts of children are splendors in the eyes of God, who basks in them with delight. An innocent heart obtains everything from God! And when it's a matter of scandalizing even one of these little ones, Jesus, normally so merciful when faced with human weaknesses, does not mince his words: "If anyone causes one of these little ones who believe in Me to stumble, it would be better for him to have a large millstone hung around his neck and to be drowned in the depths of the sea," (Mt. 18: 6 and Luke 17: 2).

Parents have great power over the spiritual life of their children, sometimes too great a power: they can either crush their child's innocence, or they can help it flourish and yield fruit.

I remember little Matthew, who was six at the time I heard this story about him. His mother announced to him that, this year he would still go to catechism, but he would no longer go to "Children's Adoration," because, she said, "On top of catechism, it's too much!" Matthew was used to going each week to a church in Paris, where, along with other children, he was learning how to adore Jesus in the Eucharist. He just loved that time, because the priest who accompanied them talked to them and to Jesus from the abundant riches of his heart. He opened their eyes to a marvelous God with whom they could freely speak. He introduced them to a loving God who paid attention to their little, everyday stories. Desperate at seeing this heavenly time taken away, Matthew cried out: "But, Mom, you don't understand! At Catechism, I'm learning about Jesus, but at Children's Adoration, I learn how to love Him!" Thank God, faced with such a declaration, the mother gave in and little Matthew was able to continue developing the secret layers of his beautiful soul in front of his God, who was hidden in the Eucharist… Oh, the splendor of those humble dialogues between that tiny little man and the God that made Himself so small as well! The joy of the angels, we just cannot imagine!

Even though they are rarities, there still exist some civilizations that are very close to nature and to the Creator, isolated in a distant terrain and protected from the viruses of our more materialistic society. There, among those people, you can also find rare pearls of evangelic freshness.

Here is a beautiful testimony recounted by Agostino Ricotta, a father of five, a musician, and a prayer group leader with Renewal in the Spirit in Sicily who composed many of the songs still used during Adoration in Medjugorje. Agostino studied with Father Slavko, and for seven years he voluntarily and wholeheartedly gave himself over to the service of the parish of Medjugorje.

While in Medjugorje, Agostino met an Italian priest who often accompanied groups of pilgrims. By the end of Agostino's years there, he had developed a real friendship with this priest. Then suddenly Agostino didn't see him anymore, and he wondered what had become of his friend. Three or four years later, the priest came back to Medjugorje and explained his absence to Agostino:

"I was sent by my community to a remote little village in South America as a missionary. There, the inhabitants didn't know anything about the Christian faith. They had never heard of Jesus or Mary. So, I had to give them the ABC's of the Catechism. I spoke to them about Jesus, about Scripture, about His miracles and His teachings, about the Sacraments, etc. That group of very simple people willingly listened to the Good News with an open heart and many asked to be baptized. One day, when I was celebrating Sunday Mass, a woman approached the altar right before the Consecration. She was carrying a dying child in her arms. To my great surprise, she laid the child down on the altar. Right at that moment, I was disconcerted and I asked her: 'What are you doing?' She answered: 'You said that, when you consecrate the bread, Jesus is physically present in that bread and that the Jesus who comes to us on the altar in the host is the same as the one who lived 2000 years ago. That Jesus passed among us, did good things for everyone, touched and healed the sick. If what you said is true, if Jesus is coming to us on the altar, he simply has to touch and heal my little boy! I am very poor, and I don't have the money to go to the doctor or to buy medicine.'

"In the face of such a declaration, I answered: 'It's okay. You can leave him here.' So she left her child on the altar, and after the Consecration, the child was healed! You should have seen the joy of that woman! You can easily guess what followed: the people of the village, upon hearing the news, began to bring their sick children to the altar during Mass. I let them do it, and many of them were healed.

These people lived in great poverty; they had nothing; they had barely been baptized; but their faith conquered the heart of Christ, a childlike faith, a simple faith, a faith that can move mountains."

To this astounding testimony, Agostino added: "Why isn't it like that in our churches, in our parishes, in our movements? Jesus said, 'When the Son of Man comes, will he find faith on the earth?' (Luke 18:8). I think to myself, 'Yes, He will find it, if we truly want it!'"

Children in China, © Photo Ella Poon 2015

Prayer to the Child Jesus

One excellent way to regain the spirit of childhood is to familiarize ourselves with the Child Jesus. He is a great, healing therapy for our sophisticated west. That's why I offer Him this prayer:

> O, Child Jesus, I look at you and see you so small, so innocent, so vulnerable…
>
> And yet you are my Lord and my God!
>
> With Mary, Joseph, and the shepherds of Bethlehem, I come also to adore you.
>
> Make of my heart your little crèche, come live in me!
>
> Little Jesus, Herod wants to kill you, even though you come to pardon and save.
>
> Guard me from all sin and from anything that might sadden you about my life.
>
> Fill my soul with love and that divine peace for which I long so much.
>
> Oh, how I would like to take you into my arms as Mary, your mother does, and cover you with tender kisses!
>
> You were cold in the winter of Bethlehem. I want to warm you with the songs of my soul.
>
> May each of my secret acts of love be for you like a tiny bit of straw and warmth.
>
> Come re-create love among us! You are our unity!
>
> Guard us from Satan; don't permit him to sow hatred and division among us.
>
> Let evil be crushed by your innocence!
>
> I beg You, Infant Jesus, bind the wounds of my heart and heal my illnesses!
>
> Little Divine Shepherd, may your blessing be always upon us!
>
> Guide us all along the way of salvation!

23
REALLY, EIGHT ABORTIONS?

Pierrina was trying desperately to contact the visionary Marija Pavlovic. With a gnawing feeling inside, she told herself that this meeting was her last chance. Marija received her warmly and understood that she had in front of her a bruised and broken heart.

"Marija, I've come to you today because I'm on the verge of committing suicide. I can't do it anymore. I'm completely broken. You know, I've had eight abortions. Eight, can you believe it? My husband didn't want children. But today, I feel death inside me. I can't continue like this. I'm finished. Please, when you see the Virgin Mary this evening, ask her to help me. I can't go to see a priest, because, if I tell him that I've had eight abortions, he'll throw me out of the confessional."

"No, he won't," Marija said. "No priest will throw you out of the confessional – quite the opposite! Tell him frankly all you've been through, and you'll see: he'll listen to you and help you. Don't be afraid to go to confession. And tonight, I promise you, I will speak to Our Lady about you. And I'll pray for you."

That very day, Pierrina made the confession of her life and was happily astonished that the priest received her with immense gentleness and profound understanding. But more than that: after having explained her misery, her sins, and her wounds, she sensed that Jesus Himself came to her aid and gave her peace of heart. She fully absorbed this incomparable treasure, which can neither be purchased nor fabricated: the peace of heart which every person dreams to have, and that so few experience.

She waited for Marija at the foot of the left tower of St. James Church. She knew that Marija always received an apparition at 5:40pm, that she remained for the 6pm Mass, and would be coming out of the church around 7pm. Next to the little choir door, a group of pilgrims had already gathered, but Pierrina who had foreseen the crowds, tucked herself inside the cove of the door leading out to the piazza, so that she would be the first to capture Marija's attention.

"You know," said Marija with a big smile, "when the Gospa appeared, I spoke to her about you. She didn't let me give her too many details. She was smiling while she listened to me and said, 'This woman will be an instrument in the hands of God for saving many lives.' "You see," added Marija, "you don't have to be afraid. The Gospa is going to help you, and you will walk with her on a new path. Have you been to confession?" Marija asked. "Yes, Marija, and Jesus has healed my heart. I no longer feel despair. It's the first time in my life that I feel at peace. Thank you, thank you, thank you!"

Upon her return to Italy, reinvigorated by the shower of graces she received in Medjugorje, in her body, in her heart, and in her soul, Pierrina decided to go back to the hospital where she had gone through these 8 abortions. There, with the simplicity of those who have nothing to lose, she began to talk with the women who had come to have an abortion. She didn't lecture. She didn't explain. She didn't preach. She simply gave witness to her own personal experience: how after 8 abortions she had sunk into an inner death and how, in Medjugorje, by way of a sincere confession and the personal intervention of the Blessed Virgin Mary, she had found the taste for life again and the joy to be alive.

The prophesy of the Mother of God was being realized! Indeed, after listening to Pierrina and seeing the light which emanated from her, many women left the hospital with the intention of keeping their babies.

What is so tremendous about God is that even in the middle of the greatest disaster, He always finds a way to stir up courage and rebuild life for whoever trusts in Him.

Oh, Mama, If You Only Knew Me!

During one of my missions to Kerala, in southern India, I witnessed hundreds of people crying their eyes out during an outdoor performance by the 'RexBand's Theater – Jesus Youth's musical outreach. This troupe, composed of mostly young people from India, are fervent Christians, well-formed in evangelization. They travel all over India to make Christ and the Catholic faith known, especially to young people.

That evening, the enormous audience seated themselves wherever they could find a spot – on makeshift benches surrounding the stage, on blankets, everywhere. They were completely silent except for the sound of sniffles. In fact, very few people left the performance with dry eyes. There, in that assembly, I, too, couldn't hold back my tears, and I saw that up in the front row, the bishop of the area, who came to see the performance, didn't even *try* to hold back his own.

What took place on that stage? A woman spoke with a warm and captivating voice, but this voice also had within it the complex characteristics of a unique tone that pierced the inner workings of the heart, a tenderness and at the same time joyful exultation. But then, that same voice gave way to a voice that revealed that a tragedy had taken place. There were cries of pain. A discrete orchestra echoed this new voice that pierced through the night. We were in the presence of an often-concealed drama that has violated, and that continues to violate to this day, thousands of little human beings.

That night it was Beena who incarnated one of those little beings, giving voice to their silent screams. It is simply impossible for me to re-create here on paper, the tone which gave this drama such profoundly human significance! But you will know how to read between the lines the message of the love song that Beena sang, which transports us into the pure, naked reality of the most tiny of human beings.

"I am a child who has never seen the light of day,

and I am speaking to you from Eternity.

I was created in love, but they killed me with cruelty.

When I was still a tiny embryo of three months,

they condemned me to death.

My father became the author of my death,

and the womb of my mother my deathbed.

Oh, how I envy all of you who are alive!

Oh, how much I would love to sing with the birds in the sky!

I want to dance in the wind with the lilies of the field!

I want to laugh! I want to cry!

I want a taste of the wonderful life of which I was so unjustly deprived.

All that is left for me now are memories … wonderful memories of those three months I spent in my mother's womb.

Let me live! Let me walk in the brightness of the sun!

Let me live! Let me nestle in the arms of my mother!

Let me nestle in her embrace. Let me feel the love of my father.

Let me be part of God's creation!

Let me live!

I have been in my mother's womb for a month.

I float in this warm little corner, which is dark and intimate.

I hear soft sounds all around me. Is that my mother? I wonder.

My mother doesn't know yet that I am here.

Oh! How happy she's going to be when she becomes aware of my presence!

Now, I am two months along, and I continue to grow each day.

My heart is the biggest part of me, and now it's beginning to beat.

Oh! How happy I am to be alive!

My hands and toes are completely formed, and now I have a tiny mouth.

Today, I am three months along and I can smile.

I can wrinkle my eyebrows.

I can kick and even punch.

Mama! I am here! I am alive! Mama, I am alive!

Yesterday, my father and my mother killed me.

They thought I was only a collection of cells.

Me? A collection of cells?

Oh, how can I explain the pain I felt, when I learned that I wasn't wanted?

How can I describe the horror that came over me, when I discovered that I was headed for execution?

Who would understand the agony and the horrible pain I had to endure, when the doctor's instruments pierced my body and cut me into pieces?

My little hands, my little feet …!

Can anyone tell me what's wrong with me?

Why don't they want me anymore?

Oh! Mama! Mama, don't you know me?

Don't you remember me?

I'm your child! The flesh of your flesh!

You carried me in your womb for three months.

I shared your life and your blood … and then you killed me.

Why, Mama? Why?

All I wanted was to live. To be part of the family.

Tell me, dear Mama, how did the idea come to you to take away a life given by God?

Does being something you can dispose of seem right to you?

Oh, Mama, if you only knew me!"

Then Beena turned to the audience. "Remember: every one of you is alive today, simply because your mother didn't kill you when you were still in her womb. Are you going to listen to me? Is someone going to hear my silent scream and my supplication? All I ask is the right to live …"

Give a Name to the Child

An abortion is always dramatic for the parents. It is a profound wound, whether they are aware of it or not. The Lord, in His Mercy, gives these mothers and fathers the means of healing, the means of binding up this wound. Several steps can be taken, one after the other:

1. Be cognizant of the fact that this child exists in Heaven. Marthe Robin used to say that aborted babies made up the crown of Glory of the Blessed Virgin, and that they spent their time in Heaven interceding for their parents. They continue to grow in the womb of Mary, until they

reach the size of a "perfect adult."

2. Give a name to this child. This step is very important, because a name is an identity. Thus, the tiny one will no longer be anonymous for its parents, or "a collection of cells," but a perfectly identifiable being, with whom it is possible to experience the communion of saints. The baby will fill the empty abyss which has formed in the womb of the mother.

3. Ask for God's forgiveness in the Sacrament of Reconciliation. Normally, this task is reserved to the bishop, but faced with a plethora of cases, the bishop often delegates to his priests the power to pardon the sin of abortion.[25]

4. Ask forgiveness from the baby, too. Now that he has a name, an identity, his parents can speak to him, because he can hear them. We have to be aware that the child is probably the first person they will recognize when they enter Eternity! For parents to experience asking for pardon from their child, and receiving that pardon, is very healing.

5. The last step in the process is to forgive one's self. For many people, this is the most difficult task. The awareness of the seriousness of this sin can lead to profound and intense guilt. For some mothers, it is their self-image which is damaged; they feel shame and deep humiliation. I have noticed that many mothers who have gone through an abortion confess it over and over again. In reality, they haven't forgiven themselves and therefore don't

---

[25] During her near-death experience, Gloria Polo saw that each abortion unleashed a horrible kind of satisfaction in Hell among the demons, who are so full of hatred toward human life. Jesus showed her that abortion is a form of worship on the altar of Satan. Each time a baby is killed, the gates of Hell are breached and the demons who come out attack priests in particular. There would be, therefore, a direct link between the plethora of abortions today and the fall of so many priests. Of course, we don't have to accept that as Gospel truth; it remains a private revelation, (See the testimony of Gloria Polo, Chapter 5).

find peace in confession. When I suggest doing this, they sometimes answer me: "But how can I forgive myself for such a terrible act? That baby will never come back!" So, I exhort them to prove their humility by saying to themselves: "It's true. I was once capable of doing that!" Saint Thérèse the Little Flower herself says that, without prevenient grace of Divine Mercy, she would have been capable of committing many mortal sins.

Happily, once this sin has been confessed with true repentance, the evil is pardoned by God, once and for all; it becomes engulfed in the ocean of His Mercy. In a way, it no longer exists as a sin; only its consequences live on and need to be treated with inner healing in mind. The two parents can enter, therefore, into the joy of knowing that a child, their child, is waiting for them in Heaven; that he is truly living and that he loves them infinitely, without any kind of bitterness! Like God's love!

How Does a Woman Feel After an Abortion?

Benedetta Foà is a doctor of psychology in Milan.[26] She leads inner healing sessions for mothers who have gone through the loss of an unborn child. Her experience is enlightening! She writes:

"It is problematic to affirm that women who have voluntarily aborted their child, feel the same suffering and loss, for the simple reason that every woman is different and reacts in a unique way. Some will feel badly immediately after the interruption of pregnancy, others years later (often on the occasion of the birth of another child). I have encountered women, who, after having aborted, continued their lives as before, as if nothing special had taken place. That isn't because they are not religious, but because they lack awareness. It often happens

[26] Dr. Benedetta Foà (Milan): info@benedettafoa.it

that uneasiness begins when parents realize that a child is missing, and if they become aware that it is their own doing, their suffering intensifies.

Parents seeking psychological support to endure this grief suffer from the global pathology of post-abortion stress, which is characterized by a syndrome with a great many associated symptoms, including:

i. Depression: self-pity, dark thoughts, sadness, anguish, constant tears, guilt, and shame;

ii. Anxiety: at its core, it can be both positive and stimulating, but anxiety can devolve into anguish and panic attacks;

iii. Fits of anger: against the partner, the parents, the doctors;

iv. Obsessive ideas: fixation on the event of abortion;

v. Trouble sleeping: insomnia, lethargy, nightmares;

vi. Denigration of self: to the point of thinking one is no longer worth anything;

vii. Cognitive difficulties: attention deficit, memory loss, trouble concentrating;

viii. Relationship troubles: ending often in a rupture with the spouse and a withdrawal of the woman into herself, into her inner grief, with a progressive isolation from the world and others.

ix. Sexual problems: disinterest, or on the contrary, frenetic sexual activity without protection, in a way that would cause another pregnancy (an unconscious process);

x. Dark ideas: suicide attempts."

I asked Dr. Foà if it is possible to find one's way out such great pain. Her response was that, yes, a woman can and should extricate herself from this immense suffering. Everything is rectified in Christ and everything can be immersed in His Merciful Heart. There is no greater sin than doubting the forgiveness of God! It is imperative to take a number of steps, beginning with the recognition that the abortion of a baby constitutes a traumatic event in and of itself. It is a complex conflict which requires professional support. Abortion is a wound which involves the body, the mind, and the soul: the healing of each part is necessary. Just as you go to a doctor to care for your body and your mind, you must go to a competent priest, informed on the subject, for your soul."

24
THE EXORCISM OF A PRIVATE CLINIC

Father Jozo Zovko, O.F.M., used to say: "A country which kills its children has no future."

In the city of Rockford, in the state of Illinois, where Barack Obama was Senator before becoming President of the USA, one of the clinics specializing in abortions was the scene of some exceptional crimes against women.[27]

Since its opening in 1988, innumerable babies have lost their lives in this sinister place. It is *The Rockford Women's Center*, which reportedly stood out among other "clinics of death." Unique in its services, it offered clients a simplified procedure that allowed the physicians to perform an abortion more quickly. During this procedure, however, medical precautions were not respected, and the hygiene practiced in that clinic left a great deal to be desired, which fatally threatened the lives of the mothers!

Medical reports revealed that instruments were not properly sanitized, some remained stained with blood, and medical professionals ignored risks of infection from one patient to the next. Abortions were botched because of a lack of competent staff, and preliminary pre-operative procedures were unreliable. Six women died as a result of violations of elementary rules

---

[27] When ex-President Obama was a senator for the state of Illinois, he continually opposed laws which might have protected unborn children. To learn more, see the link in Italian: www.lalucedimaria.it/esorcizzano-la-clinica-degli-orroi-succede-lincredibile/

of sanitation, and four thousand were maimed for life. Moreover, like many other clinics in Illinois, the clinic falsified the number of abortions that were performed, and, of course, kept the number of victims quiet.

In the USA, there are many private initiatives that fight against the atrocity of abortion. Patricia Bainbridge is the president of one such organization called *Human Life International*. She also worked for the diocese as Director of the Office of Respect for Life. When she read the reports of this clinic, she thought she was dreaming! It was horrifying! She could not understand how the state could protect this kind of operation. Worse, how the media could ignore such behavior! Nevertheless, she rejoiced to see that, little by little, an army rose up, an army of people defending life. These people gathered around the exterior of the building and offered the mothers the use of a mobile unit where they could not only find psychological assistance but also verify the health of their babies with sonograms.

It is common in the USA to see people assembling for prayer in front of clinics that perform abortions. Their goal is threefold: first, to implore God to spare the lives of the babies; second, to convert the staff engaged in abortion; and finally, to give the mothers the light of the Holy Spirit, which might encourage them to say "yes" to life.

Thanks to the continual prayers of this fervent group of Christians in front of that horrible building, the situation of the women has already been ameliorated. Kevin Rilott, a member of the Pro-Life Initiative of Rockford, explained that prayer was the cornerstone of their work. He specified that it was prayers of a special nature which radically turned things around during an unprecedented event in 2009.

With the approval of their Bishop, Monsignor Thomas Duran, and accompanied by faithful pro-lifers, four priests, among them Father Kevin Butler, a vicar from a parish in the diocese, placed themselves at the four corners of the clinic. There they recited prayers of exorcism and repeated the ritual on many occasions. The prayers were not directed toward people within the building, but had as their goal to dislodge the evil which had taken hold inside those walls.

After years of legal battles against the clinic, battles which had proven fruitless, a change finally came about as a result of the exorcisms. In the two or three weeks following the prayers of the priests, the number of abortions began to diminish. Within several months, the number had been cut in half, while the requests for help from pregnant women at the Rockford Pro-Life Initiative doubled.

The clinic, which had performed between 25 and 75 abortions per week for many years, was forced to reduce its number of days of operation. The employees were frustrated because their working hours and salary was cut. In September 2011, the clinic had to close temporarily because it was no longer able to afford its employees the number of work hours required by the government. In January of 2016, although the department had suspended the sanction, the clinic had to pay a fine of about $5,000. Immediately afterwards, the celebrated Rockford Women's Center, declared its definitive closure.

It took six years for these four courageous and motivated priests to win the victory! How many lives were saved because of them? They will only find out in Heaven! But we can easily imagine that the angels of God and all the elect danced for joy for each child saved, because, according to the words of Our Lady in Medjugorje, "Never forget that each one of you is a unique world in the eyes of the Heavenly Father!"

Could this story inspire other priests to become motivated to support the pro-life movement in such a dramatic way?

25
Maryam Still Knocks

Rome, May 17, 2015. Along with several Croatian and French friends, I was seated right in the middle of the highest stage of St. Peter's Square, less than 50 meters from Pope Francis who was celebrating the Canonization Mass of Maryam of Bethlehem. We were baking under a torrid sun, but we were full of joy. Little did I suspect that just a few rows in front of me was a woman, a stranger to me, who was crying out with all her heart for help!

It was Martina from Tarascon, France. For 27 years she had battled against the impossible, and she made the entire journey to Rome, by bus, just to come and fling herself into the arms of Maryam, her great friend, who was being canonized this day. Maryam's tapestry had just been unfurled in front of the façade of St. Peter's, and Martina cried out to her with every bit of passion that could emanate from a person being crucified: "Maryam, I can't do this anymore. Take Lawrence. I'm giving him to you. Take care of him, do something! I've tried everything. I'm at the end of my rope."

Who is this prodigal son, this villain, Lawrence? Abandoned at the age of two and a half by his father, he managed to grow up in a household with almost no parenting. His mother, Martina, constantly worked hard to provide for her 4 children. Lawrence's consolation came from his older brother Jacques, whom he admired and never let out of his sight. Then, at the age of 18, Jacques was suddenly the victim of a terrible car accident and he ended up in an emergency room more dead than alive.

After an exhaustive examination, the doctors declared Jacques was brain dead, with no hope of improvement. His electro-encephalogram displayed a flat line. In the face of this incontrovertible evidence, Martina was presented with a fateful choice: "If you want to donate his organs after the machines have been turned off, to give life to someone else, you have to do it within a matter of hours because the law forbids you to donate his organs after tomorrow. If you want to keep him on the ventilator, you will have to take him back home where he could remain in a permanent vegetative state, hooked up to machines, for years." Martina, already overwhelmed with pain at the shock of the accident, felt pressured into making the terrible decision right then and there, without delay.

Because she worked in the pathology lab as a technician in a hospital, she was aware of the value and rarity of human organs donated by young people to save lives through transplants. In her generosity, she hoped that her son's accident might at least help another person on a waiting list for an organ donation. She asked that the machines keeping her son Jacques alive, be unplugged. She donated his entire body: "heart, liver, and lungs." At eighteen years old, Jacques' heart was practically new.

When he learned of his mother's choice, Lawrence couldn't comprehend her motivation. He saw only one side of the issue: "Mama had my brother unplugged. Jacques is dead, and my mother killed him." There grew inside of him a ferocious hatred towards her. "You gave him life, and now you killed him!" Those were the words that he threw in her face. There were never enough of those words to insult her, and he screamed the worst insults, hoping somehow to alleviate the pain that the loss of his brother, and his life's companion, brought upon him.

For Lawrence, this violence toward his mother, driven by the unconscious cruelty of a 15 year-old adolescent, was just beginning. The events which followed were beyond anyone's imagination. He began to hang out with bad friends, and to drink. For her part, Martina's body was being ravaged by three different types of cancer. She was often absent from the house and was sometimes even transported by emergency helicopter to Paris. Lawrence felt doubly abandoned. Then he began sniffing the gas from his moped. When she noticed all this caustic behavior, Martina moved him to different schools, but nothing seemed to work. He was engulfed in the labyrinth of self-destruction. It was a descent into hell.

He began to inject himself with drugs and contracted hepatitis. In the meantime, Martina remarried, this time to a good man, and, thanks to his faith in God, she endured the charges of her son with an almost angelic patience. For 27 interminable years, Lawrence tortured his mother. He went as far as burglarizing his parents' house. "If my husband had not been there," she told me, "he would have destroyed me." She sometimes had to spend colossal sums of money to rent lodgings near various hospitals where Lawrence would land because he had drunk too much alcohol, and to repair the apartments he trashed during his crises of insanity. By the grace of God, her husband supported her in her battles and managed to pay the bills. It seemed that with Martina, maternal love had no limits. Lawrence had tried in vain to fight her off, striking her, stealing from her, injuring her, but the maternal heart of Martina, surely profoundly wounded and in pain from each blow she received from him, never flinched. It seemed that Lawrence's hate would drown in the ocean of love that his mother felt for him. She never closed her door.

How did Martina endure it all, the amount of pain in her wounded maternal heart, the constant fear of public scandal, the risk of incurable debts, and the torturous thought that Lawrence might end up dying from an overdose? From where did she draw such love?

When I asked her, "How did you maintain hope that he would come out of this someday, when you had, under your very eyes, constant proof that he was heading to the bottom?" Her answer sprang forth in one word: "Prayer!" She drew her love from the immense heart of God, whose love knows no limit. For that, Martina utilized the most efficacious means: she drew her love with a bucket of confidence, as Jesus had taught Saint Faustina. She believed with her whole being that God would save her child from the grips of destruction. The idea that He would not save him never entered her mind.

Lawrence had several motorcycle accidents, which required numerous operations. He was given a transplant, and the surgeon told Martina that under anesthesia he heard Lawrence speaking with Jacques, his father. "No, Jacques is his brother," Martina replied to the surgeon. She now understood that Jacques had been constantly at the side of his hospitalized brother. What encouragement!

Among her close friends, she counted a priest who was working to spread the spiritual message of Saint Maryam of Bethlehem, and who had connections in Bethlehem and in Pau, France where the Carmelite had lived for several years. This man with a good heart and an erudite mind, kept those around him in a constant state of marvel at that little Carmelite from the Holy Land. Martina was familiar with her and spoke to her often with an open heart. She adopted Maryam and even went so far as to tell me, "You know, Sister Emmanuel, I love the Blessed Virgin a lot, but I love Maryam even more." It seemed that Maryam and Martina were somehow joined together in the simplicity of child-like hearts.

Each morning, Lawrence began his day by downing (swallowing in one gulp) an entire liter of Vodka. That often made him pass out. Now an excess of alcohol in the blood can burn through the sheaths of nerves and produce enormous suffering. That is why the doctors often induced an artificial coma in Lawrence, to spare him this torture. Those who were near to her began to wish that her son would die and that this nightmare would finally end, so that Martina could begin to breathe. Each year, Martina went to Lourdes with several friends to look after the sick pilgrims. Her friends shared with her their anxieties about her son, telling her without hesitation, "Martina, stop dreaming. Don't even think of taking him out of the hospital, he's septic, he has a temperature of 107, and he doesn't have enough vital nutrients in his body. Let him go so that he can finally be happy, so he'll be at peace!" Whenever the whole world told her he was a lost cause, Lawrence would come out of his coma. The doctors could never understand. But Martina, the unshakeable, spent entire hours each day at his bedside and never stopped her confident prayers.

Unshakeable? Seeing her heroic trust in Him, God comforted her with a sign that she will never forget: She went on a pilgrimage to St. James of Compostela, Spain. Inside the cathedral of Saint James is a statue of the apostle, the patron saint of her lost son, Jacques (James in French). Pilgrims are invited to walk behind this statue, which dominates the main altar, go up onto a small platform, and embrace the statue from behind, while praying to the saint. So, that's what Martina did, and there, a beautiful consolation was bestowed on her: her son Jacques, who had died many years earlier, appeared to her, and without saying a word, smiled at her. He was very handsome and seemed to be saying to her, "Mama, it's all good, continue!" It hardly needs saying that at that moment Martina received such a dose of light, joy, and courage that she was ready to continue the struggle, with the certitude that Lawrence would one day be saved, despite all appearances to the contrary! In reality, the thought that God couldn't save her son never entered her mind.

Then came the blessed day of Maryam's canonization. Guided by her priestly friend, Martina arrived physically and emotionally exhausted. When the portrait of Maryam was unfurled in front of St. Peter's, she repeated interiorly this prayer that Maryam used to say constantly:

"Holy Spirit, inspire me; Love of God, consume me; on the right path, guide me; Mary, my mother, look down on me; along with Jesus, bless me; from all harm, from all illusion, from all danger preserve me. Come, my Consolation! Come, my Joy! Come, my Peace! My Strength, my Light, come, enlighten me in finding the fountain where I must quench my thirst." (This prayer can be found in my book on Maryam. You may copy it.)

And Martina called out to her in her pain and pleaded with her, crying from exhaustion: "I can't take it Maryam. Do something for Lawrence. Take care of him for me. It's too much."

I have often heard that the Saints, on the day of their canonization, grant very special graces to those who pray to them. And, indeed, a beautiful gift was waiting for Martina. A week after her return from Rome, Lawrence arrived at her house and calmly announced: "Mom, I have stopped drinking. I will never drink again, starting now. I've made up my mind." Martina looked at him. He had undergone a META-MOR-PHOSIS. A miracle had occurred!

What had happened? Lawrence was very sober in his explanation: "I had a sudden transformation. I didn't want to drink any more. I didn't want to take pills. I didn't want to do drugs. But I needed someone to help me." Martina, who had always seen her son overloaded with problems, couldn't get over it. She was standing in front of a different man. "He was a man I didn't recognize," she said. "It was the real Lawrence returned from Hell. Recently he met a substance abuse counselor who had taken him under his wing, and Lawrence came out of it a changed man."

Another joy awaited Martina. On December 25, 2015, Lawrence arrived at her home with a large package under his arm. It was Christmas. "Listen Mom, I'm going to give you a gift. A gift that no one will ever give you and that you will keep forever." Martina opened the package and found a large, beautiful statue 60 centimeters high. "Look Mom, it's me! It's your son Lawrence, a new man!" Martina knew nothing of this new technology. With a voice full of emotion, she explained: "He got into a machine that turned like this: 'tchouk, tchook, tchouk,' and the statue was made. It was him! With his favorite jacket, his pants … Unbelievable! It was totally him!"[28]

---

[28] 3-D printing like this is relatively recent. It allows those who desire, to create a three-dimensional clone of themselves in the form of a figurine which seems more real than nature itself. Although the general look of it already seems realistic, what astonishes one the most about these reproductions are the myriad details in staggering realism found in the clothing, the hair, and even in facial expressions. www.gentside.com/imprimante-3d/une-imprimante-3d-capable-de-fabriquer-un-mini-clone-de-vous-meme_art52572.html

Upon seeing the statue Martina broke down in tears. Overwhelmed, she couldn't contain her joy and trembled with emotion.

Since Lawrence had been a brilliant student, and because Martina had made sure that he followed the best academic path possible, despite his deviations he was able to resume his job with the national railway. All the benefits that went along with being an engineer, the position he held before his descent into Hell, came along with the job. He resumed living in his company apartment and today oversees the security of train stations from Marseille to Monaco.

He knows that he owes his life to the unconditional love of his mother and to her prayers. Martina had far surpassed all quotas of patience. She had even surpassed Saint Monica, who prayed for 22 years for the conversion of her son, Augustine. In their case, the result for the Church was two saints: the person of St. Augustine and St. Monica! Perhaps in the case of Martina and Lawrence, we will have two more to give us the example of perseverant prayer.

It is true that after all those years that were so difficult for Martina, Saint Maryam of Bethlehem, the little Arab, knew how to deliver! Will she stop there?

Dear Maryam, during your life you went from victory to victory. Now, continue to pour out your blessings on the family of Martina, but not only on her. Do you know how many young people today live like Lawrence? To put it another way, your work has only just begun. Get on with it! We're counting on you. Please listen to the cries of fathers and mothers, who, when they read this testimony, are going to bombard you with appeals for help![29]

---

[29] To purchase the book on Maryam of Bethlehem, go to www.sremmanuel.org click on store.

26
I KILLED MY FATHER!

For Natalia, this was a first! She decided to experiment with the depths of horror, and she succeeded! There she was, standing in front of the most brutal scene imaginable: her father tortured to death by two men.

She didn't cry. She didn't feel any sadness. Her affect was flat and her face remained emotionless. It was exactly the way she imagined it when she ordered his assassination. She was just thirteen years old and already her past was quite colorful.

Natalia was born in a poverty-stricken area of Brazil that was rife with violence in 1983. People fought for space and were surrounded by rats and garbage. She was the result of one of the multiple relationships her mother had at just seventeen years old. As was common in these favelas, her mother depended on prostitution to furnish her own addiction to crack: the drug of the poor, that wretched drug, worse than heroin, which utterly destroyed her. Incapable of taking care of her daughter, she abandoned her to the mercy of the streets. Natalia was raised by relatives in a neighborhood just as rife with drugs, so the change of guardianship did not improve matters. In fact, it made them worse. Natalia ended up in a family of traffickers, where drugs and violence ruled.

The heart of little Natalia was quickly filled with hatred and rebellion. At the age of nine, she went to live with her father, who was also a drug addict. He treated Natalia with coldness; a coldness that was made even worse by his deliberate meanness, even though he was very affectionate with his other children, who were born from his union with the woman who shared his life. You can probably guess the kind of anger that secretly rumbled beneath the surface of the heart of this child, increasing day by day.

But she hadn't yet reached the depth of this horror. One morning, her father asked her to massage his back. She did. But during the course of the massage, the true motive of the father revealed itself, and he raped his own daughter. From that moment on, Natalia lost all will to live. An enormous emptiness filled her heart. She began to rebel against God and against the whole world. Violent hatred of her father intensified her revolt. A nagging desire began to germinate within her and soon became a fixation: kill him!

At the age of thirteen, she was arrested for committing assault. Prison only increased her interior violence and reinforced her decision: to go through with the act and kill her father. One day, she won R$ 50, the equivalent of 12 €, and ran to purchase the services of two hired killers. But she didn't have to spend a cent. The killers asked her what her motivation was, and, when they learned that her father had raped her when she was nine years old, they decided to do the job for free. Natalia was anxious to see with her own eyes the suffering and death of her aggressor. Natalia, the violated child, became a murderer. Would her soul be lost forever? To think the answer is yes would be to misunderstand the mercy of God!

The arrival in the favela of young missionaries radically changed the course of her existence.[30] They radiated a joy which Natalia had never seen or experienced in her life!

They cared for the sick, removed garbage from houses, and put themselves at the service of the residents. Why did they

---

[30] Alleanza Misericordia (Covenant of Mercy) is a Catholic community born in the archdiocese of Sao Polo in Brazil which welcomes street children and evangelizes in slums and very poor areas. They have now new foundations in Poland, Portugal, Columbia, Venezuela, Mozambican and Belgium.
Their contact is: www.alleanzadimisericordia.it and alleanzadimisericordia@gmail.com

do all that? And for free? Natalia had trouble believing it. Could a love so expansive, so unselfish even exist? Natalia was overwhelmed by so much light and love. The missionaries revealed to her that they were Christian and that they were risking their lives out of love for Jesus.

'Jesus? Who was that?' she wondered. She had hardly heard of Him during her childhood, but for her He was so far away!

Everything changed for Natalia when she heard this living testimony. A fire, a warmth, entered her heart along with enormous hope. The beginnings of life began to fill her heart! Completely mesmerized, in her enthusiasm, she ran to Father Henrique, who was accompanying the missionaries. In three words, she outlined the pattern of her life: addiction, hatred, and murder. She added that the love of the young missionaries had turned her heart around and allowed her to come to know Jesus. "I want to become like them," she said to him. "Can you baptize me?"

"For me", Natalia said, "a new pathway opened up. I understood how the devil could destroy a life, but, also, how love can give us new life. I was born again! I began to visit and become acquainted with the community of the Covenant of Mercy, and there I discovered the living presence of God, just as He said. Some words that Jesus spoke to Sister Faustina touched me in particular: "If the greatest sinners only trusted in my Mercy, they would become the greatest saints of their time."

Thanks to the "Yes" of Natalia, her entire family found salvation. That fulfilled for her the words of the Lord that we read in St. Paul: "Believe and you will be saved, you and your whole family." The community welcomed Natalia's sisters and brothers, and her mother was, from that point on, freed from her addiction to crack.

Today, Natalia has become a missionary and has dedicated her life to evangelization. She bears witness to the power of that merciful love which transformed her and that can transform us all.

One lasting memory is engraved in her mind: the former little murderer was chosen to sing on stage for the World Youth Day in São Paulo during the visit in 2013 of Pope Francis. Another one of those gifts from Heaven that God delights in giving His lost and re-found children.

27
THE SECRET VISITS OF FATHER SLAVKO

Father Slavko Barbaric, who prayed and fasted a lot, undertook some secret endeavors that only a few people witnessed. He used to love going to the homes of families in the area, especially where there were children. He brought them chocolates and strawberries, played with them, laughed and prayed with them.

One of the families who was close to him went through a serious crisis. The father had begun to drink, and the atmosphere had become unbearable. One day, at the tomb of Father, the visionary Marija told us that when the holy priest was still alive, he had taken it upon himself to save this family from destruction and ruin.

He asked the mother what time her husband began to drink each day. Then he decided to visit the family at exactly that time, so he could engage the man in conversation. He told the man stories, brought some strawberries, prayed with him, and found a thousand ways to hold his attention. Later, by the time he left, cocktail hour had passed, and sobriety had scored a point. Fr Slavko visited that family every day. His faithfulness, his friendship and his luminous presence filled the emptiness that this countryman felt in his heart, so much so that one day, he forgot all about alcohol and engaged in normal life again, by assuming his responsibilities as father and educator of the family. He was cured!

28
GO AND DO LIKEWISE!

He was lying in his own blood. He had lost consciousness from the violence of the blows. They had thrown him into a ditch, the way you get rid of garbage after rummaging through it. He was slowly dying, all alone.

Fortunately, a priest passed by, on his way from Jerusalem, and he saw the injured man lying in the ditch in agony. Certainly he would stop and care for him! After all, for a consecrated person, this was a golden opportunity to live out the most beautiful precept of the mitzvoth: that of unselfish charity toward another. As the priest passed by, he took one look at the man, walked around him and continued on his way. He found the perfect excuse: the formal commandment for Jews not to touch the dead. In the meantime though, while walking around him, he hadn't wanted to hear the voice of the Holy Spirit that whispered to him, 'perhaps the man is still alive and needs immediate help.' Now, for Jews, the protection of human life ranks above any other precept.

Thankfully, a Levite from that area came upon the same place and saw our friend lying in the ditch. Without a doubt a man of God, a cleric who sang the praises of the Lord every day in the Temple, could not remain unmoved! But, horror of horrors, he also passed him by, leaving one to wonder how it is possible, what excuse could the Levite possibly find to shy away from the misery of his brother? Surely he had an appointment. Or, maybe he didn't want to get himself dirty and arrive disheveled in the Temple for evening prayers. Or, perhaps he told himself that if the man was in that condition, it was probably because he went out looking for it! He may have thought, 'with strangers, you just never know.'

Time passed by, and the condition of the man in the ditch worsened.

Unfortunately, the next passer-by was a Samaritan, a stranger to the Hebrew community. The Samaritans and the Jews didn't speak to one another; they weren't in agreement on certain fundamental points of religion. Furthermore, he was traveling, people were waiting for him somewhere. In short, nothing good could come out of this.

But, what a surprise! When the Samaritan saw the dying man in such a pitiful state, he was moved and filled with deep compassion. Contrary to every expectation, he approached the man without hesitation. He was shaken by the sight of open wounds. To him, that was unconscionable. When he saw the suffering of this man, he made it his own.

So, without asking himself any questions, without permitting any excuse to enter his mind, he did everything in his power to aid the wounded man as if he were his own son.

He leaped into action, because true compassion doesn't consist in experiencing a feeling or a strong emotion; it pushes us to act. That is the sign of authentic mercy.

So he began to put into action a series of interventions that would give this unknown man the best chance at survival. He omitted nothing: he bound his wounds, he poured oil and wine on them, he put the man on his own horse, he took him to an inn and looked after him, he took out two denarii, and gave them to the innkeeper, saying, "Take care of him, and if your expense is greater than this, I will pay you back when I return."

Among all of the Samaritan's many actions, the last good deed stands out in a particular way, because the Samaritan took a real risk: the innkeeper could have taken advantage of the situation to abuse the Samaritan's trust and fill his own pockets.

Without the Samaritan's slightest knowledge, it was the

Holy Spirit who inspired this burning compassion in his heart. The Samaritan didn't calculate any of the eventual consequences of his wild generosity: not the potential cost in money and time, not even the possibility of being swindled. We understand through his action that compassion is the polar opposite of indifference.

But our carnal nature, goaded by the devil, resists this movement of the Holy Spirit. The minute our hearts erupt in a burst of charity, of mercy, of forgiveness, he bombards us with thoughts that block it, such as: you don't have the time! This isn't really the right moment! That's going to be expensive! Who knows what consequences there might be? Does this person really deserve it? You aren't capable! It's too late! It's too early! He's going to take advantage of you! You don't even know this person, etc.

This parable magnificently edifies our human spirit! Jesus, in conclusion, purposely asks his questioner, a lawyer, to take this Samaritan as an example and do as he did: "Go and do likewise!" Likewise? It's not a matter of doing simply a tenth, or a quarter, or half, but all! And what promise is attached to this invitation? Nothing less than Eternal Life.

Jesus Returns!

And that's not all! The symbolism in this story opens our eyes to a great and profound mystery that leads us concretely, even this very day, to Eternal Life. It is the mystery of the Church.

Who does our friend, lying in the ditch of death, represent? A fallen man, wounded by original sin, disfigured by his own sins. A man whose soul is nearly dead. In other words, he is every one of us, you and me!

What do the priest and Levite represent? The powerlessness of the Law of the first covenant, and of the ancient priesthood, to save humanity by themselves alone.

Who does the Good Samaritan represent? Jesus Himself! The Samaritans were scorned by the Jews. Jesus, the most scorned of all, is the only one able to take charge of the injured man and care for him.

What is represented by the inn, where the wounded are left, and the innkeeper, who receives all the money he needs to care for the man? Surely they illustrate the Church, which is both a house and the people in it. She receives from Christ the power to guide souls to salvation and all the means to do so, particularly through the Sacraments, symbolized by the oil, the wine, and everything the innkeeper had to buy before the Samaritan returned.

And this return? It represents, of course, the return of Christ in all His glory, a return the whole Church is waiting for. When that time comes, Jesus will bestow on each person the reward reserved for him.

Sins of Omission, or Non-Assistance to a Person in Danger

One day, in catechism class, the teacher was explaining to the children the different kinds of sin. To determine if they had understood it all, she questioned little Clément:

"Can you tell us what a sin of omission is Clement?"

"Yes, ma'am," he said. "It's when you have a chance to commit a sin and you don't do it!"

This little one-liner furnishes us with an excellent mnemonic: we sometimes retain a bit of humor better than something serious! However, let's keep in mind that little Clement's definition is certainly not the correct one.

What will happen when we present ourselves before the Lord at the time of our passage to our new life? In the clarity of the instant of death, we will see our lives and our souls in their pure reality. No detail will escape us. According to some Christian mystics, it appears to be even more painful and more serious to see the good that we didn't do, when it was in our power to do it, than to see the evil we did commit. This is the crux of the sin of omission, exactly as Jesus speaks about it in the description of the Last Judgment (Mt. 25: 41-46): "Truly I tell you, whatever you did not do for one of the least of these; you did not do for me."

In essence, in the twilight of life, we will be judged on love, as St. John of the Cross teaches us. That's precisely what the priest and the Levite in our parable forgot. They preferred a false and legalistic vision of the Torah, disconnected from brotherly charity in action, to love. They allowed themselves a clear conscience for leaning on badly interpreted precepts of legal purity. Their downfall happened so fast!

Thank God everyone doesn't go down that slippery slope! Today, we see so many examples of people who choose mercy in action over their own security, or any other consideration. A beautiful example comes to mind:

A French religious saint, Mother Yvonne-Aimée Beauvais, sometimes referred to as Mother Yvonne-Aimée of Malestroit, managed a hospital in Brittany during the Second World War. She emanated great compassion for all who were at risk of ending up in concentration camps, to the point that she disguised many of them as patients in order to foil the Nazis. She knew she was exposing herself to torture or death if she was discovered, but she never quit when faced with the desperation of these men. She simply found a way to save them from a shameful death.[31]

The engine of mercy is compassion. Let's not be afraid: true compassion doesn't make anyone weak. Our Blessed Mother stood at the foot of the Cross. Padre Pio remained for hours in the confessional and not in his bed, not moaning about the violent pain of the stigmata he endured because of

---

[31] For more information about Mother Yvonne-Aimée Beauvais and the Malestroit Augustinian Monastery see: www.augustines-malestroit.com/a_index.php

sinners. On the contrary, he worked relentlessly, and it was really sharing the suffering of others that got him through life with joy, and even humor. His profound compassion gave birth to his enormous hospital at San Giovanni Rotondo "for the relief of suffering." The indefatigable Mother Teresa of Calcutta saw only Jesus in the broken man; rather than wondering if she had or didn't have the strength to help him, she rolled up her sleeves and threw herself into the work of aiding him. She went as far as nagging God, who was then obligated to send her the strength she needed!

True compassion ennobles the soul. It offers us the beatitude of the merciful. People who live it have at heart a certain light, a particular tenderness, a special beauty. They have obtained mercy!

29
WILL YOU GO TO HEAVEN WITH NIVALDO?

Nivaldo before his death in Brazil, © Photo Alleanza di Misericordia

Collapsed in tears on the sidewalk in front of a church, Nivaldo was completely done in. This young, illiterate Brazilian had known nothing in this life but extreme poverty and extreme violence. He had descended into drugs at the age of 12, then into delinquency and criminal activity by the age of 15. A member of one of the numerous gangs that pollute the slums skirting the edge of the suburbs of Sao Paolo, he had just lost his best friend to a gang who was trying to settle scores. This friend died in his arms, killed when mistaken for Nivaldo.

Nivaldo felt himself plunging deep into despair. He did not know why his steps took him to a spot in front of a church, but he felt incapable of going any further.

At that moment, two young people approached him and said: "Jesus loves you!" Nivaldo, who had never heard of Jesus, retorted: "But I'm not gay! Who is this Jesus?" The young people proclaimed to him the Love of God, who, through Jesus, revealed Himself to all the world; then they invited him to go into the church to pray in the Chapel of the Holy Sacrament.

Nivaldo accepted, persuaded more by his despair than by faith.

Inside, he knelt and began to think: "Lord, if You really exist, if You truly love me, demonstrate Your love to me, show me that You are God!"

Instantaneously, he felt a desire to pick up the Bible, and he opened it by chance. His eyes fixed on a passage from Isaiah. Imagine his amazement when he realized that he, an illiterate (he only knew how to read the bus numbers), began to spell out, then to read rapidly those words which proclaimed: "I am the Lord; there is no other: apart from me, there is no God. I will strengthen you, though you do not know Me, so that from the rising of the sun to its setting, people may know that there is none besides Me," (Is. 45:5-6). The words, and his tears, fused with one another into a fire that Nivaldo felt in his entire body, as if those words were alive, as if they filled him up, embraced him and re-created him.

He felt invaded by this fire, a fire he would understand later as that of the Holy Spirit. He felt cared for, washed, and restored. When he got up, he was no longer the same man. Everything in him seemed new.

With the strength of those words, which had penetrated his despair, Nivaldo completely changed his life. He threw away his revolver and took up as his only weapon: a large crucifix, which he kept with him always and that he used as veritable armament in his most difficult battles against the powers of evil. He succeeded in conquering the demons of impurity and drugs, and never, after that effusion of warmth, fell into those vices again. Nivaldo became, as the words which he had heard proclaimed to him, an inspired preacher, extremely generous and simple. He suffered from violent headaches, a consequence of being under the influence of drugs for so long, but despite that, he applied all his strength to studying. Joyous, pure, always smiling, he was always available, ready to serve and to welcome.

He worked for a number of years in a rehabilitation center.

One day, he felt a desire to dedicate his entire life to God by proclaiming the Gospel. He got involved in a community, The Covenant of Mercy (Alleanza di Misericordia).

He gave his life over completely, with the unique objective of growing in love. He had changed so much that from that time on he chose not what was easiest, but what cost him the most, in order to be more like Christ.

Shortly after his conversion, Nivaldo read a book by St. John of the Cross. He underlined these words: "Love neither rests nor grows tired." He decided to take as his motto this very beautiful expression that he changed a little without wanting to, because of his difficulty in reading. He said, "Love neither grows tired nor rests." Those words were for him a veritable fountain of life, and he had no idea to what degree he was actually going to live them.

On September 15, 2001, he led a retreat in a prison for juvenile offenders. His theme was that of *The Good Thief*. That talk, which turned out to be his last, touched every heart. Not only those of the young prisoners but also those of the prison guards. The words he spoke were prophetic.

"Beside Jesus on the Cross," said Nivaldo. "There was a robber who had been condemned to crucifixion. Faced with death, he was able to recognize the Son of God, and, with humility, he said to him: 'Jesus, remember me when you enter into your kingdom,' (Luke 23:42)." Nivaldo continued: "I also was a thief, maybe like some of you. I participated in robberies; I was on drugs; and I was a dealer. I was part of a criminal organization. I carried a weapon, and that gave me a sense of power. But one day, in the depths of despair, I, too, said to Jesus with good intention and with humility: 'Lord, remember me!' And He remembered me! He led me out of the abyss into which I had fallen, because I invoked His Holy Name with a sincere heart. Yes, I want to go to Paradise, but not alone!"

Beginning to point to some of the juvenile delinquents, he added, "And you, do you want to come to Paradise with me? And you, too, do you want to come? And you?" He repeated his question a number of times so that the young people would feel personally loved in a unique way. At the end, he added, "Because being consecrated means not going to Paradise alone!"

At that time, Nivaldo was the coordinator of The Covenant of Mercy's house of welcome, open to the young people who had left the streets and wanted to escape from drugs. With the help of the intense love which was poured out to them, they were able to find their dignity again and begin a new life.

That particular night, returning from the prison after his talk, Nivaldo learned that one of the young people they had welcomed just ran away from the house. Nivaldo asked his spiritual father for permission to search for him in the streets of Sao Paulo: "He is weak, and he will not have the courage to come back if no one goes to look for him," he entreated.

Believing it would be dangerous, the priest refused. In an outburst of love, of generosity, and of "evangelical folly," Nivaldo soon responded: "Father, you taught me that the Good Shepherd gives his life for his sheep, (John 10:11). Let me go look for this lost brother. Tomorrow will be too late!" The priest was so touched by these words that he allowed Nivaldo to leave with two other missionaries.

On their way back, they were victims of a serious car accident. At the scene, only a few meters from the house, Nivaldo rendered his beautiful soul to God. He was 26. Nivaldo, an ardent witness to the Mercy of God, returned forever to the House of the Father. He was the first consecrated missionary of his community.

He alone died in the accident. He was found on the front seat, curled up as though he were in the arms of the Blessed Mother. With the two other brothers of his community, he had just finished saying the rosary. The final prayer of his life was the Magnificat: “He remembers His promise of mercy, the promise made to our fathers, to Abraham and his descendants forever,” (Luke 1:54-55).

The next day, during the wake, the “lost sheep” came back. The young man who had fled from the house of welcome in a moment of weakness, wanted to stand next to the casket, and he stayed there the entire night. Nivaldo, his shepherd, had given his life for him. Although he had not found him that night in the bars of Sao Paolo, he succeeded, from Heaven, in bringing him back to the fold. He had gone beyond the very limit of mercy!

The brothers of his community preserved Nivaldo’s crucifix as the most precious and most talked about remembrance of his total offering of self to God. Beside the cross, they placed part of his clothing, stained with the blood he had lost in the accident, with a passage from the Gospel that explains so well the meaning of Nivaldo’s short path in life and the fecundity of his mission:

“If a kernel of wheat falls to the ground and does not die, it remains only a single seed. But if it dies, it produces many seeds,” (John 12:24).

30
MOTHER, HE IS YOURS!

Jesus is an excellent story-teller. Raised in a little village of Galilee, off the beaten path and nestled among pleasant hills full of surprises, he was able to observe creation. He saw man grappling with nature, and the hard work he had to do to master it. "There is a tree," he tells us, "that bears no fruit. It's using up the soil; it's becoming harmful. It needs to be cut down." 'But,' we think to ourselves, 'why should the tree be cut down? The land of Israel is no Normandy and it takes many years to grow a tree in that soil which has so little water! Surely all of the work of the grower will be lost.' But, "No!" Jesus assures. "I will give the tree one last chance. He can dig around its roots, give it a solid dose of fertilizer, and it will revive. If it still produces nothing, then it will have to be cut down," (Luke 13: 6-8).

And that parable reminds me of a story:

Fredonia, Kansas, USA, October 18, 1985. Father Stephen, pastor of Sacred Heart parish, had to admit the truth: he had gotten it completely wrong, and he ruined his life.

He had arrived at a place of despair, an awful crisis of conscience. It all began on a well-traveled road in Kansas. He collided with a pick-up, was thrown from his car, and landed in a nearby field, never having fastened his seat belt. As Providence would have it, a very competent nurse was behind him; she saw him fly through the windshield and then the air, stopped her car and ran to help him. Thanks to her quick diagnosis, she was able to direct the emergency medical team who arrived on the scene who took great care in moving him, conscious that the smallest shock could have paralyzed him for life. She realized that the man was suffering from serious brain injury and a spinal fracture. If they moved his head even a little too much, he would die of asphyxia. He had already lost consciousness.

Since the nearest hospital could do no more than stitch up his scalp, the doctors decided to transport him by helicopter to the trauma unit of a larger hospital in Wichita, while quietly acknowledging that he probably wouldn't survive the trip. In fact, they gave him a 15% chance of survival. However, they didn't take God's grace into account! Father Steven was placed in the hands of a neurosurgeon who specialized in the treatment of cervical fractures like the one he suffered from, the ones known as Hangman Fractures. He was immobilized in two devices for eight long months. Four screws were attached to his skull, so as to surround his head from top to brow, with a sort of metal crown. Four metal rods came out of the crown and extended to a vest, which supported his thorax. These two devices had to keep his neck in alignment with his thorax and prevent any movement on his part, so that his spine would repair itself. He had never suffered so much in his life! The doctors thought he would remain in this position, lying on his back, for the rest of his life, paralyzed from head to toe. But the Lord had other plans!

The evening of the accident, one of his parishioners happened to be in the same hospital in Fredonia, and saw his pastor in this critical state. He sounded the clarion to get the entire parish to pray for him. The church remained open all night so that his parishioners could pray for Fr. Stephen. The faithful knew their pastor was hanging between life and death, and they lifted him up to God in incessant prayer. The rosary was recited twice a day for his recovery. Even Protestant churches – Methodists and Mennonites – began to pray intensely for him.

Even after his return to Fredonia, his convalescence lasted about a year.

His Memory Returns

One day, when he was celebrating morning Mass as usual, an entirely supernatural phenomenon surprised him. He was about to read the Gospel of the day, a Gospel that he knew by heart, the parable of the fig tree which was using up the soil, in Luke 13:6-9. It's about a landowner who wants to cut down his fig tree because, after three years, it hasn't produced any fruit. The intercession of the gardener saves it from destruction by begging for a second chance. He promises to put fertilizer on it to give the tree new life. At the moment of the reading, Father Steven started to remember a conversation he heard. Then, the page of the lectionary lit up, grew larger, and detached itself from the book, coming towards him. Overcome with emotion, he tried to finish the Mass as normally as possible. Then he hurried off to his presbytery, sat down, gulped down four cups of coffee, and searched his mind for why that particular Gospel brought back so many memories. But what were the memories?

Enlightenment was not long in coming. With stunning precision, he relived the moment of the accident, when, gravely wounded and unconscious, he had had a near-death experience. He was at death's door.

Father Steven's story contains a very rare element. At that crucial hour of definitive choice, he could hear the incredible dialogue between the Lord Jesus and the Blessed Virgin Mary, His mother, concerning Father's eternal destiny. He was aware that he deserved Hell.

Let Him Tell the Story!

"I was before the Throne of Judgment. Jesus Christ was the Judge. I didn't see Him, and I could scarcely hear Him. Everything happened in a fraction of a second, if you were to compare it with our idea of time down here. The Lord laid out my whole life before me and unveiled my many sins of action and omission. Not only had I not confessed those sins, I hadn't even repented for them. Consequently, they couldn't have been forgiven. When presented with the evidence of each of these offenses, I would say, 'Yes, Lord!' In fact, sometimes foreseeing that moment of my personal judgment, I had already planned a whole bunch of excuses to give the Lord. For example: 'Um, well, Lord, you know, this parishioner was really annoying. She caused everyone to lose their patience!' But then, when you address the Truth in person, you don't have any excuses, and all you can say is: 'Yes, Lord!'

"When Jesus got to the end of my judgment, He told me: 'Your sentence is Hell.' And there again, I said, 'Yes, Lord, I know!' It was the only logical conclusion He could come to. It didn't shock me at all. It was as if the Lord respected and honored my choices, my decisions. I had really chosen my own sentence.

The hour came for Father Steven to enter his eternity. Facing the immense Divine light, he realized that he couldn't even pretend he would enter Heaven, because during his years on Earth, he had opted for the dark side. Hadn't he lived for a long time, day after day, in a state of mortal sin, he, a priest?

"It was at that moment," he said. "After that terrible sentence, that I heard a feminine voice."

"She asked Jesus, 'Son, don't you want to spare his life and his eternal soul?'

"I heard the Lord answer her. 'Mother, for twelve years he was a priest for himself and not for me. May he reap what he has sown.'

"She answered, 'But, Son, if we give him some grace and special strength, we could see if he bears fruit. If not, may your will be done.'

"Then there was a pause of a short instant and I heard Jesus say: 'Mother, he is yours!'

"Settled in the armchair of my presbytery, I was overwhelmed by the memory that came back to me. All the pieces of the puzzle came together harmoniously. Saved in extremis by my Mother in Heaven, I became truly hers both naturally and supernaturally in the years that followed.

"I was amazed… How could I have lived without her for all those years when she was absent from my existence and from my spiritual life? People often ask me: 'But you must have had a special devotion to the Mother of God before the accident, so it's not that astonishing that she interceded for you, right?' "To that I respond, 'No, not at all! Certainly, when I was little, I sometimes joined my mother in saying the rosary on Wednesday evenings, nothing more.' But later, even though I was a priest, my faith in the angels, the saints, the mother of God was just about nil. Okay, I believed in their existence, but only in my head. It was an intellectual knowledge, not at all one from the heart. For me, the angels and the saints were nice friends from imaginary games. But they weren't real. It was only through my accident that I discovered just how real they are. I had to have that accident to focus my attention on the Lord.

"Remember the day when Jesus died on Calvary. Mary, his mother, and John, the disciple who loved him were at the foot of the cross. When Jesus saw his mother, he said to her with love: 'Woman, behold your son,' then to the disciple he said: 'Behold your mother.' At that precise moment, Jesus gave us all to His mother, as her sons and daughters. She took that very seriously. She comes to the aid of every person and intercedes for him the way she interceded for me. I was nothing exceptional. Since the accident, I have learned a very important truth about Our Lady, the Father, the Son, and the Holy Spirit. Everything the Blessed Mother wants – whatever it may be – neither God the Father, nor the Son, nor the Holy Spirit can resist. It's impossible for them to say no."

What power there is in the intercession of the Mother of God on behalf of her favorite sons! She obtained for Father Steven a return ticket to Earth! And to give her even greater joy, a second chance was offered!

After experiencing the true light of the life beyond, Father

Steven became a different man and radically changed the direction of his life. In his soul, the night gave way to day.

God Yields to Our Freedom!

Recently, I was able to ask him a few simple questions: I started, "Father Steven, a second chance is given to so few people after they've received a particular judgment; why did it happen to you?"

"I understood that, after the accident, I was saved from physical death and spiritual death for two reasons. One, to say that Hell exists. Two, equally important, to say that even priests are susceptible to going there. And I'll add one more reason: to say that we are all supposed to keep God's commandments, and we are responsible for doing that."

Father Stephen continued, "In our era, a lot of people have a tendency to reject the fact that God is just. They think that, because God is love, no one can be punished for all eternity. This is a false idea. Each of us is called to keep God's commandments and to use the sacrament of Reconciliation for the forgiveness of sins. If we think we don't sin, we had better make a more complete examination of conscience. At the time of my accident, I learned an important truth: it's not God who sends someone to Heaven or Hell. We ourselves choose our eternal destiny. God yields to our freedom. That decision comes from us. God only honors and confirms our own choice, out of the infinite respect He has for each of us. It's not as though a priest enjoys some guarantee for Heaven. Just the opposite! A priest has to be even more responsible than any lay person at keeping God's commandments. He must represent the kind of priest ordained to serve the people of God and to incarnate Jesus Christ. The Blessed Virgin Mary asks us often to pray for priests and not to criticize them. Now more than ever, in these times, it is easy to criticize a priest or a bishop when we believe they have left the Church's path of orthodoxy."

Father Steven told me that he sometimes makes this significant gesture: he takes off his Roman collar in front of the people and declares: "This little piece of white plastic that you see is no guarantee of Heaven!"

He Changes His Life

Father Steven used to live in a state of mortal sin, that's clear. I didn't dare ask for details about the sins he committed. What had he done that was so serious, and how had he broken communion with God? He willingly admitted 2 things:-

1. He endeavored more to please the faithful of his parish than to watch over their souls and protect them from sin. He kept quiet about the commandments of God and the true demands of the Gospel, which would have led them to conversion, because he was afraid of losing their approval. Since they donated money to him, he wanted to keep their friendship. Basically, he wanted to keep their money.

2. He didn't pray and never recited his Breviary even though that is a daily duty for every priest. It is in faithful prayer that the priest draws from God the light and love he needs to exercise his ministry for the people of God. That is where he recharges his batteries. Without prayer, what can he give others? Besides, this lack of prayer trains his conscience to go to sleep. He doesn't hesitate to sin gravely, then continue to celebrate Holy Mass anyway. Venerable Marthe Robin confided to Father Finet (her spiritual director) that she saw, in a mystical way, so many priests ascend the altar in a state of mortal sin, and she sobbed from the pain. It's a question of an extremely painful sacrilege to the Heart of Christ, because it's the result of the "choices" of those who are supposed to love Him in a special way and take care of his flock.

During the interview that he granted me, I found a priest very solid in his faith, to the point that it was difficult for me to imagine him lukewarm and mundane before his accident. I asked him: "I suppose you are very happy now to be back in this world, to finally experience a true union with the Lord?"

His answer gushed out: "Oh, yes! But here, the Earth … it's not our true place. The true life is after death. Here, we are living only a shadow of the life that lies ahead of us."

"Have you seen God?" I asked.

"No, I haven't seen Him. I was in a state of mortal sin. You don't see Jesus when you are in a state of mortal sin. On the other hand, I heard His voice clearly."

So as not to get in the way of that humility, I questioned a couple of very dear American friends, Bill and Mabel, who lived in his diocese, about him. I wanted to learn about his manner of living both before and after the accident.

Mabel revealed to me: "One day when I was surfing the net, I came upon the story of this priest who had had a near-death experience and was given a second chance. I did everything in my power to meet him. Following our first encounter with him, seeing the light that emanated from him, Bill and I asked him to be our spiritual guide. Subsequently, he got us "on board" with the Marian Helpers, who propose daily Mass for members. On the first Fridays of the month he instituted Adoration in his parishes, and he himself participates. He encourages the Marian devotion on the first Saturdays of each month.[32]

---

[32] The five first Saturdays of the month: on the evening of December 10, 1925, the young postulant, Lucia of Fatima, received a visit from the Blessed Mother in her cell, and, next to her, borne on a luminous cloud, the Child Jesus. The Virgin showed her a Heart surrounded with thorns, which she held in her hands. The Child Jesus said: "Have compassion on the Heart of the Most Blessed Mother surrounded by the thorns that ungrateful people inflict on her at every turn, without a single person doing an act of reparation to take them out". Then Our Lady said: "See, My Daughter, my Heart surrounded by thorns that ungrateful men inflict on me every minute by their blasphemies and their ingratitude. You, at least, must try to console me, and tell all who go to confession on the first Saturdays for five months, receive Holy Communion, recite a rosary, and keep me company for fifteen minutes meditating on the fifteen mysteries of the Rosary in a spirit of reparation, that I promise to help them at the hour of death with all the graces necessary for the salvation of their souls."

"Occasionally, in the middle of our consternation about how to handle a difficult situation, he would say, 'Only God knows, and right now, He's not talking!' That remark helped us abandon our troubles and place our trust in God.

"Before his accident, he admits, he used to seek above all else to be loved and appreciated by his entire entourage, his parishioners, and other priests. He worked hard for that. He reveled in the advantages of being a priest, without having the least concern for souls. Even as a child, he had developed the habit of achieving his purposes by winning over the religious nuns at his school through sentimentality and charm; he would tell them that he wanted to be a priest, which merited special favor from them. In short, he was already adept at making himself loved and spoiled.

"As an adult, he gave the world and the spirit of the world top priority in his life. The esteem and opinion of others were primordial for him, which inexorably led him to doubtful compromise. As a priest, he was sacrificing the duty of pleasing God to that of pleasing men. That is what almost got him lost! It explains Christ's remark about him, "He was a priest for himself and not for Me." Such an attitude explains the darkness which inhabited him. Didn't Saint John say clearly: "If any man loves the world, the love of the Father is not in him," (1 John 2: 15).[33]

"After the accident, his first concern was to please God. He was finished with deadly compromises! Father Steven became a free man, delivered from the slavery of others' opinions. Time and time again, he doesn't hesitate to proclaim the truth of the Gospel of Christ, even if he is occasionally a little sharp-edged. He proclaims the naked, unvarnished truth. Whether it pleases his audience or not doesn't matter! He has become his own valiant defender.

---

[33] "If any man loves the world, the love of the Father is not in him," (1 John 2: 15). And also: "Whosoever, therefore, wants to be a friend of the world makes himself an enemy of God," (James 4:4).

"Doing the will of God at all costs, that's what counts for him, because he touched the splendor of that will. He has done a 180° turn! His honesty and sincerity are remarkable! For him, obedience to God and fidelity to his role as a shepherd of souls is essential.

"The Blessed Mother has become very dear to him, and he repeats constantly: 'Jesus can refuse her nothing!' He makes the first Saturday prayers very special. He has put the Holy Mass at the center of his life, and he is anxious to celebrate it every day, even on his days off."

Mabel added: "A lot of us who live in Great Bend have been driving 50 kilometers to get to Bushton and attend his First Saturday Masses. Because, in our diocese of Dodge City, no Mass is celebrated on Saturday mornings. In good weather, to welcome us, he stands outside in front of the church door, or in the vestibule if the winter is less clement, and there, he offers an anointing of oil to all those among us who are older than 65, sick or not. Because, he says, we run a greater risk of dying unexpectedly. It's true that, for him, sudden death is no longer a mystery. He wants to give us the favor of this extra grace. After the Mass, the rosary and the litanies of the Virgin Mary are recited. He was dressed in the most beautiful vestments for the Feast Day of Our Lady. He made sure to put very beautiful flowers on the altar. He was wearing an enormous rosary with a large cross, and this contained a relic of the True Cross."

Another anecdote demonstrates that he has received some charisms. Bill, Mabel's husband, tore one of his biceps. Severe pain radiated down his entire arm. He consulted one of their friends who who was a doctor. Bill's surgery had been scheduled, and Father Steven had inquired as to the exact time of the operation. He arrived at the hospital and remained seated next to Bill while the nurses busied themselves with preparatory care. After his final examination of Bill, the doctor did not hide his pessimism about the success of the surgery he was about to do. In short, the atmosphere was not reassuring! The time came to roll the gurney into the operating room, but

Father Steven stopped it and began to pray over Bill, inviting Mabel and anyone present to do the same. Upon seeing that, the doctor asked Mabel: "What's this priest doing here?" "He's a very dear friend who came to give support to Bill," Mabel replied.

Then Father Steven looked Mabel right in the eye and affirmed: "It's going to be okay. Everything's going to go well for Bill!"

Between the preliminary examination and the surgery itself, the whole thing was to last around five hours. In the waiting room, to curb the intrusion of fear, Mabel recited to herself these words of Father Steven: "Pray and have confidence!" Three hours later, the surgeon, red from emotion and dripping with sweat, bounded out of the operating room and ran towards Mabel, shouting: "Mabel, I was successful! I have just done the operation of my life! I don't know what happened in there, but I succeeded in taking hold of the muscle, stretching it out, and fastening it with two screws. The repair is solid. I simply can't believe it! With the right therapy, Bill should have a good, stable shoulder. I know it was Father Steven's intercession that blessed us with this result."

Father Steven was endowed with the genuine gift of healing, which has manifested many other times. Today, at 69, he lives in a retirement home for priests, because he is very sick. He is kept on oxygen, since he suffers from serious cardiac insufficiency, and he is hanging onto life by a thread. We can easily guess just how much he wants to see, with his own eyes, his dear Blessed Mother and to fling himself with confidence into the arms of Jesus, his King of Mercy!

Thanks to Mabel, I had the joy of knowing this priest, who, by his testimony, corroborated what the Church, like all the mystics, have always taught us: God is love and mercy. He puts no one in Hell. He sent His son Jesus to offer Eternal Life to all His children: "God wants all men to be saved," (1 Tim. 2:4). We choose for ourselves our eternal destiny by the decisions we make day by day during our lives. Our little yes in each moment is preparation for our great and final YES, and our little no for our great and final NO, because the tree falls in the direction in which it is leaning. Don't be fooled if Our Lady has powerfully interceded with her Son. It is He, Himself, her Son, who has inspired her prayer, in order to have once more the joy of granting His mother's plea and saving that soul.

Is it difficult to Go to Hell?

The striking testimony of Father Steven conforms, in a way, to that of Gloria Polo. Both found themselves at the gates of Hell and received a second chance. Some might question whether God is truly satisfied that justice is being done in the case of a sinner who has not repented, considering the way human justice is meted out. We sometimes imagine the condemned soul as pleading desperately for the Lord not to send him to Hell. It's exactly the reverse! It is God, Who, up until the very end, pleads with the soul to accept His mercy and to demonstrate a surge of trust in it, so that that soul may be saved forever.

Let me quote here from a poignant dialogue between Jesus and the little Vietnamese Marcel Van, Servant of God, who shows us to what degree God thirsts for our unwavering trust in His mercy.[34]

Jesus: "If men could only comprehend that Love loves them infinitely, there would never be a soul who fell into Hell…Truly, the devil has no power to take a soul out of My hands. All he can do is lead people to fall into sin. However, if a soul no longer trusts in My infinite love, then, naturally, it is very easy for the devil to capture that soul.

"Alas!! Marcel, is there, for Love, any pain that compares

[34] The cause for beatification of the Servant of God Marcel Van of Vietnam is open. See the association Friends of Van: www.amisdevan.org

with losing a soul? Naturally, Love being infinite, it loves out of infinite love as well. But this infinity of Love can only take firm hold of hearts where genuine trust is found. Without that genuine trust, can infinite Love still hold onto the heart, when there is nothing there to grasp onto?

"Oh, sinful souls, My little sisters, the only thing I ask of you and the only thing that is sufficient for me to press you against this heart overflowing with love, is that you truly believe that Love loves you infinitely. Poor, wretched little Sisters, do you think I am completely ignoring the fact that you are miserable? Even if your misery is infinite, you must believe, even then, that My love is infinite and infinite. Even if your sins could condemn you to Hell an infinite number of times, you must not, for that reason, lose confidence in My Love... But, alas! The sad thing is that people don't have confidence in My Love; there is absolutely nothing that offends My Love more than lack of confidence in My Love...

"Marcel! Marcel! Oh, little brother, pray so that sinful souls, so very numerous, do not lose confidence in My Love. As long as they hold onto this confidence, the Kingdom of Heaven will never truly cease belonging to them."

Marcel: "But Little Jesus, if people continue to sin deliberately, what will happen? Will you still give them Paradise?"

Jesus: "Little brother, you don't understand that I know the extreme weakness of man! Even if men offend Me deliberately and as seriously as you can imagine, their sin is nothing compared to even a shadow of Love... Love is infinite. Say it loudly to people: 'yes, infinite and infinite'. Have confidence in Me, and never, never for eternity, will you be separated from Me. Even the devil has to despair of a soul in which the word "confidence" is found... Later, in Heaven, people will surely be surprised to see, ranked with the saints, a great number of souls that they believed to be damned...

"Love loves infinitely. It is infinitely just. It is because it is infinitely just that it loves infinitely, and it is because it loves infinitely that it is infinitely just... A simple look of confidence directed towards Me is enough to wrest sinful souls from the grip of the devil. Even if a soul finds itself already at the gates of Hell, waiting for his last breath to fall into it, if in that last breath there is the slightest degree of confidence in My infinite Love, that will be sufficient for My Love to pull that soul into the arms of the Trinity; that is why I say that it is very easy for people to go up to Heaven, while it is very difficult, even infinitely difficult, for them to fall into Hell; because Love will never suffer a soul to be lost easily.

"However, little brother, these words must not be shown to all souls indiscriminately; it must be done with prudence, for fear that some souls, knowing this, will only harden themselves in evil… And, consequently, lose confidence in Me and no longer have any confidence at all."[35]

This last sentence is of prime importance: sin, as pardonable as it is by God, blinds us progressively to the goodness of the Lord. It keeps us in the dark, like Father Steven, who no longer believed in mercy and who didn't even ask for it during his encounter with Jesus! Ah, if Mary hadn't been there… But she was there, and she will be there for us all!

One of my friends, very close to God, revealed this to me: after having committed a sin, he was plunged into profound pain and he felt guilty for having wounded Christ. It was then that, in his heart, he heard these words: "Your sin? Look at my body covered with wounds. You have confessed your sin, so the past no longer exists. Your sins are in my wounds and no longer in you!"

[35] Extracts from the book: MARCEL VAN, Collection, § 646-650, Saint Paul Editions/Religious Editions

31
Hiroshima and the Victory of the Rosary

Hiroshima after the explosion of the atomic bomb

It was August 6, 1945. At 9:15 AM, a giant mushroom cloud rose over the city of Hiroshima, Japan. In just two minutes, it reached an altitude of 10,000 meters, and nothing could resist its devastation. Within a radius of two miles, 10,000 buildings were destroyed by the blast of the explosion and 50,000 more by fires. Thousands of victims died instantly inside the 1200-meter diameter of the impact of the explosion. Beyond that circle, because of radiation, Japanese soldiers, charged with gathering the dead, died themselves, one after the other, within a few weeks. In spite of everything, several hundred meters from the center of the explosion, one house remained standing, as if it had never been touched by the bomb, even though it was of typical Japanese construction, made of light materials which should have been destroyed in the blink of an eye. What happened?

This house was none other than the presbytery of eight German Jesuits. One of them, Father Hubert Schiffer, gave a stunning testimony at the great Eucharistic Congress of Philadelphia in July of 1976, an event I was able to attend along with Pierre Goursat and several members of the Emmanuel Community. None of the seven other Jesuits who were living with him were harmed by the bomb, and all were spared from any radioactive contamination. They emerged from the drama not only alive but in perfect health. They died from old age many years later. Father Hubert Schiffer was 30 years old when the bomb exploded. He lived another 33 years in good health before dying in Frankfurt in 1982.

Experts were puzzled for a long time over this enigma. They investigated it with the help of the best equipment and researched intensely whether there was some hidden strength in the construction of the house. They could not figure out how it was possible for this little house to resist such a cataclysm. Moreover, the Jesuits themselves endured physical examination by more than 200 scientists and specialists. Their conclusion remained the same: they were surprised not to see in the men any effect of radioactivity and couldn't understand how these men could have survived in the middle of this utter disaster in which thousands of other living creatures had perished.

When science came up with no answer, it was the Jesuits who finally revealed the key to the mystery. They explained that it was thanks to their daily praying of the rosary, recited together, that had miraculously protected them. Father Schiffer said later: "The scientists didn't understand anything. They didn't believe our explanation when we told them that we were living out the message of Fatima, that we had prayed the Rosary together each day in that house." The Queen of the Rosary had kept her promise. During World War I, May 13, 1917, she told the three little shepherds of Fatima: "Recite the rosary each day for peace in the world and for the end of the war."

A similar thing happened in Nagasaki. Before World War II, Father Maximilian Kolbe had planned to construct, in Japan, a Franciscan monastery dedicated to the *Immaculate*. When he told his superiors that he wanted to build this monastery just behind a small hill overlooking Nagasaki, the men mocked him and tried to prevent him from doing it because the site had neither water nor electricity and was in an extremely inconvenient place. They questioned why he did not want to build in the city and use urban amenities? Father Kolbe, inspired by the Virgin Mary, prayed intensely and waited for his superiors to change their minds. He won his case and constructed his monastery dedicated to Immaculate Mary on that very hill. There, in that Franciscan monastery, the brothers also prayed the rosary together each day. They could not have imagined what was going to take place before their very eyes! Three days after the bombardment of Hiroshima, on August 9, 1945, the bomb H known as "Fatman" was dropped on Nagasaki. It miraculously spared the monastery. The little hill had protected it, even though 80% of the city was destroyed.

Our Lady endlessly reiterates that peace can only be achieved by returning to God through prayer, especially praying the Rosary. She always keeps the promises that she makes to those who confide in her. So, let us not forget the promise made to Saint Dominic and the Blessed Alain de la Roche: "Those who confide in me and pray the Rosary, will never perish" and "Those who spread the Rosary will receive my help in all their needs." Facts often speak louder than words! Entire books would not be enough to contain all the testimonies of graces and miracles obtained through the Rosary!

Here is another story from the United States, told to me by a friend named Linda. Her child attends a primary school and as part of their curriculum, a few new age books promoting witchcraft had been introduced. During the parent-teacher conferences, the promoter of these books was invited to speak about them over the loudspeaker. Seeing this, Linda and her friend Mary decided to silently pray the Rosary. At a certain point, while speaking through the microphone, the promoter of these books started stuttering. One after the other, the parents who were attracted to the promotion table where these books were being sold went back to their seat. The children were protected! "Give me an army that prays the Rosary and I will conquer the world!" said saint Pius X. Also, Adrian VI said: "The Rosary is the whip against the demons."

Like any other form of prayer, the value of the Rosary does not depend on the feelings that one experiences, but rather, it depends on one's good will and one's firm decision to devote this time to God to become closer to Him. For the rest, the Lord will provide! One day while Saint Faustina was feeling sad about being distracted in prayer, Jesus said to her: "When you feel consolation in prayer, it's Me consoling you. When you experience dryness, it's you consoling Me!"

The Virgin Mary's Prophet

All kinds of prophets prophesize about the future, but there is one whom I'd like to quote here, because he is canonized: Saint Louis Marie Grignon de Montfort (1673-1716). His prophecy is strangely accurate in our present days, particularly in Europe.

"Jesus Christ will come, just as the whole church anticipates, to reign over all the earth, in a time and manner that men least expect."

"At the end of time, perhaps sooner than we think, God will raise up great saints in order to establish the reign of His son over a corrupt world, by means of devotion to the Most Blessed Virgin."

"In the last times, the power of Mary will be manifested to all. She will extend the Kingdom of Christ as far as the Muslims."

"Mary must shine forth more than ever in mercy, in strength and in grace in the last times."

"The friends of the world will persecute more than ever those who belong to the Most Blessed Virgin. But the humble Mary will always have the victory."

"The power of Mary will shine forth over all the demons, particularly in the end times."[36]

Sister Lucia of Fatima Explains

The little shepherdess of Fatima, who became Sister Lucia of the Carmelite Convent in Coimbra, Portugal, returned to the House of the Father three months before John Paul II in 2005. She left some very powerful writings on the Rosary, because, even after the six apparitions in 1917 with her cousins, she continued to meet with the Blessed Mother and to receive enlightenment from her about the Church and about our times. Let's not forget that it was to these little shepherds with no education that Our Lady entrusted the most beautiful prophecy of all regarding herself: "In the end, my Immaculate Heart will triumph." What Mary did not specify was, at the end of what?! But these letters on the Rosary clarify it to us: they recall that the victory of love is won with the simplest of means, and that the enemy allows himself to be conquered by those who pray like children.

In Fatima, Our Lady recommended the Rosary "to end the war." But a hundred years later, why have we abandoned that devotion? Why have we allowed the enemy to take away from our families and our churches a practice which disturbs him so much?

In 1957, Sister Lucia wrote to Father Fuentes: "The Most Blessed Virgin Mary wanted to give, in these last times that we are living, a new efficacy to the praying of the Holy Rosary. She wanted to reinforce its efficacy so much that there would be no problem that could not be resolved by praying the Rosary. No matter how difficult that problem might be – whether tem-

---

[36] (Extracts from the book "The Secret of Mary").

poral or, above all, spiritual – in the spiritual life of each of us or in the lives of our families, be they our families in the world or Religious Communities, or even in the lives of peoples and nations. I repeat, there is no problem, as difficult as it might be, that cannot be resolved by praying the Holy Rosary. With the Holy Rosary we will save ourselves, sanctify ourselves, console Our Lord and obtain the salvation of many souls.

In 1970, to one of her sisters, Sister Lucia wrote: "The Rosary is the prayer of the poor and the rich, of the educated and the simple. Take this devotion away from souls, and you take away their spiritual daily bread. The Rosary is what sustains the little flame of Faith that still has not been extinguished in many consciences. Even for those souls who pray without meditating, the very act of taking up the Rosary to pray is already a remembrance of God, of the Supernatural. A simple recollection of the mysteries of each decade is one more ray of light to sustain in souls the still-smoldering wick. This is why the devil has made such war against it. And what is worse is that he has succeeded in deluding and deceiving souls who have a great deal of responsibility because of the positions they occupy … They are the blind leading the blind …"

To all the Marian Communities in the world, Sister Lucia wrote in October 2001: "The Blessed Virgin exhorts us to pray the Rosary with more faith, more fervor, while contemplating the Joyful, Sorrowful, and Glorious Mysteries of Her Son, Who united her to the mystery of our Redemption… When you say the prayers of the Rosary in your hands, the Angels and Saints unite themselves to you. That is why I exhort you to recite it with great reverence, with faith, meditating with profound piety on the meanings of the mysteries. Recite it in private or in community, in the house or out-doors, in a church or in the street, with simplicity of heart, following step by step the path of the Virgin with her Son. Recite it always with vibrant faith for those who are being born, those who are suffering, those who are laboring, and those who are dying. Recite it in union with all the just of the earth and with all the Marian communities, but, above all, with the simplicity of children, whose voices are united with those of the Angels. Today, as never before, the world needs your rosary … Very often, the recitation of a single rosary has appeased the anger of the Divine Justice, and has obtained for the world the Divine Mercy and the salvation of so many souls."[37]

One of the most astonishing miracles that occurred in France through the praying of the Rosary, was the one obtained by the visionary Jacqueline Aubry, from l'Ile Bouchard.[38] Ever since an apparition she had at the age of 11 in 1947 of "Our Lady of Prayer" (recognized by the church), she prayed intensely for France. Inspired by the Holy Spirit, she interceded in particular for Georges Marchais, the leader of the Communist Party from 1972 to 1994 and Deputy from 1973 to 1997, and she wrote him a private letter. Marchais was dying of cancer. The result was really not unexpected: before dying on November 16, 1997, Georges Marchais received inner enlightenment and converted on the spot. He asked for his Confession to be heard and to receive Holy Communion.

Father Manteau Bonamy, O.P. (1916-1999), a great Marian expert and friend of Medjugorje, wrote: "The divine maternity

---

[37] On December 10, 1925, the Blessed Virgin appeared to Lucia of Fatima, and next to her, suspended on a luminous cloud, the Child Jesus. The Most Blessed Virgin put her hand on Lucia's shoulder and showed her at the same time a heart surrounded by thorns that she held in the other hand. Then, the Most Blessed Virgin said to her: "Look, My Daughter, at my heart surrounded by thorns, which ungrateful men pierce me with at every moment with their blasphemies and their ingratitude. You, at least, try to console me, and announce that I promise to assist at the hour of death, with all the graces necessary for the salvation of their souls, all who for five months, on the first Saturday of each month, go to confession, receive Holy Communion, recite the Rosary, and keep me company for fifteen minutes while meditating on the fifteen mysteries of the Rosary with the intention of making reparation to me.

[38] On December 8, 1947, the Virgin appeared to four little girls, Jacqueline, Jeannette, Nicole, and Laura and asked them to "pray for France." Basically, after the Second World War, the country was on the brink of civil war, and the Communists were ready to assume power. The prayers of the children and of the entire parish caused the enemy's plan to fail. Jacqueline died on March 15, 2016, after a beautiful life of witness. On December 8, 2001, Monsignor Vingt-Trois, the archbishop of Tours, authorized pilgrimages and public worship to be celebrated in the parish church, Saint Gilles de L'Ile-Bouchard, to invoke Our Lady of Prayer.

has graced the Blessed Virgin with a splendor that has no equal, either on earth or in Heaven. She gives to it, through her participation, the power that God has by nature, and we could say that nothing takes place on earth or in Heaven without her intervention. The divine maternity has given to the Blessed Virgin, in her interactions with us, the comforting tenderness of a mother and the incomparable authority of a queen. Mary, Mother of God, Mary, Queen of Love, participates in the mediation of Christ and all the graces that Christ has acquired for us. She has merited becoming the distributer of them. It is she who distributes all the gifts, all the virtues, all the graces to whomever she wants, when she wants, in the manner and measure she wants."[39]

On December 2, 2016, in Medjugorje, Our Lady said: "Dear Children, my maternal heart cries when I see what my children are doing. The sins keep multiplying: purity of soul is of the least importance; my Son is forgotten, less and less honored, and my children are persecuted… That is why, Dear Children, return to the prayer of the Rosary. Pray the Rosary with feelings of goodness, of sacrifice, and of mercy…"

[39] Father Manteau-Bonamy, O.P. Extracts of the book (in French) "Marthe Robin sous la Conduite de Marie." Ed. Saint-Paul.

32
I Want to See Maïti!

Maïti's hands ran over the piano masterfully. A magnificent melody rose into the air with her touch. The effect was almost magical. She was 12 years old. A brilliant career awaited her. Maïti had no doubt: music would be her life!

In 1922, Maïti Girtanner was born into a large, Catholic family of German origin, in the German area of Switzerland. During the 1930s, one could already perceive, with some disquiet, the rise of Nazism. Maïti's father died when she was 3, and since her mother was French, they both went to live in a trendy part of Paris. There, she undertook her studies with great gusto at the Paris Conservatory of Music and became, little by little, a talented pianist. The little girl already had an intimate relationship with Christ and dreamed of making Him known through her use of the piano. "I understood that the truth was a person, Jesus Christ, and this realization made me burn with desire to transmit and proclaim this truth." When France was invaded by the German army in 1940, the family took refuge in their holiday home in Bonnes, near Poitiers, very close to the line of demarcation which separated unoccupied France from the part of France occupied by the Germans.

Shocked by the demands that the Nazis placed on her people, and endowed with a rebellious nature, Maïti very quickly joined the Allied powers who fought against Nazism and established her own network. She had just turned 18. In forming her little group of rebels, she carefully gathered together students who were totally inconspicuous. They helped soldiers, Jewish families, English people – all sorts of clandestine groups

– to flee into the free zone. They traveled many miles by bicycle to pass information and manufacture false papers. Faced with the grave danger that these actions exposed them to, many of them were afraid. Maïti was also afraid, but she encouraged them with a firm voice: “Do you believe in God? Then pray to Him, and move on!” Her faith and determination destroyed all human limitations. Nothing stopped her momentum. In spite of her youth, she decided to pursue this work to the end. Later, she would ask herself “Just where is that end for me?” It would lead her much further than she could have expected.

In 1943, as the line of demarcation became erased with the advance of the Germans into the free zone, Maïti decided to leave for Paris by herself, in order to continue her activities in the Résistance. She was 21 years old!

In Paris, she continued to help friends obtain papers, and to ensure that comrades arrested by the Gestapo were set free. She always utilized her “weapons”: her mastery of the German tongue and her art of cajoling and persuading. She even went as far as agreeing to play the piano for the Nazi officers. She connected particularly with a music-lover, a general, who appreciated her talents and who trusted her completely.

The Time of the Nightmare

Toward the end of 1943, Maïti was arrested by chance during a roundup of prisoners in the capital. For Maïti, this was the beginning of the horror. When the general found her name on the list of people who were chosen randomly, he was indignant: “Release this young girl immediately. She’s our little pianist.” Unfortunately, the arresting officers proved to the general that Maïti was a leader in the Resistance. Alas, her involvement was proven beyond a doubt, and her activities had been discovered. The general was aghast with anger at having been deceived by this young girl. He decided to inflict a horrendous punishment upon her that would be an example for others.

So Maïti was transferred with 19 other rebels, both male and female, to a secret site where no one emerged alive. There, torture doctors made every attempt to do the worst possible harm to their victims.

Maïti was handed over to one man. His name was Léo. For days without respite, this doctor struck her with diabolic brutality and precision. The blows caused great harm to the bone marrow of her spine, a damage which would destroy her sensory nervous system. Her torturer intended to imprison her in unbearable pain forever. Like her companions, Maïti was certain of only one thing: she was going to die.

In February of 1944, after a new series of tortures, she was left to die. At the last minute, she was liberated and saved, but the after-effects of her torture were irreversible. It took eight years of care and hospitalization to put her back together again. The suffering never left her. The beautiful future that lay ahead of her fell apart. She would never be a pianist. "It was over," she recounted. "That surrender was terrible to accept. For many years, hearing the piano played made me cry and rage with regret." Along with renouncing the piano, Maïti also gave up the idea of ever getting married and having a family.

"But in spite of everything," she said, "I wasn't mad at anyone. For all intents and purposes, anger wasn't going to get me anywhere and wasn't going to give me back my fingers. I didn't at any moment transform my pain into hatred, nor did I nourish any personal resentment towards this Léo and his colleagues."

Not only was she not angry at her torturers, Maïti was not angry at God either. "When I discovered that I had this personal relationship with Jesus, I realized that God hadn't wanted me to walk that path of suffering and horror. I understood that in the midst of that suffering, He had been joining me, almost physically, with His presence, His proximity. He had joined me in undergoing an evil that men were sadly and completely capable of creating themselves. God didn't desire this evil just so that I would be closer to Him at the end. Instead, God joined me in this awful evil perpetrated by men, in order, first of all, to help me extricate myself from it and reconstruct myself, and then to carry, with my consent, a message to others."

Despite her profound faith, Maïti admitted: "I wasn't too sure about the notion of forgiveness. That, also, is a long journey." For forty years, every day, without exception, Maïti prayed for Léo. She held him up in her prayers. She said, "I always thought that the evil was worse for the torturer than for the victim. Man is not cruel by nature."

40 Years Later, Léo Telephoned Her

Maïti had to interiorly reform herself, and accept her new state of life. "I had to accept what I no longer was and accept it fully." She became a tutor in philosophy, got her driver's license, and deepened her Christian faith, which helped her find a new direction: giving of herself always and growing in love. She arrived at that point not by the strength of her fist, but by calling for the help of grace.

40 years later, that grace may have allowed an unimaginable meeting with Léo. At least, Maïti thought so. She said, "Rather quickly, I had the crazy desire to forgive that man." But it took many graces to make it happen.

It was he who telephoned her one day in 1984. Yes, this man who had destroyed her resurfaced. He said he was in Paris and wanted to meet her. Maïti was overcome with emotion. She had nothing prepared, nothing planned. She didn't even know if she could truly forgive him. She said yes. She was going to try to take the high road, as she had always done. She herself told the story of this meeting on television.[40]

She said that he came to find her in 1984, when he was at the point of dying. Léo had become an old man of 72, and he

---

[40] Direct testimony of Maïti during the telecast "The Day of the Lord" (in French).

was terrified of death. His doctor had given him only a few weeks to live. Léo felt an inexplicable need to find this young girl whom he left to die after his torture in 1944. Maïti, like the others, should have died a few hours later, but this former SS agent, almost intuitively knew she was still alive. When they first met, Léo was 26 years old. Maïti had asked him how he got there. Seized by Hitler Youth members at the age of 8, he was torn from his family. Then, like all the others, he had been brainwashed into becoming a torture-doctor, a war criminal. He was very proud of the fact that he had been personally chosen by Himmler.

Léo remembered hearing Maïti speak about God to her comrades, the 18 other Resistance fighters imprisoned with her in a tiny, little room, where he came to find them when he took his turn at administering torture. She used to talk to her cellmates about this 'Love' which awaited them after death. Those who had not died under torture were brought back to that tiny space, and Maïti used to help them to accept death. Léo not only heard everything she said, but he also remembered it. As his own death was approaching, a very deep apprehension seized him and he wanted to be certain: Does life after death exist, or am I going to fall into a black hole?

At first, Léo only wanted to see Maïti for one thing: to be reassured. He found her in her Paris apartment, and this was the first thing he said to her: "I came to talk to you about death. It's urgent!" The discussion ended up lasting nearly two hours. Maïti spoke to him about death, affirming him that God waits for all of us, with arms wide open, even for the greatest of sinners, as long as they repent. Upon hearing those words, Léo's memories of the atrocities he committed came back to his mind. The notion of forgiveness began to germinate in his spirit. His face changed suddenly. Until that moment, his vision of death had been that of an iron curtain that slammed down brutally and behind which he would be eternally imprisoned, with no chance of communicating with anyone. Maïti explained to him that the greatest torture in hell was the absence of any communication with God, the absence of God Himself. Maïti saw the flame of regret growing gradually in his eyes.

At the end of an hour, Léo unfolded his legs, straightened up in his armchair, lowered his head and asked Maïti with great humility, like a little, lost child, “What can I do?” And there it was: grace had just come through! Then, Maïti spoke to him about God, about Love. “Talk to God – stammer and stutter. God lives inside all creatures, even the darkest ones. Now you have nothing to live for but love, since you have only a few weeks to live. You should accept the challenge and be nothing but love for others.”

“I can’t,” Léo answered. “I’ve cut all connections with my family, and no one knows what I experienced. Everyone is ignorant of the fact that I was a torturer. I made new friends. I became the mayor of my city. I’m a good citizen, a remarkable friend, esteemed by everyone.”

Léo and Maïti had just experienced unforgettable moments. But the most beautiful fruit, the unimaginable, was yet to come: “At the moment of our parting,” Maïti recounted, “Léo was standing at the head of my bed. An irrepressible movement raised me up from my pillow even though it hurt me terribly, and I kissed him, so as to place him in the heart of Jesus. And he said to me very quietly, ‘Forgive me.’ It was the kiss of peace which he had come to find. From that moment on, I knew that I had forgiven him.”

Léo had been experiencing an inner earthquake. He was transformed! His wife related after his death that the moment he returned to Austria he gathered his family together and revealed everything, because they knew nothing of his past as a Nazi torturer! He finished his confession by saying to them: “And now, I want to spend the time I have left, loving you.” He gave each person particular and concrete attention. He reunited with his old friends of the past, and his present friends, and renewed his confession. He declared that, beginning recently, he no longer felt in his heart any hatred towards anyone, and he did not even feel the ideological hatred injected in him by Nazism. Then he continued: “I have only one idea, only one desire: that is to spend the last weeks of my life in acts of love and tenderness towards you."

The guests couldn't get over it. Léo had followed to the letter all that Maïti had told him. Could it be that for him she was the only way, the only person who, during all his life, had shown him the path of light?

Moments before dying, Léo did not request a priest or a pastor. Surprised, his wife asked him, "Who do you want to see?" He murmured, "Maïti!"

33
Comparison Comes From the Evil One

The Desert Fathers always amaze us with the clarity and sobriety of their testimonies. There once was a monastery in the middle of the Egyptian desert. One of the monks went to find the hegumen (the elder priest of the community in the first Oriental Christian churches) to complain to him, because, he said, he had witnessed an injustice and a breaking of the community rule. Apparently, a new postulant, Brother Antoine, had placed a cushion in his cell. Now all the other cells had only a mat on the floor. Why did this new arrival have the right to a cushion and not the others?

The hegumen, discerning very quickly the trap into which his brother had fallen, asked him several questions:

"Before entering the monastery, did you have servants at your home for working the fields and doing domestic tasks?"

"No, that was out of the question for us. It never occurred to us to have servants," the monk said.

"And before entering the monastery, did you have enough food to eat every day?" the Hegumen asked.

"No," answered the monk, "some days we didn't have anything. My family was very poor, and I was often very hungry."

"I see," said the Hegumen. "And today, here in the monastery, have you eaten every day?"

"Yes," answered the monk. "Thanks be to God!"

"Before entering the monastery," the hegumen continued. "Did you have a roof over your head?"

"The roof we had was very precarious. Water leaked in, and, often, my father didn't get there to protect us from bad weather."

"And now, do you have a roof over your head?"

"Yes, now it's the roof of the monastery."

"You see, in the world you had practically nothing, but upon entering the monastery, you were enriched. The quality of your life was greatly ameliorated, and now you lack nothing, even though we live simply. Brother Antoine, in the world, was a very rich prince; he lived in a palace, where servants took care of all his needs. He enjoyed a rare kind of comfort and could buy for himself anything he wanted. He ate well every day. In short, he lived in the lap of luxury. Upon entering the monastery, he renounced all his worldly goods to follow the poor Christ. Which of you two is experiencing poverty more profoundly?"

The monk quickly understood and thanked his hegumen, who had helped him detect the trap in which he had lamentably fallen by judging his brother.

Let us keep our eyes open to this danger! Comparison comes from the devil. God doesn't compare. Each person is unique in His eyes. Comparison often plunges us into bitterness, frustration, feelings of injustice, and jealousy. It pushes us to ignore the goodness of God towards us and the specific and unique beauty that He places in us when He created us. Jesus once said to Saint Mechthild, "He who rejoices in a gift that God gives his brother, and that he himself does not possess, will receive the same recompense as he who possesses this gift."

The Holy Monk and the Prostitute

Contained in the Eastern tradition of the Desert Fathers, in the first centuries of the Church, we are reminded of a similar aphorism. In an Egyptian monastery there was a hegumen reputed for his mercy, because everyone who went to see him returned full of joy, even after shedding many tears over their sins. The hegumen surprised those surrounding him with his profound humility and by the burning love he had for Christ.

His charism of converting the most hardened of sinners was well known, so one day people brought to him a prostitute from the city. This woman wore a prodigious amount of makeup. Her hair was braided and decorated with pearls, and a bewitching perfume emanated from her, indicating that this woman had a great desire to please men. The hegumen welcomed her with kindness. He let her speak a moment, then he began to cry. A profound sadness had come over him to the extent that he couldn't speak. Of all the people who had met with this hegumen, this woman couldn't get anything else but his tears. When they saw him crying like that, his friends murmured among themselves: "Oh, what great compassion he has for sinners! How beautiful it is to see how much he is in communion with Christ when encountering sin."

When the woman withdrew, the hegumen continued to sob. He seemed inconsolable. At that point, one of his brothers thought that there must have been something else going on, and he asked the hegumen, "Father, why so many tears?"

The hegumen responded, "When I saw that woman, I guessed that she had spent many hours in front of the mirror to make herself beautiful in the eyes of men. And I, a consecrated man, haven't spent as many hours as she did to make myself beautiful before my Lord!"

The Eastern tradition of the Church teaches us that the most desirable of gifts of the Holy Spirit is precisely the gift of tears, when the heart is grieved at wounding a person whom one loves, or perhaps a person one does not love! Before considering the sadness of Christ at the prostitute's sin, the holy monk managed to see something remarkable in that woman. As he might have seen in a mirror, with the help of his humility, he saw that he himself was not capable of experiencing the same degree of passion for God that this woman experienced preparing her body for men.

Such a story urges us to make a real examination of conscience: what passion have we put at the center of our hearts? Which of our sins, our judgments, our omissions of charity, even our condemnations would we cry over?

34
Hugo, Rise up and Walk!

Ugo Festa and Pope John Paul II

There are people on this earth who we could say: "Having a picture of them on the table is better than actually having them at the table." Or, "All our visitors bring us joy, some when they arrive, others when they leave."

Admittedly, Hugo was a first-class grouch. He never missed an opportunity to demonstrate his aggressiveness or worse, to utter his blasphemies against God. He was angry with all of creation and especially the Creator. But in his defense, if we were to examine the root cause of his attitude, we would find immense suffering; physical and moral. From his early childhood, Hugo was afflicted with an incredible series of illnesses.

Contrary to the Good Thief, he had no opportunity to meet

the stunning gaze of Jesus on the cross, the gaze that turns one's soul inside out in a few seconds, and which lightens the worst of crosses.

Here is just a glimpse of the physical suffering Hugo endured from the time he was a baby into middle age:

From the moment of his birth in Piovene Rochette, a little village in the north of Italy, Hugo suffered abandonment by his mother, and immense physical suffering. After his adoption, at the age of ten months, Hugo was afflicted with bilateral otitis, which caused him to lose his hearing. At the tender age of five he contracted tuberculous meningitis, and was later hospitalized with encephalitis. Sometime later, after undergoing an adenoidectomy, he was struck with vision problems caused by hemiplegia and strabismus. When he was thirteen he was again hospitalized and doctors surgically removed his appendix. At fourteen years old, he was hospitalized for a hiatal hernia where his stomach pushed up into his chest. That's when he had a bit of a reprieve until he was twenty-two. Then doctors operated on a second hiatal hernia. At twenty-three, he contracted viral hepatitis and was transferred to a psychiatric unit for delirium. At twenty-four, he was attacked by a syndrome with dizzy spells leading to nervous depression. Because he was continually hospitalized, he suffered from neuro-circulatory asthenia. At twenty-five, he suffered from duodenum erosion (inflammation of the small intestine). At twenty-six, he began to fall into the slavery of alcohol and tobacco. At twenty-eight, he suffered from lumbar sciatica (pain originating in the lower back and traveling down the sciatic nerve). The nerves in his foot were involved causing a muscular deficit, which made it very difficult for him to walk. He developed arthritis, and the hospitalizations continued. Around the age of thirty, the list of pain he endured did not shorten! He began to show symptoms of muscular dystrophy, epilepsy, convulsions, deformation of the spinal column, along with troubles only people with chronic pain would think of – difficulties involving insertions of catheters, etc.

To summarize, Hugo Festa suffered from organic damage

to the nervous system, which brought about mild paralysis of the lower extremities, multiple sclerosis, depression, frequent epileptic seizures, unsteady pupils and trouble with vision and with the pupillary sphincter, psychological problems, as well as urinary incontinence. He had many, many pathologies which condemned him to a wheel chair, with no hope of healing. For many years, he went from hospital to hospital and consulted with a great number of specialists. All in vain. Medicine admitted to being totally powerless. Hugo Festa was incurable!

Despair is Defeated

At thirty-four, in understandable despair, Hugo took the advice of a former mill worker, who was married and the father of two children, and went to Lourdes. Very skeptical, he went to France not so much to find a cure there as to find a mother, since the abandonment of his own earthly mother had so deeply wounded him. The emotional and physical obstacles he had to overcome to get there were not easy for him: for a long time, he was profoundly rebellious toward God, whom he held responsible for his terrible situation. But after being bathed in the miraculous waters of the pools in Lourdes, Hugo Festa, the inveterate blasphemer, could not utter a single obscenity. He went to confession for the first time in a long time, and was able to make peace with God in the sacrament of Reconciliation.

Our Lady was also waiting for him with a wonderful grace: as soon as he was seated at the Grotto and was thinking about his birth mother, he heard the voice of the Immaculate Conception: "I am your first Mother," she said to him. "And all other mothers are your mothers." It took these tender, maternal words, this very special balm, for which Mary alone possessed the secret, for Hugo's life to begin to change. He experienced at that time an authentic conversion; he began to pray and decided to offer his suffering up to God.

Despite these first steps, Hugo still suffered a great deal, and he remained paralyzed, which caused a deep spiritual crisis that sometimes plunged him into despair. Fortunately, a new divine gift was waiting for him and not a small one!

The decisive turning point came about when he traveled to Rome to have a few icons of the merciful Christ blessed. He became acquainted with Mother Teresa, who blessed him and greatly comforted him.

John Paul II Passed in Front of Him

The next day, April 29, 1990, at St. Peter's square, Pope John Paul II passed in front of him and, in a marvelous moment, stopped at his wheelchair, blessed the images, and asked him how he was doing. Hugo took the opportunity to describe his sadness, his despair, and his rebellion.

"But how can you be in despair," John Paul II asked him, "when you hold in your hands the Merciful Jesus? Abandon yourself completely to God and trust in the intercession of my Sister, Faustina Kowalska!"[41]

The Holy Father recommended that Hugo go to Villazzano, in the diocese of Trente, to the "Villa O Santissima," a sanctuary where the Alleanza Misericordia (Covenant of Divine Mercy) had its headquarters.[42]

Without much conviction, Hugo decided to follow the recommendation of the Holy Father and made his way to "Villa O Santissima", not too far from where he was born. He arrived just when there was a week of evangelization and spirituality

[41] Saint Faustina Kowalska (1905-1938) was a Polish nun who received numerous mystic graces. Jesus, who called her "the secretary of My mercy," dictated to her many messages about the Divine Mercy, which she faithfully inscribed in a published diary entitled 'The Diary of Sister Faustina' available in every Catholic bookstore. The story of Hugo was used to support the canonization of Sr. Faustina.

[42] "Villa O Santissima" is a sanctuary where the Alliance of the Divine Mercy has its headquarters. It is run by a community of prayer and study directed by Father Renalto Tisot, who took Hugo under his wing.

taking place in the sanctuary. Hugo didn't expect to receive any particular graces. He had the impression he was surrounded by fanatic evangelicals. The first day of prayer was traumatizing, but he allowed himself to be persuaded by people there and decided to stay. In this place of recollection, the state of his soul was considerably soothed, to the point that he found the strength to forgive his mother and to thank her for having given him life. He was able to forgive during a prayer for the healing of life, of memory, and of wounds experienced in the womb of his mother. All the hatred he had built up since his infancy exploded inside him with great force. Then he calmed himself and received, because of the forgiveness he had given, a profound healing of the relationship with his mother. The effect of the forgiveness sparked an ardent desire in him to meet her and embrace her with love. The huge knot of his life had just been undone! The initial source of all his misfortunes and that hatred which had held him captive in his body and soul since infancy, had just vanished, thanks to the strength of forgiveness. From then on, Christ could freely deploy in Hugo the power of His love and His life.

God Adds to It!

On the fourth day of the session, Hugo ended up in the first row of the chapel, praying with the others in front of an icon of the Merciful Jesus. Suddenly, he had a strange sensation: the figure of Christ in the icon in front of him began to stir! Hugo saw Jesus' garment move and saw Him reaching out his arms. Hugo was afraid and tried to avoid this gesture from the Redeemer. He didn't want to accept what was happening. But God is patient, and the vision came back five more times. In the end, Hugo decided to accept the incredible grace being offered to him. The sixth time, the figure of Christ came out of the icon and approached him. The ailing man felt someone touch him. Then he heard the voice of Christ saying to him: "Get up, leave your wheelchair!" Before he even had time to reflect, Hugo found himself standing, his arms raised in front of the icon of Jesus.[43]

It was August 2, 1990. Hugo Festa regained the use of his legs, the epilepsy disappeared, and his visual deficit was greatly healed. From that moment on, Hugo spent his time praying and thanking God. He never returned to his wheelchair! On August 29th, he met with the Holy Father again to inform him personally about the grace he had received, and this time, he arrived before him standing firmly on two legs.[44]

The Ex-Rebel Did a U-Turn

Let's move on now to the fruits of Mercy. After his spectacular healing, Hugo traveled the entire world to proclaim the goodness of God in even the worst cases, like his own! He had become the privileged witness of the mercy of Christ. In India, Mother Teresa wanted to be by his side, and you should have seen how she covered him with her tenderness! Hugo signed up as a volunteer with her Foundation in India and Africa.

Back in Italy, Hugo gave his body and soul in service to the poor. As an apostle, with his stupefying story, who could listen to him without being profoundly touched by grace? Without shedding tears at such love of Christ? Though he had once spat out his venom against God and the Church, after his healing, he gave off a kind of strength that overwhelmed those around him. He never recoiled in front of any obstacle standing in the way of his testimony and of reaching those most es-

---

[43] This community of "Villa O Santissima" in Trente has given the gift of the icon to the parish of Medjugorje. It is found in the little church of Surmanci, 15 kilometers from Medjugorje. Many pilgrims go there on foot to honor the Divine Mercy.

[44] The miracle was attested to by a neurologist according to the severe criterium required in Lourdes before a miraculous healing is declared. This doctor was providentially present at "Villa O Santissima" that day. He witnessed Hugo's miracle which took place in front of the icon of the Merciful Jesus. This doctor had himself been healed of a cervical tumor which was declared incurable.

tranged from God. Because of this, Hugo was exposed to many perils in the toughest areas of the cities amidst the most disadvantaged of people. One day, May 22, 2005, when he had finished a difficult mission, he was savagely assassinated by a youth who did not respect Hugo's love for Jesus. To end his earthly story in beauty, he shed his blood for the One who had shed His own before him and had saved him from the worst, Jesus. Hugo thus became a martyr for Mercy.

On the occasion of his death, an Italian journalist wrote: "The story of Hugo Festa demonstrates how, for God, no life is useless or undignified. So, the life that Christ loves the most and is for him the most precious is the one which most resembles a disaster, the one that today's dominant mentality would like to suppress. He can do great things with this life. And the one place in the world where the exceptional is produced daily is the Church. The privileged place of the Divine Mercy."

35
THE DEATH OF A SON

Under the harsh July sun, the small group of Apostles moved slowly forward along the roads of Galilee. Jesus was with them moving from synagogue to synagogue, from house to house. He loved so much to talk to those who crossed his path, whether healthy or sick, rich or poor, sincere or hypocritical. He was particularly attentive to the soul that he saw, with his Divine sight, behind each face. He had just given a powerful teaching on loving one's enemies, which was not well received by everybody. What would you expect! Up until then, the Torah said 'An eye for an eye, a tooth for a tooth', which was much more palatable. But his extraordinary power to heal fascinated the crowds. Everyone did whatever they could to be near him. A simple encounter with his gaze illuminated and transformed them. In fact, he always surprised people with his compassion and unique way of discerning the true needs of others and giving life back to them. As they walked beside him, the Apostles were often disconcerted and asked each other: "What is he going to find for us next?!"

That day, accompanied as usual by a large crowd, Jesus and his disciples approached the little town of Naïn, near Nazareth. At the entrance gate of the town, they crossed paths with a funeral procession. A poor widow was about to bury her only son. The Apostles, already tired from their long walk under a blazing hot sun, and the endless demands of the people, feared the worst! There was no doubt that Jesus would stop; he would not remain unmoved by the pain of these people who mourned. Maybe Peter even muttered under his breath, "Hey guys, it's not bedtime yet!"

He was not mistaken! In fact, deeply moved by compassion, Jesus crossed through the crowd seeing only her – the widow, in tears, all in white, the color of mourning in the East. He knew how much she already suffered from the death of her husband. This new death completed her misery. How would she manage without him? He was the last person she had in the world. Jesus looked at her, she looked back at him, tears streaming down her face. Both were silent. "Do not weep", he said to her, gently.

Then he moved to the coffin and touched it. The bearers halted. Without hesitation, in His power as Creator, Jesus spoke directly to the deceased, "Young man, I order you to arise!" In Greek, the literal translation is: "Awake." Then, the young man sat up and began to speak. What did he say? We will only find out in Heaven.

Jesus then gave him back to his mother. Astounded, she could not believe her eyes. Everyone was caught up in wonder. How joyfully they glorified God! Finally they were convinced that this Jesus is a very great prophet, as great as Elijah, who had also raised a son from death. They no longer doubted that it was God Himself who had come to visit them in Jesus. They thought to themselves that it is only He who could raise people from the dead!

Mercy For Those Who Mourn

The loss of someone close is particularly painful. Who better than Jesus to understand it? Gazing at this widow who had just lost her only son, what was He feeling? His heart was shaken to its core. He could see his own Mother in the future. It was the same situation: The Blessed Mother would have already lost Joseph, her husband, and she was about to lose her only Son. Jesus was shaken to his foundations. He, the Creator of maternal love, also wanted to have a mother on this earth. He wanted to be born of a mother's womb, and to know the mutual affection of a loving human home with his Mother. For thirty years, Jesus had known a truly warm family life.

Through his mother, he also saw all those mothers who throughout history have lived, are living or will live through the piercing pain of the loss of a beloved child. Moved by compassion that was both human and divine, Jesus feels these same feelings in His Heart, He participates in our sufferings; He sees them and, in the face of all our tears, He intervenes.

The Gospel makes it clear that He asked the women looking for him at the tomb, particularly Mary of Magdala: "Woman, why are you weeping, whom do you seek?" In the same way at Bethany, faced with Martha and Mary sobbing after the death of their brother, Lazarus, Jesus was moved to tears. We should know that he is just as overwhelmed before each one of us, when we are weeping for a loved one.

Before The Open Wound

When we experience a struggle like mourning the loss of a loved one, the demon intervenes and tries to push us into despair, encouraging us to revolt against God and doubt His love, to think that our fate is unjust. This widow from Naïn could have thought: "I am much older than my son, it would have been fairer for me to die rather than him." We may also be assailed by fear for the future when the family support disappears. We could be taken over by jealousy when we see a woman who still has her husband and son with her, while we are so terribly alone. This is how envy starts growing, depression overwhelms us, or we are even plagued by the desire to die. We may feel anger at God, anger which could push us to shut Him out of our life. And there, the Evil One is waiting with delight! Seeing the open wound caused by the loss of the loved one, he tries to inject his own poison into our hearts, the same poison that constantly torments him. But, seeing this open wound, Jesus has a powerful remedy to eliminate the despair: he applies to the wounded heart a comforting balm, His love, which gradually transforms and transfigures suffering.

Jesus does not limit himself to helping the widow, he also helps the son. We know that at the time of our death, God reveals Himself to each one of us, we will see Him face to face and we will also see the film of our life pass before us. Let us take the example of Brother Daniel.

Brother Daniel Natale (1919-1999): The Second Chance

In the 1940s, an Italian Capuchin monk was living at San Giovanni Rotondo, Italy, and was much loved by Padre Pio. Brother Daniel was suffering from a serious tumor in his stomach. When the doctors predicted his imminent death, and warned him that surgery would only hasten his death, Padre Pio told Brother Daniel: "Go and get an operation in Rome with this particular surgeon!" Trusting the advice of this great prophet, and against medical advice, Brother Daniel went to Rome to have the operation. The operation lasted eight hours and, at first, was successful. But a short time later, Brother Daniel fell into a coma for three days, and then died. Padre Pio, shocked by the news, prayed intensely for him, and made a sort of private deal with Our Lady. (You know how saints have their own private dealings with God.) In fact, Brother Daniel's friends said to him: "Father, you're the one who insisted on the operation against the opinion of the doctors, now you must pray for him to come back to life!" Padre Pio was answered very quickly. Suddenly, Brother Daniel got up from his deathbed. He was well and truly alive, walking, talking, he could even see through the walls of the clinic!

Obviously, he was bombarded with questions on what he went through at the time of death! The details that follow were reported to me by a priest and some lay people who knew this brother well. Also, Brother Daniel's own nephew, Father Remigio Fiare, gave a private account that was sent to me by friends in Rome.

Brother Daniel recounted that when he died he had a marvelous meeting with Jesus, and that the Blessed Mother was also there. He said: "On this earth, we have no idea of what God's love is! It seemed to me as though I was, for Jesus, the sole object of His love. I had the wild desire to be united with Him, so strong was His love, and, what is more, He was actually inviting me." At that moment, Daniel saw, in a split second, the film of his whole life unravel before him, and he realized that he deserved to go to Purgatory, as he was not ready to enter into God's embrace. In fact, he had not confessed certain sins, particularly certain failures in his vow of poverty for which he had not felt regret. He had to pass two or three hours in Purgatory, but this purification seemed to him to last a whole century!

Brother Daniele Natale, Italy

He also testified that in Purgatory he had endured two terrible sufferings. The first was that he could no longer see Jesus, because at that point he was seized by an unspeakable longing. It is what one calls the pain of loss, when one can no longer see God, while having a frantic desire for Him, the Supreme Good. One feels one is far from Him and finds it impossible to see Him and enjoy His presence. But the hope of seeing Him consoles the soul. The second suffering was even more painful. The Lord made him understand the great degree of holiness he had planned for him. Brother Daniel even saw all the graces that his Creator had offered him throughout his life, to enable him to come to the fullness of this state of holiness. For Daniel, this was dazzling! What beauty there was in that high degree of holiness! What magnificent glory! What splendor! But when he saw what he had actually accomplished on earth, he saw that he had only carried out a part of it. He was seized by intense suffering, which he described as a sword piercing his heart. 'It's too late,' he thought. 'And we have only one life down here!'"

Indeed, he had passed up a part of the dream that God had conceived for him.

It was then that he saw Padre Pio appear in Purgatory! He also saw the Blessed Mother, and began to beg of her: "O Blessed Virgin Mary, Mother of God, ask the Lord to give me the grace to return to earth, to live and work there purely for the love of God!" He also implored Padre Pio: "By your terrible pains, by your blessed wounds, my Padre Pio, pray to God to free me from these flames and grant me to continue my Purgatory on earth!" Then he realized that Padre Pio was talking with Our Lady. She bent her head, then smiled at Brother Daniel. It was then that he took back possession of his body. Padre Pio told him: "I promised you that I would always be with you!" In fact, Padre Pio's prayer had obtained from the Mother of God a second chance for Brother Daniel. That is how Brother Daniel came back to life. Needless to say, the hospital staff at his bedside were terrified and began to scream! They thought they were seeing a ghost, so much so that they locked his door for several hours!

From the moment of his return to earth, Brother Daniel was radically changed. In the certainty of what he had seen and understood in the other world, he spent the rest of his life in prayer, his rosary always in his hand. He had an extraordinary compassion for the little ones, the poor, the handicapped and suffering of all kinds, and welcomed them tirelessly; he saw Jesus suffering in them. He was filled with joy, despite very poor health and numerous operations, because he had come to realize how much suffering, offered to Jesus, can bear fruit in the plan of Redemption. In a word, he did not waste his second chance!

Brother Daniel was declared Venerable on November 5, 2016, and his beatification case has been opened in Rome. Let us pray to him! He might perform a miracle among us, and that would hasten his cause.

Let's come back to the son of the widow of Naïn. Once he was raised by Jesus, he would certainly also have reconsidered his life on earth, understanding that only love counts, and all the rest passes away. Like Lazarus at Bethany, like Brother Daniel in Italy, this young man of Naïn, from that day forward, had many insights to share with his loved ones on the future of the soul after death, and one can only suppose that his witness shook his own mother. She had lost a son, but she found in her son a witness to mercy!

36
His Hair Smelled Like Incense

Why did Our Lady say that "death doesn't exist," as though she had never witnessed the death of her husband Joseph, her son Jesus, the first Christian martyrs, and so many others?[45]

It's because, as Father Cantalamessa says, "Death is not a wall but a door." According to the Talmud, when Moses died on Mount Nebo, a multitude of angels were sent by God to take up his soul. But, faced with the greatness of Moses, none of them dared to go near him. Hadn't he spoken with God face to face? So, God decided to go and bring Moses' soul back Himself, and it was through a kiss on his mouth that he aspirated. That's why it is written: "Moses died on the mouth of God."[46]

Happy and blessed are they who die in the peace of God, because, in reality, it means they are born into another life. In one of her numerous, "shocking" messages in Medjugorje, the Blessed Mother made a surprising remark to us: "No, dear

---

[45] Message given to the prayer group in Medjugorje, according to Jelena Vasilj.

[46] Read Deut. 34: 5 where we are present at the death of Moses: "And Moses, the servant of God, died there in the land of Moab." In reality, the Hebrew text adds: םיהולא לש הפב (on the mouth of God), which nearly every Bible translates as "according to the order of God!" But the genius of the Hebrew language allows Jewish Tradition to affirm that – even if it is ordered by God that Moses died on Mount Nebo, after having seen but not reached the land he had hoped to set foot on for forty years, - he had benefitted from a singular honor. Basically, this text can also mean: and there Moses, servant of God, died in the land of Moab, on the mouth of God.

children, you don't know how to celebrate the death of your dear ones the right way! You ought to celebrate the death of your dear ones with joy, the same joy you have at the birth of a baby."

Sometimes God takes drastic action, not unlike a surgical incision, in order to elevate His children into dimensions they couldn't even have dreamed of before the divine intervention. Florence lived near Lisieux, France. She and her husband had six children. When her first little boy was born in 1988, she was so awe-stricken at seeing within him the splendor of life that she turned towards her Creator and, in profound gratitude to Him, was constantly giving a flood of thanksgiving from her heart. She had given birth to an immense treasure.

Florence was already a practicing Catholic, even a fervent one, but motherhood was another milestone in her intimacy with God which brought joy to her life in Him. She felt tiny in front of such a marvel, this new, little baby lying in her arms. Her maternal sensitivity awakened in her the feeling that the life of her little Emmanuel didn't belong to her, but that the life was entrusted to her by the Creator and that she had to collaborate with Him to help this child become fully what he was in the eyes of God: A saint. Other children were born into the family, and Florence grew in her love for all of them.

One day, at the age of eleven, Emmanuel experienced severe convulsions at school, and, after exhaustive examination, the diagnosis came down like a guillotine: he had three brain tumors, one of which was inoperable.

Only parents who have lost a child can imagine the shock. There were only two possibilities: God would accord their child a miraculous healing, or He would not. Florence and her husband stormed Heaven with their prayers. The very idea of his being taken away from them pierced their hearts.

As the news of the illness spread, their friends began a chain of prayer and fasting for the child. One person in the group was familiar with Medjugorje and handed out one of the messages of Our Lady during their prayer assembly. That's how Florence and her husband discovered Medjugorje. This improvised group of prayer and adoration resulted in conversions back to God which had previously seemed unachievable.

As for Emmanuel, he was joyful and comforted by all those who came to his house with knots in the pits of their stomachs. His parents revealed the reality of his condition to him very delicately.

Florence understood that the Lord was going to take her son. She developed a deep understanding and intuition, and it was incontrovertible. She renewed before God her act of abandonment, the same one she had made spontaneously at the moment of Emmanuel's birth.

Although she cried a great deal, it was pain mixed with glorious praise, as it was for Jesus at the time of Lazarus' death. Her child had achieved his mission on this earth. She had to let him go. "The Lord gives, the Lord takes back, blessed be the name of the Lord!" she said to herself. She and her husband consecrated Emmanuel anew to the Immaculate Heart of Mary and to the Sacred Heart of Jesus, so that when he passed away, he would be carried by them to eternal happiness.

On the night of Emmanuel's passing, the whole family was reunited with him in the intensive care unit (special permission obtained surely from Our Lady), and his passing was very simple, like a departure for a trip. Emmanuel had already been given to God; he had not been torn away. His hair smelled like incense! According to everyone, the funeral service was more like a celebration of birth into Heaven than a burial. Smiles and tears mingled together.

On All Saints' Day, November 1, Florence was present in Medjugorje when I suggested to a group of pilgrims that they go through all the four stages of consecration for any death, their own or that of their dear ones. At the end of the talk, she ran towards me and said: "That's exactly what happened to me! I understand now why we got through Emmanuel's dying in such peace! No anguish, no frustration, no rebellion… In prayer, we were literally transported. Emmanuel has not disappeared; he remains with us, and we speak of him quite often in the family. Through him, the peace of God is communicated to us!"

For this very Christian family, Emmanuel is their link to Heaven, their dear treasure! He helped them grow in their faith and aspire to the things which don't pass away. Just as Mary invites us to do, they experienced the death like a birth. Tears, yes, but gentle tears. May we all experience true love, and rejoice when our beloved dead enter real life. "If you loved me," Jesus says, "you would rejoice that I am going to the Father," (John 14:28). As Saint Bernard of Clairvaux used to say: "When we are on Earth, we are not yet born. We are born when we enter Heaven. On Earth, we are carried in the womb of the Mother of God."

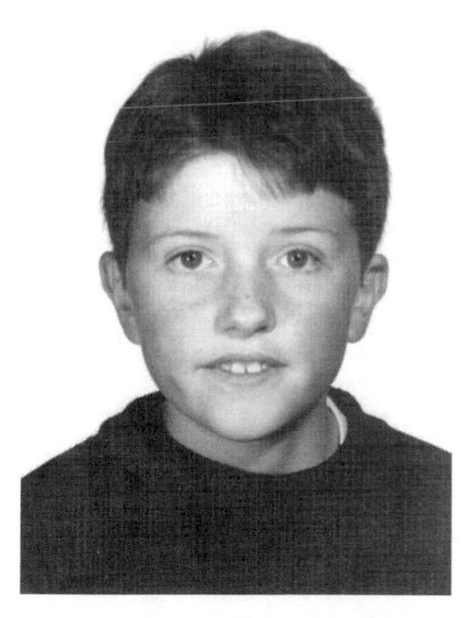

Emmanuel de Villequier, France

Consecrate Your Death!

The prospect of death is there for every person, and many are afraid. However, it's simply a matter of passing from this life to another life, a true birth. That's why the Blessed Mother tells us that death doesn't exist. When she spoke about Father Slavko, who died on November 24, 2000, she didn't tell us in her message the next day: "He died a holy death" but rather: "Rejoice with me, because your brother Slavko was born in Heaven and he is interceding for you!"

Consecrate your death! Living fully in the womb of the Mother of God means banishing all fear of death, fear of this mysterious birth with its promise of a leap into the unknown, which comes along with it. Every good mother prepares for the birth of her child with great care and infinite tenderness. How much more would the Blessed Virgin Mary do for us! I love Vicka Ivankovic's comparison: "Death is nothing. It's like going from one room to another in the same house!" She then thinks again: "No, not even that. It's like going from one corner of a room to another corner of the same room!" "If people knew just how good God was, they would never fear death."[47]

But, in our world, so shrouded in the fog of materialism, we have lost this ultimate perspective of our lives! We often see death as merely a departure with no return, a pitiable descent, a limitless black wall, when it's not a matter of a wall but of a door, the door that opens up to us the life for which we were created.

That's why, as sons and daughters of the Virgin Mary, it is good to consecrate our deaths to her Immaculate Heart and to the Heart of Jesus, so that this crucial moment of our existence belongs fully to God by way of Mary's hands. To be certain of

---

[47] Read about the journey of Vicka Ivankovic and Jakov Colo, when, in 1981, Mary takes them to see Heaven, Purgatory, and Hell in: *Medjugorje, Triumph of the Heart*, which can be found at www.sremmanuel.org.

chasing away fear and all insidious anguish which might disturb us, here are four steps that people can follow, each at his own pace:

1. Thank God with all your heart for the moment He has chosen to bring you back to Him. Whenever that moment is, tomorrow or in fifty years, tell God that you are confident, knowing that He will have chosen the best moment for you, from the perspective of your eternity.

2. Go even further, and thank Him for the way He has chosen to bring you back. Don't let your imagination create a movie! If you do that, you might suffer by anticipating something that will never happen! On the contrary, quiet down the silly voices in your head – your imagination – and make an act of total abandonment of self into the hands of the One who knows, far better than you do, what you need.

3. Keep going to another level, and thank God for the moment He has chosen to bring back to Him the person who is the dearest to us. Tomorrow? In fifty years? May He be blessed for it, because this divine choice is the best for that person, for his eternal happiness. At this stage, your trust in God is great, because it finds its source in abandonment to His holy, loving will.

4. Finally, thank God for the way He has chosen to bring this dear soul back to Him.

This process requires profound interior work. It doesn't always flow like a fountain, because you might meet strong resistance. This is an opportunity to let go, with the confidence of a child towards his Father… For us adults who have suffered some blows and want to maintain control of our futures, this may take some time! But, with genuine determination, aided by the grace of God and by a vibrant faith in His love, we can finally give our "Yes." And the great gift which flows from this "Yes," this confident surrender to divine plans, is the healing of our fears and anguish, over death. It's serenity in the face of any event, pleasant or unpleasant, because we know in whom we have believed. We have reached a safe investment! In the hands of such a Father, of such love, how could fear still penetrate us? How could anguish dare predominate in us? If Jesus, in the garden of Gethsemane, took on all our anxieties, wasn't it to help us to overcome them?

37
An Unexpected End to a Coma

In Texas, Father Tim Deeter was a parish priest at St. Mary's Parish, and also night chaplain of a large Catholic hospital. There, he worked during the nighttime hours after the doctors have finished the examinations and tests of the day and when the visitors, families and friends have return to their homes. Given the number of sick people to visit, the responsibility is huge. The patients who must undergo surgery the following day are placed in single rooms and remain alone. It's at that time, more than at any other hour of the day, when they ask for a priest.

Each evening, Father Tim used to visit any number of sick people, but he never missed dropping in to see Helen, whose coma had lasted several weeks. He knew that a person in a coma could still hear, because hearing is the last of the senses to disappear. Every night, he recited an Our Father, a Hail Mary, and a Glory Be at Helen's bedside, then, quite naturally, offered her a little synopsis of the latest news of the day, including the sports, weather, arts and entertainment, noteworthy events, etc.

But one evening, the list of people to visit was so long that Father Tim thought he'd put off his visit to Helen until the next day. "Besides," he said to himself, "she doesn't really respond to me being there, so if I skip going there one evening, it won't matter." However, after finishing all the other visits, the thought that he ought to go see her just wouldn't leave him.

At 3 o'clock in the morning, he entered the room without turning on the light, because the moon was shining enough to illuminate it. Sitting on a chair near Helen's bed, he began to recite the usual prayers rapidly, thinking it would suffice. Nevertheless, he had a feeling deep within that his task had not finished. Something (or Someone) told him that he should ask her if she wanted to receive the Sacrament of Reconciliation: he thought, perhaps she hadn't had the chance to make a confession before she became ill.

So, leaning down close to her, Father Tim murmured in her ear: "Would you like to receive sacramental absolution for your sins? I'll give you a moment of silence during which you can confess your sins to God in your heart." A little bit later, Father recited slowly the Act of Contrition and asked Helen to pray along with him in silence. Then, he put his hands on her and gave her absolution for all her sins. (Let's remember that "absolution" doesn't signify "pardon" but "deliverance."[48])

Father Tim never forgot the shock he received next! While he was uttering the last words of absolution, Helen suddenly sat up in bed! With eyes wide open, she threw out her arms, and, smiling widely, cried out, "JESUS!" Father Tim was overcome with fear. He directed his gaze to the wall at which Helen was staring so intently, and in the shadow of the moonlight, he perceived a small wooden crucifix. Turning again towards Helen, he saw that she had fallen back on her pillow and had died. It took Father Tim several minutes to understand what had happened and to regain his composure. Something

[48] Absolution takes away sin, but it does not remedy all the disorders sin has caused. Raised up from sin, the sinner must still recover his full spiritual health by doing something more to make amends for the sin: he must "make satisfaction for" or "expiate" his sins. This satisfaction is also called "penance". The penance the confessor imposes must take into account the penitent's personal situation and must seek his spiritual good. It must correspond as far as possible with the gravity and nature of the sins committed. It can consist of prayer, an offering, works of mercy, service of neighbor, voluntary self- denial, sacrifices, and above all the patient acceptance of the cross we must bear, (Paragraphs 1459 and 1460 in the *Catechism of the Catholic Church*, published by Doubleday, 1995).

in the life of this woman had been preventing her from passing away, but once delivered of that bond, she was free to go to Jesus.

On the day of the funeral, Helen's sister met Father Tim. She had heard that he was present at the moment her sister died. Father Tim clarified that he had given Helen absolution, even though she had been in a coma. Full of gratitude and with tears in her eyes, this woman revealed to him something about their childhood: "When Helen and I were young, our parents taught us to ask the Lord every night in prayer for the grace of a good death (that is, a death in the state of grace). Now I know that God heard our prayers, and I thank Him that my sister died in peace."

In addition, Father Tim revealed to me that sometimes he says to patients in a coma: "Here, I'm taking your hand, and if you want to receive absolution from your sins, give me a sign by squeezing my hand a little." Often with their meager strength, these patients answer with a little bit of pressure, indicating that they have heard and understood everything and that they want to receive this sacrament. These stories should be proclaimed from the rooftops today!!

38
THE SOULS IN PURGATORY CRY OUT FOR HELP

We must never forget that praying for the souls in Purgatory is indeed one of the most noble works of mercy. We certainly remember to honor our deceased loved ones with a beautiful funeral, with flowers and other tokens of our affection. However, once a soul has left this world, only one thing is needed: God's grace. That is why we have been given many spiritual tools to obtain these graces from God for those departed souls. Our prayers, our sacrifices, the celebration of masses, the offering up of our own sufferings for their intention and the obtaining of indulgences offered by the Church are just some of the spiritual help at hand.

As for me, I enjoy praying in our local cemetery which is only a 10-minute-walk away from our house. It is the final resting place of Father Slavko Barbaric, Nado, Iva and a few other beloved friends. It is easy for me to go to this quiet place so dear to me, where our invisible friends lay resting. Once at the cemetery, I openly talk to the souls who could still be in Purgatory:

"Dear souls in Purgatory, I am aware of your dire need of help and how ardently you desire our prayers to go to Heaven. So, with great joy, here I come to your assistance. For my part, I do also require your intercession, as I know that it is powerful. So please remember me and obtain for me this grace..., I implore you."

Then, for nine consecutive days, I pray the rosary as a novena for their intentions in the cemetery. I can say from experience that, no matter the nature and size of my requests, seldom are they not granted! In fact, Purgatory is a place of great mercy. So, let us try to deepen our understanding of the reality of Purgatory. Today, the very existence of Purgatory is indeed too often forgotten and even denied among some Catholics and Clergy.

The Transforming Fire

Father Slavko Barbaric's encounter with Cardinal Ratzinger in Vienna

In *Eschatology: Death and Eternal Life*, Cardinal Joseph Ratzinger declared: "Purgatory is not a third intermediate way between salvation and damnation. Purgatory definitely belongs to salvation. It is intended for the soul who still needs some final purification to be capable of God."

In another part of his book he wrote, "Purgatory is neither a waiting room or a kind of concentration camp set up above where chastisement would be imposed to souls in a rather negative way…Purgatory is an internal transformation process of the soul which is necessary to make the soul capable of Christ, capable of God and afterwards, to be able to unite itself to the whole communion of Saints."

Let us be clear about it. When we will see Christ face-to-face after our death, two choices and not three will be placed in front of us. Either we agree to His salvation or we reject it. If we reject it, this is damnation. However, some of us will accept His salvation but will fall short of the grace to live in His presence. Consequently, this very presence, while loving, will also be painful to us. This is the purifying fire mentioned by St Paul. Thus, Purgatory is neither a waiting-room, nor a preliminary penance before seeing God. The suffering of Purgatory does actually emanate from the sorrowful vision of God experienced by the redeemed soul who feels contrition for its remaining sins. Cardinal Ratzinger presents it as follows: "In Purgatory, the vision of God is felt as both sorrowful and beatific. Our own impurity is literally violated by God's vision. This intense and deeply hurtful contrast cleanses the soul from its impurities."

There is now a growing number of theologians who believe that the soul is purified by the very presence of the Lord, rather than by waiting for His presence in a separate place from Heaven. This belief has also been supported by the Tradition.

Pope Benedict XVI develops this theme in His Encyclical, *Spe Salvi*: "Some recent theologians are of the opinion that the fire which both burns and saves is Christ himself, the Judge and Savior. The encounter with him is the decisive act of judgment. Before his gaze all falsehood melts away. This encounter with him, as it burns us, transforms and frees us, allowing us to become truly ourselves. All that we build during our lives can prove to be mere straw, pure bluster, and it collapses. Yet in the pain of this encounter, when the impurity and sickness of our lives become evident to us, there lies salvation. His gaze, the touch of his heart heals us through an undeniably painful transformation "as through fire". But it is a blessed pain, in which the holy power of his love sears through us like a flame, enabling us to become totally ourselves and thus totally of God."[49]

[49] Paragraph 47

Earlier, as Cardinal Ratzinger, he also observed in *Eschatology: Death and Eternal Life*: "In Purgatory, the soul would feel temporarily but painfully dazzled."

Truly, if we had spent a long time in complete darkness and suddenly we were stepping outside in the midday sun, we would surely be dazzled. Our eyes would hurt and would need some time to adjust to the broad daylight. The blindness could last a long time and could be very painful. The intensity of the pain would vary in accordance with the depth of the darkness to which our eyes were previously accustomed to. In Purgatory, Christ's presence fills the soul with a joy which is somewhat tinted with pain. This isn't intended as a punishment by God but it happens because the soul isn't fully prepared to bear His light.

Mystics Shed Some Light on Purgatory

Many Saints have had interesting encounters with Purgatory. Each mystic brings something personal to the heart of Doctrine, which will never change. How astonishing it is to see their individual revelations intersect and reveal the same realities, even though they didn't know each other in this world. May their writings enlighten us and nurture our hope.

Saint Mechtild of Hackeborn (1241 – 1299) One Sunday, Saint Mechtild had just prayed for the souls in Purgatory when a vision presented itself to her. A great number of souls, filled with an immense joy, were praising God for their liberation. Mechtild rejoiced with them, especially when she learned that someone had died. She hastened to say five 'Our Fathers' in honor of the five wounds of the crucified Christ. She wished to know how effective her prayers had been to bring relief to that soul. Our Lord responded to her one day:

"The soul received five favors: on its right, the soul was covered by the protection of the angels. On its left, it was comforted by them. They placed hope in front of her, trust behind her and celestial joy above her."

Then, Our Lord added: "When compassion and charity urge someone to intercede for a deceased soul, all the goodness bestowed by this person will be of benefit not only to themselves but to the whole Church. When this intercessor leaves this world, the same favors will be ready to relieve their own sufferings and to save their soul."

Saint Bridget of Sweden (1303 – 1373) As Saint Bridget was praying one day, she heard voices from Purgatory saying: "May graces be poured out on those who bring us relief in our sufferings. Their power is infinite! O Lord, render a hundredfold to our benefactors, who conduct us sooner into the sojourn of your divine light."

Saint Catherine of Sienna (1347 – 1380) Jesus confided to Saint Catherine: "And if you turn to Purgatory, you will find my sweet and priceless Providence toward those little suffering souls. Being now separated from the body, they do not have any more time to be able to earn any merits. For them I have provided, by way of you, of you who are still in the mortal life and have time for them and, by means of almsgiving and the divine office that you have had said by my ministers (the Mass), together with fasting and orations done in a state of grace, you can shorten for them the time of penalty, trusting in my mercy."

Saint Catherine of Genoa (1447- 1510) teaches us in her "Treatise on Purgatory" "No happiness can be found worthy to be compared with that of a soul in Purgatory except that of the saints in Paradise; and day by day this happiness grows as God flows into these souls, more and more as the hindrance to His entrance is consumed… But they endure a pain so extreme that no tongue can be found to tell it, nor could the mind understand its least pang, if God by special grace did not show so much… The soul separated from the body finds itself not being any longer as clean as it was created. As it also sees in itself the impediment to its union with God, the soul understands that this can be taken away only by means of Purgatory and casts itself therein swiftly and willingly. For it sees that sins for which no atonement was made prevent it from drawing near to God. It casts itself therein because it understands that Purgatory is God's great work of mercy.

"And it sees by the divine light that God does not cease from drawing it, nor from leading it, lovingly and with much care and unfailing foresight, to its full perfection, doing this of His pure love. The soul is being drawn by that uniting look with which God draws it to Himself. Its beatific instinct grows unceasingly, so impetuously and with such fierce charity towards God. Could the soul who understood find a worse Purgatory in which to rid itself sooner of all the hindrance in its way, it would swiftly fling itself therein, driven by the burning conforming love between itself and God.

"Its need to be transformed in God kindles in it a fire so great that this is its Purgatory. But feeling its instinct towards God, aflame and thwarted, that is what makes Purgatory. It is true that love for God which fills the soul to overflowing, gives it a happiness beyond what can be told. But this happiness takes not one pang from the pain of the souls in Purgatory. So that the souls in Purgatory enjoy the greatest happiness and endure the greatest pain; the one does not hinder the other.

"I see the souls suffer the pains of Purgatory, having before their eyes two works of God: First, they see themselves suffering pain willingly, and as they consider their own deserts and acknowledge how they have grieved God, it seems to them that He has shown them great mercy.

"The second work they see is the happiness they feel as they contemplate God's ordinance and the love and mercy with which He works on the soul. Because they are in a state of grace, they are aware of these sights and understand them as they are, in the measure of their capacity. They are far more intent on God than on the pains they suffer, and of God they make far greater account, beyond all comparison, than of their pains."

Saint Frances of Rome (1384-1440) This saint was also privileged with visions of Heaven, Purgatory and Hell. She described Purgatory as a place ruled by sorrow and divided into different regions, where the penalty of sorrow varies in accordance with the seriousness of the offences. She also observed that prayers and good works offered up for one Holy Soul are certainly of immediate benefit to that soul, but not exclusively. In fact, other souls gain from it too. If that soul has already entered Heaven's glory, the merits gained through prayers and good deeds bring solace to other Holy Souls.

Saint Teresa of Avila (1515 – 1582) The famous Teresa of Avila recalled in her writings one of the greatest graces she had been granted. One day, in a vision of Hell, God showed her the actual place which had been prepared for her, should she have persevered choosing a lukewarm and superficial life, even in religious life. From then on, she was seized by an infinite desire to save souls from this abyss. In her book *The Interior Castle*, she explained that the soul's ardent desire for the beatific vision of God causes a great agony. This suffering can reach considerable heights because it is not felt by the body but in the intimate core of the soul. An ardent thirst for possessing God consumes the soul, whereas it is still unable to quench it.

Saint Mary-Magdalene de Pazzi (1566 – 1607) This holy woman was a Carmelite nun who had frequent ecstasies. She had a vision one day of her own deceased brother, Alamanno, in Purgatory. She cried to him: "Oh, my poor brother, I can see that you are suffering terribly. May you receive consolation. You know that these sorrows open to you the gate to eternal happiness. I can see that you are not sad. You voluntarily bear these great sufferings and you are filled with happiness. When you were still in the world, you rejected my admonitions and advice. Now you need my attention. What can I do for you?"

Her brother asked her to offer a certain number of masses for him and to receive Holy Communion for his intention. St Mary-Magdalene hastened to fulfill these requests for his deliverance. On a side note: she was also shocked to find members of religious orders in Purgatory.

Venerable Orsola Benincasa (1547 – 1618) This mystic was also greatly devoted to the Holy Souls. Sometimes she even went to the extent of taking their sufferings on herself. Once, as Orsola was at the bedside of Cristina, her dying sister, she suddenly watched her sister being seized by a terrible fear of Purgatory. Orsola wished to bring her comfort and freedom from her anxieties. So she asked God to draw to her the pains of Purgatory and to let her bear them instead of her sister. Our Lord obliged. At that moment, all agony and fear lifted from Cristina who died in peace. Conversely, Orsola was overcome by great sufferings which remained with her until she died.

Teresa Musco (1943 – 1976) This young woman was born in the Italian village of Caiazzo to a humble family of farmers. As a consecrated member of the Franciscan third order, she nurtured a special love for the souls in Purgatory. On All Souls' Day 1962, she was unable to go to the cemetery. Instead, in her room, she united herself in prayer with the Holy Souls. While absorbed in prayer, she suddenly saw her room filled with people and cried for joy. They were greeting her by saying: "You have freed us from the sufferings of Purgatory!" before disappearing from her sight. She was greatly heartened by this encounter and endeavored to work even harder for those souls. Not only did she offer up her illnesses for them, but also dedicated half of her modest income to the celebration of masses for the Holy Souls.

Natuzza Evolo (1924 – 2009) From the age of 14, Natuzza showed signs of mystical gifts. Despite being illiterate, she became like a new Padre Pio for all Italy. Deceased people appeared to her to converse with her about Heaven, Purgatory and Hell. The souls still in Purgatory continually begged her for prayers, alms (although she was very poor), intercessions on their behalf and especially offerings of masses, all this to shorten their sufferings. Natuzza encouraged everyone to develop a deep understanding of the nature of sin. In her opinion, complete loss of the meaning of sin is precisely one of the biggest misfortunes of our times. She said that there were a great amount of souls in Purgatory. Firstly, we ought to understand this is because God's mercy endeavors to save as many souls as possible. Secondly, we should also realize that even the best souls have flaws and deficiencies and might need purification.

Saint Faustina Kowalska (1905 – 1938) Saint Faustina often witnessed apparitions of Christ who referred to her as "the secretary of My mercy". The messages she received from Jesus have now reached the whole world. Jesus invites all faithful to trust unconditionally and without any reserve in God's infinite Divine Mercy. Saint Faustina recorded Jesus' words in her diary, later titled: "Diary of Saint Maria Faustina Kowalska, Divine mercy in my soul". This bestseller certainly makes a great bedside book. Below are two extracts from her diary:

"Souls who spread the honor of My mercy I shield through their entire lives as a tender mother her infant, and at the hour of death I will not be a Judge for them, but the merciful Savior.[50] At that last hour, a soul has nothing with which to defend itself except My mercy. Happy is the soul that during its lifetime immersed itself in the Fountain of Mercy, because justice will have no hold on it."[51]

"Write this: Everything that exists is enclosed in the bowels of My mercy, more deeply than an infant in its mother's womb. How painfully distrust of My goodness wounds Me! Sins of distrust wound Me most painfully."[52]

Saint Therese of the Infant Jesus (1873 – 1897) Finally, let us finish with a word from Little Flower. It happened that one day, in the Carmel of Lisieux, Therese and Mother Febronie were having a lively discussion. While Mother Febronie was certain that she would go to Purgatory, Therese was defending the infallible trust in Divine Mercy because, through that trust, we could be spared from any purification time in Purgatory. But that was to no avail. Mother Febronie was adamant that

---

[50] § 21

[51] § 1075

[52] § 1076

her view about Divine Justice was right. At that moment, Therese replied to her: "My sister, you want God's justice, don't you? Then, you will get God's justice! God gives to the souls exactly what they expect of Him"

As a matter of fact, Mother Febronie died not long afterwards. Therese had a dream about her and later told her community: "Sister Febronie is asking for prayers. She is in Purgatory because she has not relied enough on our Good Lord's mercy. Her imploring looks and deep gaze seemed to tell me: 'You were right, God is applying His Justice to me. But I can only blame myself for it. If I had believed you, I would have gone straight to Heaven.'" Therese would also later say: "One never trusts enough in the Good Lord. He is so powerful and merciful. One receives from Him as much as one hopes in Him."[53]

---

[53] A beautiful illustration of trust in God is told by Maria Simma from Austria. It shows how "love covers over many a sin". Although this story has already been published in my book *The Amazing Secret of the Souls in Purgatory: An Interview with Maria Simma*, it is a striking example which is worth mentioning again. Find the book at www.sremmanuel.org.

Another beautiful example of this is related by Maria's Simma. It shows how a good action makes up for a whole life of sin. Let's hear it from Maria herself: "I knew a young man of about twenty in a nearby village; this young man's village had been cruelly stricken by a serious of avalanches which had killed a large number of people. One night this young man was at his parents when he heard an avalanche just next door to his house. He heard piercing screams, heartrending screams, save us, come save us, we are trapped beneath the avalanche. Leaping up he rose from his bed and rushed downstairs to go to the rescue of these people. His mother had heard the screams and prevented him from leaving. She blocked the door saying, "No, let others go and help them, not always us. It's too dangerous outside; I don't want yet another death." But he because he had been deeply affected by these screams, really wanted to go to the rescue of these people. He pushed his mother aside, he said to her, "Yes, I am going, I can't let them die like this." He went out and then he himself on the path was struck by an avalanche and was killed. Three days after his death, he comes to visit me at night and he says to me, "Have three masses said for me, through this, I will be delivered from purgatory." I went to inform his family and friends. They were astonished to know that after only three masses, he would be delivered from Purgatory. His friends said to me, "Oh, I would not have liked to be in his place in the moment of death, if you had seen all the bad things he had done." But this young man said to me, "You see, I have made an act of pure love in risking my life for these people. It is thanks to this that the Lord welcomed me so quickly into His heaven. Yes, charity covers a multitude of sins..."

39

Jacqueline and Mother Teresa: A Creative Union of Hearts

Jacqueline de Decker is floating in happiness and joy! Her deepest, heartfelt wish, her dream and heart's desire finally came true. She just landed in India! Her warm native Belgian clothes were replaced by a simple cotton sari that contrasts a little with her light Nordic complexion. Of aristocratic origin, rich and highly educated; she's content with very few material possessions. She eats like the poor, sits on the ground and sleeps on a floor mat surrounded by big green lizards and other visiting night animals. Her washing is done at a brick wall mounted tap. Let's not mention electricity, a luxury that is rarely available.

It all started in Patna, capital of Bihar state, located in the North-East of the country, one of the poorest areas in India. Although both her roots and culture are of Belgian origin, Jacqueline feels completely at home in this part of the world.

There are usually two reasons to feel at home in a country: either one is born there, or one is called there.

Jacqueline received a deeply intense call from God to move to India. That call was confirmed by her spiritual father, a Jesuit priest that gave her all the support and encouragement she needed. However, on December 31st, 1946, the moment she set foot in India, this wonderful priest died unexpectedly and left Jacqueline with no spiritual guidance or support. Even on a financial level, she came empty handed and was left in a state of total poverty.

In Patna, inside the chapel of a Christian Medical Center, she met a nun from Albania whose English was very simple and basic, and who kept rolling the letter "r". After spending years at the Loreto nuns congregation in Darjeeling, and prior to actually starting life in the slums, recognizing that hope and unlimited compassion alone were not enough to meet the needs of Calcutta's poor community, this small, energetic and determined woman came to Patna for a short course in nursing and dispensary work. Her name? Teresa. So, it transpired that both women received a vocation to give their lives to God while still young. Jacqueline de Decker's calling to India was shaped by a similar desire to Mother Teresa's: to serve the poor and by the conviction that God needed human hands to reach those who most needed Him.

They connected right away. They were both consumed by the same fire: Their passion to serve the suffering Jesus hidden in the poorest of the poor, and their goal was to quench Jesus' torturing thirst of love concealed in the rejected and lonely souls. Their call was undeniably strong and powerful. Their huge compassion for the suffering members of this broken population is the reason for that deep bond that they shared. They happily exchanged their visions, their hopes and dreams, and decided to collaborate.

Jacqueline considered joining Mother Teresa's new congregation, and together, they flew to Calcutta.

Calcutta! Why is Jacqueline attracted to this city? A city built poorly by the British people and located in one of the most unhealthy and unsafe zones of Bengal? Is it the strong humidity that sticks to the skin? Definitely not! Is it the touching, sweet and humble Indian population? No. Is it the devoted Christian community that John-Paul II described as being the most fervent community in the world? Not even that!

What then?

As soon as she landed in Netaji-Subhash-Chandra-Bose Calcutta International Airport, the strong humidity, along with the unbearable heat hit her hard. Not to mention that unique and indefinable smell. She understood in her heart that despite the obvious inconveniences the pull she felt to work and live with the poor would be here. She felt she finally reached the destination God intended for her!

Calcutta! The urban slum areas were full of weak children, of elderly people lying on the ground in the corner of the streets, of fortune tellers trapping innocent people, of women looking for some food thrown by the rich in the piles of garbage, and finally of barefooted beggars desperately trying to draw attention and inspire pity by mutilating or cutting a child's arm to ensure the survival of their other children. It was a world of misery! This is precisely the world Jacqueline landed in, and precisely the place she said to herself, 'This is my place, this is my call'.

There was the glowing Jacqueline working next to Mother Teresa! By daily watching the saintly nun, full of life, accomplishing so much for the poor, and being so persuasive to those likely to help her in her task, Jacqueline learned more every day about helping the dying by restoring their dignity as children of God, children of the King! She was filled with the key secret that fuels all actions, the key secret that is the main source of this incredible kindness: hours spent daily in Adoration of Christ present in the Blessed Sacrament.

However, the daily routine and the long working hours affected Jacqueline's physical health. While her will power and determination were still very strong, her physical resistance was fragile due to a soft and comfortable background. Still, the perfect harmony between the deep call resonating in her soul and this life totally and radically offered to God, in serving the poor, under the guidance of this remarkable little Mother Teresa, filled Jacqueline with an indescribable joy. The union of souls that she had with her was so intense, and their collaboration so harmonious, that the future "Calcutta Saint" would recognize in Jacqueline her "second self".[54] The little foundation grew in the midst of all the obstacles thanks to this profound unity.[55]

However, as the days went by, Jacqueline's health continued to deteriorate. At the age of fifteen she had a diving accident at a swimming pool. Doctors failed to identify the extent of the injury incurred at that time, but the heat and discomfort of India had aggravated the problem and caused her considerable pain. It was, therefore, decided that she should return to Antwerp for medical treatment. Back in her native country, the worst surprise awaited her.

In Belgium, it was discovered that she was suffering from a severe disease of the spine, further complicated by her body's tendency to produce abnormal fibers. Massaging a sick friend one day she noticed the beginnings of paralysis in her arms. Eventually, one of her eyes became paralyzed and so did her right leg. The reason why her right shoe was constantly worn out made itself all too strikingly apparent. Eventually she was informed that in order to avoid total paralysis she would have to undergo a number of operations. Grafts were put in her neck and two other places. She spent an entire year in plaster and then in the space of one month she had twelve further grafts added to her vertebrae.

Gradually it became apparent that Jacqueline would never be able to return to India, and that her total commitment to India's poor and diseased, and to what she had so profoundly believed to be God's will for her, was not to be. She sank into depression and seriously considered suicide. She was assailed

[54] Mother Teresa defined her "second self" as "a spiritual twin who would offer to God her prayers and suffering for Mother Teresa and the fruitfulness of her work. Mother Teresa in turn would offer her prayers and good works for Jacqueline," (*Come Be My Light*, p. 146).

[55] In Medjugorje, Our Lady places a heavy emphasis on the unity of hearts in the families and in the prayer groups. She even went so far as to say to the young people belonging to the prayer group she created in 1982: "If you are all united, your group will be more powerful than a nuclear power plant!"

with doubt and temptation to the point that she felt she had failed in her vocation. She thought she had disappointed God to the point that he had rejected her. The realization was initially a bitter one, fraught with a sense of personal failure, but it taught complete surrender to the incomprehensible will of God. It also demonstrated more eloquently than words that from every experience, however negative, something positive and constructive may spring.[56]

Thanks to her strong and persistent rooting in prayer, she came to her senses. She had most certainly not been rejected by God! Not only did He not abandon her, but he prepared a much better path for her to follow, one she never would have imagined. God rewarded her one hundred times more for what she thought she lost.

I Need Souls Like Yours

In the fall of 1952, she received a letter from Mother Teresa that returned her joy and happiness to her:

"Today I am going to propose something to you. You have been longing to be a missionary. Why not become spiritually bound to our society which you love so dearly? While we work in the slums you share in the merit, the prayers and the work, with your suffering and prayers. The work here is tremendous and needs workers, it is true, but I need souls like yours to pray and suffer for the work – your body will be in Belgium but in spirit you will be in India where there are souls longing for our Lord. But for want of someone to pay the debt

[56] Much of this chapter has been inspired by *Mother Teresa: Come Be My Light* Edited by Father Brian Kolodiejchuk, MC, published in 2007 by Doubleday, as well as a book written by Kathryn Spink in 2007 entitled, *A Chain of Love: Sharing in the work of Mother Teresa through prayer and suffering*, which was originally published in the United States under the title: *I Need Souls Like You* by Harper and Row in 1984. Kathryn Spink's book can be found here: www.lulu.com/shop/kathryn-spink/a-chain-of-love/paperback/product-1629378.html?ppn=1

for them, they cannot move towards Him. You'll be a true Missionary of Charity if you pay the debt while the Sisters – your Sisters – help them to come to God in body. I need many people who suffer who would join us as I want to have (1) a glorious society in heaven, (2) the suffering society on earth – the spiritual children and (3) the militant society, the Sisters on the battlefield. You can be in body in your country but a missionary in India, in the world. You must be happy, as you are chosen by the Lord who loves you so much that He gives you a part in His suffering. Be brave and cheerful and offer much that we may bring many souls to God. Once you come in contact with souls, the thirst grows daily."[57]

After reading this letter, Jacqueline understood what her real "vocation inside a vocation" meant. She could continue to give her life to God through the poor by cultivating her spiritual formation in accordance with Jesus' suffering, offering her illness, the multiple surgeries performed and all the pain she had endured for the success of the mission. In fact, God would go even further than she thought; her vocation became richer and more fruitful for the Kingdom of God. She didn't accept suffering because she loved suffering; but because of her love for Jesus who through her offering was able to extend His salvation to a greater number of souls. In summary, Jacqueline perceived this new call as a chance to follow the example of the Blessed Mother by becoming a "Co-Redemptrix".

In June 1953, Jacqueline laid the foundation for the "Link for Sick and Suffering Co-Workers" of the Missionaries of Charity.

Mother Teresa sent her a letter describing the core of this foundation:

"I am very happy that you are willing to join the suffering members of the Missionaries of Charity –you see what I mean-you and the others who will join will share in all our prayers,

---

[57] Spink, Kathryn. *A Chain of Love*, 21-27.

works and whatever we do for souls, and you do the same for us with your prayers and sufferings. You see the aim of our Society is to satiate the thirst of Jesus on the cross for love of souls by working for the salvation and sanctification of the poor in the slums. Who could do this better than you and the others who suffer like you? Your suffering and prayers will be the chalice in which we the working members will pour the love of souls we gather round. Therefore you are just as important and necessary for the fulfilment of our aim. To satiate this thirst we must have a chalice and you and the others-men, women, children-old and young-poor and rich- are all welcome to make the chalice. In reality you can do much more while on your bed of pain than running on your feet, but you and I together can do all things in Him who strengthens us."[58]

"There will be no vows unless some get permission from their confessor to do so. You could say a few prayers that we say also, so as to increase the family spirit, but one thing we must have in common is the spirit of our Society: Total surrender to God, loving trust and perfect cheerfulness. By this you will be known as a Missionary of Charity. Everyone and anyone who wishes to become a Missionary of Charity, a carrier of God's love, is welcome but I especially want the paralyzed, the crippled, the incurables to join for I know they will bring to the feet of Jesus many souls. The Sisters will each have one sister who prays, suffers, thinks, unites to her and so on-a second self. You see, my dear sister, our work is a most difficult one. If you are with us, praying and suffering for us and the work, we shall be able to do great things for love of Him-because of you. Personally, I feel very happy and a new strength has come in my soul at the thought of you and others joining the Society spiritually. Now with you and others doing the work with us, what would we not do? What can't we do for Him?"[59]

---

[58] Kolodiejchuk, Brian, *Come Be My Light*, 147.

[59] Ibid, 147-8. See also, Spink, Kathryn, *A Chain of Love: Sharing in the work of Mother Teresa through prayer and suffering*, 24-25.

"Smile at Jesus in your suffering-for to be a real Missionary of Charity you must be a cheerful victim. There is nothing special for you to do (claimed Mother Teresa) but to allow Jesus to live His life in you by accepting whatever He gives and by giving whatever He takes with a big smile,".[60]

Jacqueline started actively searching for the sick and suffering who would be interested in joining and sharing this beautiful vocation.

Despite the poverty and the rigorous discipline of the congregation, there were already forty-eight Missionary Sisters of Charity in 1954. There were also forty-eight 'Sick and Suffering Links' sharing in the spirit of the society and offering their sufferings and prayers.

Sixty years later, more than three thousand sick and suffering people have been given a sense of purpose to their life in joining the co- workers of Mother Teresa, and the Sisters and Brothers to whom they are linked have found new strength and companionship in the knowledge that someone is praying specifically for them. This way the sick and suffering brought energy to those who go out to alleviate the suffering of the world. To a world in which suffering represents one of the principal barriers to belief, they provide a living demonstration that it can and does at times draw people closer to God.

In Belgium, on April 3, 2009, Jacqueline went back to the Father. She had given up her personal hopes and desires in order to follow the path that God had in store for her. She joined Saint Teresa of Calcutta in a much greater adventure by becoming an example of total humility and vulnerability, while identifying herself with the poor she was longing to serve. How demanding, but how fruitful mercy is!

---

[60] *Come Be My Light*, 159.

40
Mother Teresa's Fan

Jim had always dreamed of meeting Mother Teresa. She fascinated him, and he had been waiting a long time for an opportune moment to seek her out. At 32, the man was solidly built and endowed with that strong common sense that American Marines tend to have.

The opportunity finally presented itself, and he had 10 days of approved leave. There he was, flying to Calcutta from San Francisco, where his base was located. He got a culture shock as his taxi was making its way through the humid, steamy, dusty maze of the streets in Calcutta. He arrived at the door of the convent of the Missionaries of Charity and rang the bell. A tiny little Indian sister opened the door.

"Good morning, Sister. I've come from far away, and I would like to meet Mother Teresa."

"I'm sorry, sir," she said. "Mother Teresa is not here. She had to leave for Rome."

Jim nearly fell into the poor nun's arms. He had traveled all these miles only to find his dream of meeting Mother Teresa would never be realized. He swallowed hard, trying to digest his disappointment. After a lengthy silence, he surrendered to the reality: "Well okay, but since I'm here, why not stay? Could I help you in some way?" "Of course!" She said. "There are 3 ways you could help: clean the house, cook, or care for the dying."

Taking care of the dying did not really attract him, and he couldn't cook at all, so he chose to clean the house. He was given a tiny room near the entrance to the street, but because there was so much noise, from the incessant horns of the rickshaws and people on the street, the opportunity to sleep was rare. Despite the difficulty, Jim tried his best to sleep for one week. He was far from the sanitized, gleaming surfaces of his native country, America. He tried to forget his intrinsic fear of contracting germs. After a week of cleaning, the sister's told him that he could take a day off. His excitement surprised even him.

A day off would allow him time to gather his thoughts and make preparations to leave. But just as he began to plan, the sisters asked him to answer the front door, a job which did not exactly delight him, because it prevented him from discovering the city.

That particular morning, the doorbell rang. Jim opened the door, and who did he see? Mother Teresa herself! "Am I hallucinating or what?" He said to himself. Mother Teresa raised her head (she was about half his size). She intently looked him in the eyes. She radiated love. To Jim's great surprise, she bluntly said, in that inimitable Albanian accent of hers, which he had heard so many times in news reports: "Come with me, we have work to do!" Everyone knows that Mother Teresa's "work" was to search through the slums of India looking for the poorest of the poor. Mother Teresa had spoken, he had no choice but to obey! Jim blindly followed her. She remained silent, so Jim didn't dare open his mouth, he was simply overcome with emotion. Furthermore, he didn't fully understand where he was going, or what awaited him in this truly unexpected expedition.

Mother Teresa walked briskly. On the horizon, a bridge took shape. Little by little the air became thick with an unimaginable odor. As though magnetically attracted by something, Mother Teresa unmistakably headed for the bridge. She seemed to find herself in familiar territory. But as they approached the bridge, not surprisingly the odor became more and more unbearable and nauseating. Once they arrived under the bridge, Jim saw a figure stretched out on the ground. It was an elderly man, half-naked, lying in his own excrement, vomit, and whatever else had accumulated on his miserable rags for months, if not years. Jim began to gag. But Mother Teresa, completely accustomed to this type of situation, looked at the poor wretch with tenderness and, turning towards Jim, murmured to him, "Take him!" Jim hesitated, "Take him? What did she mean by that?" But Mother Teresa had spoken, he had to obey!

Jim leaned towards the man and lifted him gently, but the stench was so strong that he turned his head with disgust. He wanted to vomit. He noticed that the man had numerous scars and that his infected wounds had attracted flies. Jim said to himself: "Whatever you do, above all, don't touch him!" So he pulled on the sleeves of his shirt to cover his hands and protect himself from contact with the man. Then he lifted him up and carried him towards the sisters' house alongside Mother Teresa. There, he placed him on a mat on the floor in a large room where the missionaries took care of the dying. At that moment Mother Teresa said to him, "Give him a bath." Jim looked at her and, turning again toward the dying man, that same thought entered his mind in a powerful way: 'No way, I can't touch that man.' But, not wanting to disappoint Mother Teresa, he complied. He took the man and laid him in a bathtub to wash him. A thought crossed Jim's mind: 'This man is going to die very soon… It would be terrible if his last memory when leaving this world were that of a young man who turned his head away with disgust! But if I treat him well, one day in heaven, he might pray for me!"

And so, Jim began to clean the man, putting his whole heart and soul into it. Using a sponge he delicately wiped the infected wounds. His dexterity however didn't keep the man from sliding several times to the bottom of the tub. Emotion filled Jim's heart. 'How could I be so self-centered? This man needs to know that he's not alone.' Placing his arms under the shoulders of the dying man, he lifted him up and let clear water flow over his wounds. Jim began to rock him in his arms. At that moment, the old man transformed. Jesus himself now lay in the arms of this great Marine and looked at him with infinite gentleness. It was Jesus who let himself be washed with gratitude. Jim trembled with the weight of what he was experiencing. He was holding the Lord in his arms! Not a vision, but Jesus Himself. He had the holes in his hands and feet. His side was pierced. His swollen face bore the traces of injury.

Jim couldn't believe his eyes and lifted his head to see if Mother Teresa witnessed the same thing. "You saw Him, didn't you?" she said to him with a very soft smile. She knew. When Jim lowered his eyes again, the man had become a poor, dying Indian man once more. The sisters of Mother Teresa then gathered around him, and Mother Teresa vanished. Mission accomplished.

Jim returned to his little room. An earthquake had shaken his very core in his thoughts and feelings. It took several hours for him to recover from the shock. 'What just happened to me?' he asked himself. He wanted to be sure. (After all, he wasn't in the military for nothing.) He had to understand. He had to find Mother Teresa again because surely she could explain it all to him.

He cornered a nun who was passing by and asked her: "Sister, I would like to see Mother Teresa before I leave. Could you tell her that Jim wants to talk to her?"

"I'm sorry, dear Brother, but Mother Teresa isn't here. She's still in Rome for a few more days."

"No, she's not. I was with her this morning in the city, and together we brought back a dying man. For sure, she's here!"

The sister was silent for a moment, and, with a humble smile, affirmed Jim, "Ah, yes," she said. "I understand. She does that sometimes."

Today, among the U.S. Marines, there is one man whose dream came true, and his life will never be the same. Under a small bridge in Calcutta, in the middle of the darkest human dereliction, he touched the face of God.

41
THE CRIMINAL NAMED DISMAS

The rending sound of the shofar rises up from the Temple of Jerusalem. All religious Jews are preparing to celebrate the coming of Shabbat. This year, it is also the Jewish Passover and the solemn moment of immolating the paschal lamb in the Temple.

At the same time, at Golgotha, there is a great disturbance. According to the Venerable Marthe Robin, two criminals are being crucified just in front of Jesus.[61] Dismas and Gesmas are both part of a band of brigands hiding out on the border of Egypt.[62]

The two robbers stayed a long time in prison before being sentenced. While the soldiers were preparing to drag him up on the cross, Dismas noticed the amazing patience Jesus had despite the terrible abuse being inflicted on him – all of hell, only too delighted to have seized him, was raging against him, with imagination that only the most violent hatred can produce. Dismas was not naturally unkind, and his heart had already been touched by Jesus' infinite meekness. He talked about

---

[61] This passage from Luke 23: 39-43 has been richly described by Marthe Robin. In fact, she relived the Passion of Christ every week, and knew every character in it. Her revelations are largely published in, "La Passion douloureuse du Sauveur" available at Foyers de Charité Publications: www.lesfoyersdecharité.com

[62] The legend says that the parents of one of them had given shelter to the Holy Family when they fled into Egypt. The child Dismas had leprosy. Our Lady suggested to his mother that she wash him in the water that had been used to bathe the child Jesus. Dismas was immediately healed.

him to his companion with respect and compassion. "They are treating the Galilean terribly," he said to Gesmas, hearing the hammer-blows and the executioners' yells.

While he was being heaved up on his cross, Dismas said to his executioners: "If you had treated us like you are the Galilean, you wouldn't now have to bother crucifying us, we would have died long ago from what you are doing to him." No one replied.

The crosses of the two thieves had been erected a little below the one for Jesus, facing one another. But space was left between them for a horseman to pass through and round easily. These two unfortunate souls on their crosses had such an appalling appearance that one had to pity them, especially the one on the left, a hideous villain who had nothing but insults and imprecations to utter. Their faces were frightful, bruised and livid. Their lips were all blackened by the drink they had been forced to take and by the blood flowing down. Their eyes were red and bulging as though about to jump out of their sockets. The suffering caused by the bonds that held them so tightly forced truly terrible screams from them.

Their whole bodies were riven with convulsive movements caused by the unremitting pain that tormented them. Gesmas shouted and constantly blasphemed against Jesus, while Dismas, already touched by grace, tried to pray and watched Jesus in silence, his heart filled with a very sweet hope.

On the cross, Jesus summoned his last remaining strength and opened his eyes. He raised them to Heaven and let this act of infinite goodness overflow from the depth of his heart that loved beyond all reason: "Father, forgive them, for they know not what they do!" In spite of the terrible cries of hatred that rose up around them, Mary, alongside her Son, repeated the same words, imploring the forgiveness of his enemies. She too prayed, "Father forgive them…" The insults against Jesus continued without ceasing, like a hailstorm.

Dismas, who had already begun to pray, was deeply touched to hear Jesus praying for his enemies. Suddenly, seized with profound repentance at the very moment when the holy Mother of Jesus was coming near to the cross, he was blessed with a great interior light: he truly knew in that moment that Jesus had intervened and entered deep into his very own soul. Dismas cried out to the crowd that was insulting Jesus: "How can you insult your savior like that when he is praying for you? He said nothing when you were abusing him, and he has patiently suffered all your attacks and your contempt, when he could reduce you all to nothing! And even now he is praying for you and you are not hearing!" He became even more animated and said: "This is a Prophet! This is our King! This is the Messiah, the Son of the Most High God! The Redeemer and Savior of all!"

At these unexpected words from the very mouth of a miserable assassin attached to his gibbet, a huge tumult arose among those present, who picked up stones to hurl at him. But Abenadar, the centurion, rebuked them severely and chased them away, then re-established order.

Dismas then said to his companion, who was still insulting the Lord, in spite of the centurion's ban: "So do you not even fear God, you who have been sentenced to the same terrible torture? For us it is justice, our crimes deserved the punishment that we are suffering, but he didn't do anything wrong. So remember you are about to die, and ask him for forgiveness!"

A Divine light now flooded the soul of Dismas, he was really touched and he confessed his sins to the Lord. Then he said to him: "Lord, if you condemn me, it will be just, because my sins deserve Hell; but have mercy on me!" Jesus said to him: "This very day you will share in my Mercy."

The example of the Good Thief who repented reveals to us all the sovereign effectiveness of divine forgiveness when it finds in a man, even the most guilty, this simple understanding: regret for one's sins. An isolated bit of comfort, these words from the good thief at this hour of Love, how sweet it must have been for the heart of Jesus and Mary in the midst of an ocean of hatred and bitterness! A single sinner converted surely gives Heaven a joy far greater than the joy received from ninety-nine just persons who do not need to repent. At least one man dared, during this universal flood of insults, to give homage to love and witness to the mission of the Son of God! … And that one man was a murderer! But his faith is contagious and will soon spring up from other repentant ones.

The divine hold that Jesus had on his apostles, disciples and innocent bystanders from the start of his ministry, was far from disappearing, even as Jesus was dying on the Cross. His enemies had hoped for complete humiliation for Jesus and his followers, but to their dismay Jesus made divine love felt to all those present at the terrible scene, and to the bewilderment of his enemies.

All this took place between twelve and twelve-thirty in the afternoon, but from that point on, there occurred great changes and transformations in the souls of the spectators, as well as in nature. In fact, while the Good Thief was denouncing his life of sin and crime, extraordinary signs were occurring in nature – signs that filled the blasphemers with terror and astonishment, and they immediately fell silent.

At about the sixth hour, according to the Jewish way of counting (approximately twelve-thirty for us), the sky suddenly darkened with a thick reddish fog, and there was very quickly an eclipse of the sun. A general terror took hold of those present, and as the darkness increased, each one became more thoughtful and either went away, or approached the Cross in fear and trembling. The animals who were out at pasture bellowed and ran away, terrified. The horses and asses of the Pharisees huddled together and whinnied as they dropped their heads. The birds looked for places to shelter, as though a storm were approaching, swooping down on the hills surrounding Calvary in great numbers. Those who had been insulting the Lord up until then, lowered their voices and withdrew. The fog was becoming more and more disturbing!

The Pharisees were still trying to explain this by material causes, but they had no success, being themselves in the grip of fear. Every person kept their eyes fixed on the sky.

Little by little, the attitudes of the crowd changed. One could feel that a very great mystery was hovering over this extraordinary scene. Something divinely great, divinely beautiful and reverent was happening on this mysterious hilltop, which became for everyone the holy hill of the love of a God for his sinful brothers.

The sky was becoming ever darker and the darkness soon covered the whole earth. The violence and hatred began to give way to fear and even repentance. Some struck their breasts and wrung their hands in despair, while others fell to their knees and begged his forgiveness.

Near Mary, the apostle John was standing, he who was soon to receive the magnificent reward for his perfect fidelity to Christ and his holy Mother. Not far from them, Mary of Magdala, filled with sorrow, had collapsed at the foot of the Cross with her arms around it. Leaning her forehead against the bleeding feet of her Beloved, she covered them with burning kisses. Very close to the Virgin Mother, there were also Salome and Mary of Cleopas, also joining themselves in pain and Love to the Great and Divine mystery of the Cross and the death of Christ.

Dismas, still in the abyss of his deep repentance, lifted his head toward his Savior and said in humble hope: "Lord, remember me when you come into your Kingdom!" Jesus replied: "Truly I tell you, this very day you will be with me in Paradise!"

When the Convict Becomes the Lawyer

Thanks to these revelations of Venerable Marthe Robin, we are allowed to penetrate more deeply into the feelings of Jesus and the Good Thief. It is clearly not by chance that the Father allowed it to be a criminal who took up Jesus' defense.

In fact, we cannot find a better representative than him! He is actually the only person who spoke openly in his favor at the hour of the Cross, and we can imagine what immense comfort this could give Jesus. Christ was giving his life for sinners, for you and me and for us all. And who was at his side? Someone whom he could save then and there! Someone in whom he can see the fruit of his Passion. Jesus, so happy to find a heart that accepts his sacrifice and receives the fruit, makes him the first saint in Christian history.

Who among us, in thrall to the atrocious pain that is suffered by crucified ones, could even say that he or she deserves their fate? The humility of this man unleashes torrents of Christ's mercy. The humility of a sinner who sincerely recognizes his sin and repents of it provokes the immense tenderness of God, always happy to wipe away our sins, however grave.

If we realize the greatness of the Heart of God and the profound depths of his mercy, we would cast ourselves blindly into his arms. Yet it is often our lack of faith in his mercy that holds us back! Jesus reminded Saint Faustina of this: "Tell the souls that they can only draw from this spring of mercy with the vase of trust. When they have great trust, there will be no limit to my generosity. What causes me the most pain, what wounds me the most, even more than the sin, is the lack of trust in my mercy," (St. Faustina's Diary § 1601).

What does the demon whisper to us to the contrary? "Leave it! It's too late for you, with all you have done, don't expect God to even look at you. You are lost forever, don't even try, you will anger God even more." How many sinners hear these poisonous words and refuse to see a priest at the time of their death, passing by the grace that is offered!

Of course, the demon is jealous of this possibility that is given us on earth to convert, to return to the burning heart of Jesus. Because God is always impatient to give us another chance, even 100 times a day, whatever our situation. God is so great!

42
Bruno Cornacchiola and the Signs of the Times

Bruno Cornacchiola with his family and Sister Raffaella Somma, Italy

Could Heaven have a particular attraction for criminals? The fact is that Jesus Himself, while nailed to the cross, canonized a highway thief. The man who was condemned to death, Dismas, became Saint Dismas, the first saint to be canonized – and by Jesus in person! "This very day you will be with me in Paradise," he said.

When it came to crime, Bruno Cornacchiola was an expert.

Bruno was born in Italy to a very poor family, with a violent and alcoholic father and a mother who had little time or tenderness to spend with him. After his marriage to Jolanda, who would bear him four children, Bruno joined the Nationalists on the side of Franco in the Spanish civil war of 1936. There, he met a Protestant, who displayed a ferocious hatred towards the Catholic Church and Pope Pius XII. After listening to this man intently, Bruno began to cultivate a monstrous plan: to eradicate the pope from the face of the earth. To make matters worse, the faith of his pious spouse agitated Bruno. One day, in an angry fit, he grabbed a crucifix and, contorting his face, threw it to the ground, where it broke into a thousand pieces. He began to write out a full discourse against the theology of the Immaculate Conception, and as he did, Bruno made the decision to kill Pope Pius XII. On a carefully-sharpened knife, he inscribed these words: "Death to the Pope!"[63]

On Saturday, April 12, 1947, Bruno was with his children on the outskirts of Rome, not far from the abbey church of Tre Fontane (Three Fountains), which owes its name to the martyrdom of Saint Paul.[64] Bruno was thirty-three at the time and his three children (the fourth child would be born later) were playing with their ball near a grotto. However, the ball got lost in a thicket, and Bruno joined the search for it. His children entered the grotto and fell to their knees in the dust, one after the other. They were frozen like statues, their hands joined, and, seemingly fascinated, all three repeated the same words: "Beautiful Lady, beautiful Lady!" Bruno called them to come out, but in vain.

At the same time that he was calling them he angrily hurried to the grotto. There he found his children on their knees, in a state of ecstasy. "What are you doing?" he barked at them. "That's no place to pray!" But the children remained deaf to his cries and didn't even turn around to look at their father.

---

[63] A year later, Bruno met Pius XII to give him the knife and ask his forgiveness.

[64] It was there that the apostle to the Gentiles was persecuted and beheaded by Emperor Nero. Tradition says that his head bounced on the ground three times and that three fountains sprung up, one in each place it struck.

Becoming more and more furious, Bruno tried to grab them, but they were rigid and heavy as stone. Then, in spite of himself, he fell to his own knees, and turned his head to the back of the grotto. The Blessed Virgin Mary was standing there, majestic, serious, extremely beautiful, and dressed in an ivory robe with a long, emerald green veil that reached the ground. Her sash was pale pink. Our Lady looked at Bruno and said: "I am the one who dwells in the Divine Trinity. I am the Virgin of Revelations. You have been persecuting me. Now, that's enough! Come back to the holy flock!"[65]

Bruno tells us that the Mother of God made a gesture with her right arm, pointing to the ground with her index finger. Then Bruno saw at the feet of the Blessed Mother a broken cross, the very same one he had thrown to the ground some time before. He also saw a piece of black fabric and a cassock tossed onto the ground.

Our Lady said to him: "You see, the Church will be persecuted, broken. That's the sign that my sons will be disrobed... As for you, be strong in the faith!" The "sons" Mary spoke of are the members of the clergy.

Then the Blessed Virgin revealed to him what was going to happen, in particular, the defection of so many priests, and how he, Bruno, had to love and serve the Church in spite of all that would happen. The broken cross, she explained, signified the martyrdom of priests who remained faithful to Christ during the persecution. "Priests," said Mary, "even if they find themselves in a hellish whirlwind, are dear to me. They will be trampled on and killed. There's the broken cross near the cassock, a sign of the disrobing of priests." The cassock thrown on the ground signified the abandonment of their vocation by so many priests. The black fabric meant that the Church would be left a widow and subject to the mercy of the world.

---

[65] This apparition has been informally recognized by Pope Pious XII when in 1956 he blessed the statue of Our Lady that can still be found in the grotto. Holy Mass is authorized to be celebrated in the little Chapel.

Bruno converted on the spot. He became an apostle on fire, a great defender of the Church, until his death in June 2001. During all those years, he received messages from the Virgin Mary, predominantly in dreams, much like those received by Saint John Bosco. These messages were prophetic. They concerned both the near and distant future of the Church, and the internal trials she would endure. Most of them referred to the times in which we are presently living.[66]

Now, on May 2, 2016, during the monthly apparition of the Our Lady of Medjugorje, the visionary Mirjana Soldo received the following message: "Dear children! My maternal heart desires your true conversion as well as a strong faith, so that you can propagate love and peace to all around you. But, dear Children, don't forget that each one of you is a unique world before the heavenly Father. That is why you must permit the constant action of the Holy Spirit to work inside you… I call upon you, dear children, 'to look carefully at the signs of the times,' 'to gather in the broken crosses,' and to be 'the apostles of the Revelation.' I thank you." Mirjana asked that I put these words in quotes. She, also confirmed that they referred to the apparitions at Tre Fontane.

Is the Apocalypse Here?

Why is the Blessed Mother speaking to us today about the broken crosses we need to gather together? It's like she's flashing her lights at those who want to serve Christ and His church in the present environment of great spiritual confusion and profound sorrow. Our world is swimming in troubled waters. It's no longer a question of a single broken cross, such as the one shown to Bruno in 1947, but of many broken crosses, those that people are breaking today in countries wanting to

[66] For those who can read Italian, these messages can be found in Saverio Gaeta's book: *Il Veggente, il secreto delle Tre Fontane*, Salani Editore, 2016. There, Saverio has collected, from the Vatican Archives, all the prophecies of the Virgin to Bruno Cornacchiola.

push Christ outside their borders. Mary describes to us also, her immense sorrow at the defection of so many Christians, both priests and lay people; at the betrayals in the very womb of the Church; at the great apostasies of our era.

Mary revealed to Bruno the name by which she wanted to be invoked in Tre Fontane: "I am the Virgin of Revelation." She was holding in her hands a small book: The Apocalypse of St. John, also called The Book of Revelations.

The Virgin of Revelation invites us today to be "the apostles of Revelation"! She specifies what characterizes the apostles who must remain faithful in the midst of tribulation. Character traits which, she indicated to Bruno, were her own during her earthly life:

"They don't complain.

They keep quiet,

And they don't rebel."

The Book of Revelation is a sacred text, partially sealed. It projects the future of humanity and the victory of God over the Dragon and the Beast, after terrible battles.[67] How can we not open our eyes and state that, now as never before, the battle against the Beast is turning out to be violent and decisive? Satan knows that his days are numbered, and he is playing his last cards with the energy of despair. Wouldn't the Blessed Mother wish to tell us that we are in a pivotal moment, an important turning point in the life of the Church? Is she not saying that this is a time in which the coming of the Apocalypse is near, and each person is going to have to take a position

---

[67] "Also, like Daniel and other apocalypses, it was composed as resistance literature to meet a crisis. The crisis was ruthless persecution of the early Church by the Roman authorities; the harlot Babylon symbolizes pagan Rome, the city on seven hills (Rev 17:9). The book is, then, an exhortation and admonition to Christians of the first century to stand firm in the faith and to avoid compromise with paganism, despite the threat of adversity and martyrdom; they are to await patiently the fulfillment of God's mighty promises," (United States Conference of Catholic Bishops).

with or against Christ? Personally, I believe so, because in her messages given in Medjugorje, Mary has never alluded to any other place of apparition, except in August 1991, to the apparitions in Fatima. Why would she now point out the sum and substance of the apparitions at Tre Fontane?

It's worthwhile to reread the Book of Revelation, particularly chapter 12, in which the Virgin appears. She told Bruno: "Before I go, I will tell you this: The Book of Revelation is the Word of God, and this Revelation talks about me. That's why I assumed the title: 'The Virgin of Revelation'."

It's important, also, to comprehend, through heartfelt, fervent prayer, how earnestly the Virgin expects us to make reparation, for sacrileges, attacks against the priesthood and for how poorly we acknowledge the presence of Jesus in the Eucharist. "My immaculate heart bleeds," she said on April 25, 2016, in Medjugorje. She doesn't ask us to "gather in the broken crosses" so that we can criticize or make negative appraisals of certain priests or prelates; even less does she do it so that we sink into despair. No, she invites us to do everything in our power to help and support priests through prayer and sacrifice. What consolation we can give her by uniting our hearts to her Immaculate Heart, which surely bleeds, but also already sees the final victory!

To make an analogy, imagine that we are on a small mountain road, narrow and badly maintained heading to the sea. The road turns and bends and never seems to stop, in fact it makes us sick to our stomachs, but we can smell the sea. We can't see it, but we inhale its familiar, iodized mist. So, we take courage; it's not far. We're going to make it! Then, at the corner of the bend, there it is, beautiful, immense, magnificent!

Victory is near, but while she waits, Mary looks for souls who simply want to be one with hers and to fight with her, until she crushes the head of the serpent. The battle is unremitting.

Jolanda Saves Her Husband

Bruno Cornacchiola's wife, Jolanda, serves as an admirable example for us of what might be a path to sainthood for a lot of spouses whose marriage is in trouble. In spite of Bruno's repeated betrayal of his wife, before his conversion, Jolanda remained faithful to the Lord, always praying fervently. So fervently that Our Lady herself praised Jolanda to Bruno saying: "God's promises are and will remain immutable. The first nine Fridays of the Sacred Heart that you were making, lovingly pushed by your faithful spouse before you went down the wrong road, have saved you!" That simple practice of piety saved Bruno from perdition![68] The Blessed Mother took up

---

[68] In Paray-le-Monial, France, 1675, Christ gave Saint Margaret Mary Alacoque twelve promises for those who venerate his Sacred Heart in a particular way on the First Nine Fridays of the month consecutively. (True devotion to the Sacred Heart of Jesus is also a devotion to the Blessed Sacrament. These promises are also for those who do an hour of adoration of Jesus in the Blessed Sacrament.) Here they are:

1. I will give them all the graces necessary for their state of life.
2. I will establish peace in their homes.
3. I will comfort them in all their afflictions.
4. I will be their secure refuge during life, and above all, in death.
5. I will bestow abundant blessings upon all their undertakings.
6. Sinners will find in my Heart the source and infinite ocean of mercy.
7. Lukewarm souls shall become fervent.
8. Fervent souls shall quickly mount to high perfection.
9. I will bless every place in which an image of my Heart is exposed and honored.
10. I will give to priests the gift of touching the most hardened hearts.
11. Those who shall promote this devotion shall have their names written in my Heart.
12. I promise you in the extravagant mercy of my Heart that my all-powerful love will grant to all those who receive Holy Communion on the First Fridays of nine consecutive months the grace of final perseverance; they shall not die in my disgrace, nor without receiving the Sacraments. My divine Heart shall be their safe refuge in this last moment.

Conditions for making oneself worthy of these 12 promises:

1. Receive a sacramental Communion under the condition that you are in a state of grace. If you are in a state of mortal sin, you must first make a good confession.
2. Receive this Communion for nine consecutive months. If these Communions are interrupted, even for a single month, whether because you have forgotten or for any other reason, you must begin anew.
3. Receive Communion on the first Friday of each month. This pious practice may begin in any month of the year.

Jolanda's defense, affirming to Bruno that she had stayed faithful and she never committed the sins of which he accused her. Actually, he used to beat her, undoubtedly to unload on her the remorse he felt for his own infidelities, until the very night before the apparition. (We might suggest to the Holy See that Jolanda be canonized at the same time as her husband!)

And the Blessed Virgin continued like this: "The Hail Mary's that you say with faith and love are like golden arrows that reach the Heart of Jesus."

What Prophecies did Bruno Receive?

Curiously, the book *Il Veggente,* about the apparitions of Our Lady of Revelation, was published in 2016, only four months before Our Lady of Medjugorje spoke about them, and alluded to the three central elements which characterized them.[69] It seems as though she was waiting for these prophecies to be made public and accessible to all before she mentioned them. Here are some extracts from a book that Bruno, himself, wrote between 1947 and 2001 while enduring great suffering:

Our Lady said to Bruno: "The whole Church will be subjected to a terrible trial in order to purify it of all sorts of carnal passions which will have infiltrated its ministers, in particular, those in religious Orders who took the vow of poverty: It will be a moral trial and a spiritual trial. At a time indicated in the heavenly books, the priests and the faithful will find themselves at a dangerous turning point and will run the risk of being thrown into the world of the damned (for example, the Satanists – note from the author), who will attack them by any means possible, through false ideologies and theologies, among other ways. Supplications will come from both sides, the faithful as well as the unfaithful, and there will be as many of them as the trials. I (the Virgin) will be among the

[69] Saverio Gaeta, Il Veggente, il secreto delle Tre Fontane, Salani Editore, 2016

elect; Christ will be our captain, and we will fight for you…"

She also said to him: "Satan's anger will not be contained, and the Spirit of God will be taken away from the earth. The Church will be left a widow. Here is the funeral pall. The Church will be left to the mercy of the world. Children, become holy, and sanctify yourselves even more. Love one another always… Take action under the banner of Christ. Working this way, you will see the fruits of victory in the awakening of consciences for the good; despite the ambient evil, you will see, thanks to your helpful and effective co-operation, sinners converted to the great Flock of saved souls," (Chapter 4, p. 81).

In another part of the book she said: "There will be days of suffering and grief. A strong people, estranged from God, will rise from the East and will launch a terrifying attack, breaking the most holy and most sacred of things, whenever they are able to do it," (Chapter 10, p. 192).

Bruno wrote: "She said, 'Look!' I looked and saw a multitude of busy people who look like ants; they come and go, do some work, and are tired… Some fall on the ground, and I see that they are pitting themselves against one another, striking blows, and I also hear their excited voices, full of anger, which blaspheme and accuse each other of the evil which exists in the world. Some have in their hands special weapons; they are making war. I see blood and death everywhere… Suddenly, I feel the earth tremble under my feet… I am agitated… I am frightened. The Virgin says to me: 'Don't be afraid. It's an earthquake, a warning sign for the entire world.' I ask: 'Are these warnings about conversion? Or maybe calls to return to the doctrine, to the Spirit of truth which they have been fighting?' Our Lady answered me: 'They are deaf and without intelligence. They see the warning signs but don't reflect on that reality. You, pray and make offerings!'" (Chapter 10, p. 195).

In the next chapter Bruno reports that on January 1, 1990 Our Lady said: "The people of God, those who are called to save others, will meet obstacles when trying to accomplish their mission: and they will not speak of God, nor of Jesus

Christ, nor of the Holy Spirit. They will no longer be able to talk about me, who am truly the Mother of God, the Spouse of God, the Daughter of God. They will be prevented from doing so, and they will not be able to speak about the Sacraments or the Sacramentals. Those who speak about those things will be persecuted, both physically and morally, and will become true confessors of Jesus Christ," (Chapter 11, p. 218).

Mary also confided to Bruno, on December 31, 1990: "False prophets are already at work; they are seeking, using any means, to poison souls, to replace the doctrine of Jesus, my beloved Son, with satanic teachings. They will do away with the sacrifice of the cross, which is perpetuated on all the altars of the world! These poisoners will take away the means of salvation: and they have already penetrated the light of the Church, which is divine, founded upon my Son, the cornerstone, the rock which was placed on the shoulders of Peter and the apostles."

But at the same time, the Virgin made clear that "Jesus has promised that enemies may ruin souls, may diminish hope, but they can never defeat the Church nor prevail against her. And Hell, with all its power, will be able to do nothing against the Church of my Son. He who lives in her will be saved," (Chapter 11, p. 221).

Bruno Cornacchiola during a mission

43
WILL WE ESCAPE THE THREAT?

He is 29 years old, he is married and a father, he is thin and nervous. His complexion is swarthy, he has black hair, his eyes are fixed and determined. Terrifying words pour forth from his mouth, they are monotone and mechanical. It is June 2016 and we find ourselves in a prison in Libya. This Kamikaze member of ISIS has just been arrested while preparing a bomb attack in Tripoli, Libya, against General Serra. In the interview broadcast on Italian television, what is eerie about this man is the absolute tranquility with which he expresses his plan to blow himself up in the name of Allah. "My fear doesn't matter," he tells the journalist of the *Corriere della Sera*. "I do what is right in the eyes of our religion, so that when I die, I will go to heaven. This is what is written, it is what the Quran demands. Soon we will arrive in Rome, the city that symbolizes the infidel's West. From there, we will take all of Europe; and from Libya, it's easy. For Christians, and all infidels, there will be three choices: convert to Islam, pay the tax stipulated by our religious law, or be killed if they do not consent."

This suicide bomber could not be more clear! Today his speech seems to be cliché, nothing new! However, to hear it live on television deeply resonates with a fear that the present times demand, and it can cause one to pause and think. To confide in God does not mean we can act like an ostrich and remain blind to the real threats facing us.

For this ISIS member, it was a question of murdering, among others, Paolo Serra, the Italian military adviser to Martin Kobler, the UNO envoy for Libya.

Our Lady of Civitavecchia

In February of 2016, I had the joy of meeting Fabio Gregori, one of the two visionaries of Civitavecchia, a place of apparitions near Rome, with his daughter Jessica.[70] There, in February 1995, tears of blood were seen on the face of a statue of Our Lady in Fabio's family garden. The Virgin of Civitavecchia, known as the Queen of the Families, warned us of the threat of a nuclear conflict between the East and the West. Moreover, she advised us that the devil will do everything to undermine the unity of the Christian family, based on marriage. She also said that without the impetus of new conversions, many priests will betray their own vocation and even cause serious scandal in the Church. She also forewarned that the Church would experience a great apostasy, that is, the denial of fundamental Christian truths that have been reaffirmed over the centuries, in the Catholic Tradition and Doctrine.[71]

Among the prophetic messages received by Fabio and Jessica since 1995, two stand out as occurring in our present time:

First, the destruction of the family by Satan, who manifests his extreme hatred for the Creator. Indeed, the family is at the

[70] As in Fatima and in Medjugorje, Our Lady calls us, and again gives us the surest way to avoid destruction, wars and all forms of evil, also promising her faithful maternal protection if we do what she says. "I can't help you," she said in Medjugorje, "if you do not obey the commandments of God, if you do not renounce sin and if you do not live the Mass," (October 25, 1993). Indeed, she cannot act if we reject God's plan for us. These apparitions have been recognized only by the Diocesan Bishop, Mgr Grillo. John Paul II had a close relationship with this exceptional family. He went personally to the parish of San Agostino where the statue of Our Lady that wept tears of blood, is available for public prayer. In his book *Diario del Vescovo*, Mgr. Grillo, also tells us that twice Pope John Paul II went to Civitavecchia incognito during his many "escapes outside the walls".

[71] Read 'The Madonna di Civitavecchia' of father Flavio Ubodi, Edizioni Ares. www.Amazon.it (in Italian). There are a large part of the prophecies of the Virgin. Other prophecies are kept secret by the local Bishop. Also, read, "The Madonna fa la strada, Civitavecchia nel tempo di Maria", of Riccardo Caniato, Edizioni Ares. .Finally: Intervista Riccardo Caniato su pubblicato Studi Cattolici nr. 652, June 2015, http://ares.mi.it/riviste-652-187.html

heart of God's plan for humanity, it is the nest of life for man created in the image of God. "On the unity of the family," said John Paul II, "depends the future of the Church and of the world." The challenge is therefore crucial!

Second, the loss of faith and a great apostasy, and many scandals within the heart of the Church. Sister Lucia, the visionary of Fatima, confirms this. Indeed, when Pope John Paul II asked Cardinal Caffarra to found the Pontifical Institute for studies on marriage and the family, the latter wrote to Sister Lucia of Fatima to solicit her prayer. To his great surprise, he received from her a long letter written in her hand, now preserved in the archives of the Institute. Here is an extract: "The final battle between the Lord and the reign of Satan will focus on marriage and the family. Do not be afraid, because all those who will work for the sanctity of marriage and the family will always be fought and hated in every way, this is the crucial point." In conclusion, she added: "However, Our Lady has already crushed his head." Lucia also warned that by touching the family, one touched the column that supports all Creation, indeed the relationship between man and woman and between generations. When destruction comes to the central column, the entire building collapses, and that is what we see today.

Under the threat of natural disasters and wars, anxiety rises more and more about the future. Peace in Europe is more fragile. Muslim extremists want to completely eradicate the Christian culture of the West. Here we are in the midst of a gigantic spiritual struggle.

In 1976, the Cardinal Karol Wojtyla openly said: "We currently face the greatest confrontation the history of mankind has ever known. I do not think that the majority of American society, any more than the whole of Christendom, grasps its full scope. We are currently facing the final battle of the Church and the anti-Church, of the Gospel and the anti-Gospel, of the Christ and the Antichrist. This confrontation is part of the designs of the divine Providence. That is why it is in God's plan. There must be a fight assumed and lead with courage by the Church…," ("Triumph of the Heart Magazine", summer 2016).

At Lourdes in 2007, for our consolation, Cardinal Ivan Dias concludes with these words of Pope John Paul II: "Anyway, one thing is certain: the final victory belongs to God and this final victory will be achieved on the intercession of the Virgin Mary, the woman of Genesis and Revelation who will fight at the head of her armies, her sons and her daughters against the power of Satan. She will crush the head of the snake."

In Medjugorje, the visionaries received secrets about the future of the world. They wept profusely when receiving one of the last. They of course did not reveal what it was, but later, Mary told them that the content of this secret was softened through prayers and fasting, but not completely removed. At the beginning of the apparitions, the Virgin had made it known that at the end of the secrets, we would see the end of the power of Satan. The visionary Ivan Dragicevic also declared: "When the secrets are revealed, we will find again the faith of our fathers."

Let us not forget that the true prophecies announcing misfortunes and sufferings are given by God not to be realized! They are always accompanied by an overture for mercy, an invitation to conversion and to return to the commandments of God. If we repent and do penance, then God will prevent evil from happening. The Bible and the history of the Church give us many good examples!

But, unless I am mistaken, our world today does not seem to come close to the Lord, at least not in the West, where it is preferred to worship the gods of money, sex, and power. In 1981, Our Lady in Medjugorje said, "I came to bring the world closer to the heart of God." But in 2012 she said, "The world departs every day more from the heart of God." Has the Queen of peace failed in her mission? No, it was we who paid too little attention to her maternal voice that constantly invited us on the true path of peace. We are too preoccupied by other objectives than that of Holiness.

Under Mary's Mantle

My intention here is neither to focus on the threats weighing down on our world, nor on the continuous flow of offences inflicted on the infinite loving Heart of our God.

Instead, I wish to evoke once again the Virgin Mary, Mother of Mercy and Refuge of sinners. She is indeed God's providential answer to our anxieties of today. Let us look closely at the life of this perfect disciple of Jesus.

She is the spouse above all spouses and, like the Disciples of Christ, she is the first to "follow the Lamb everywhere He goes," (Rev. 14: 4). Mary certainly never failed to walk the same paths as her Son and what paths they were indeed! He was born in Bethlehem in dire poverty. He narrowly escaped the murder of the Holy Innocents. He fled to Egypt with His parents, struggling to survive like so many refugees away from their homeland. Thirty years of a life hidden in Nazareth followed by 3 years of preaching. Suddenly, He let himself be arrested without any resistance, like a lamb being led to slaughter. He could have escaped, but he chose not to. His Hour had come. He was delivered into the hands of sinners and led to the most humiliating death.

This is it. The lamb is slain on the Altar of the Cross! As the world of His followers fell apart, sorrow and despair overcame them. All was finished and nothing made sense anymore. It was the utmost horror. However, there is one, single soul that didn't falter. Mary stood upright and peaceful at the foot of the Cross. She remained dignified in front of all. Only Jesus' Mother could display such a degree of magnificence in her attitude. She found support in her unfailing hope, or rather, in the certainty that the Father's plan was being accomplished in front of her. The salvation of the world was at stake on Golgotha. Her son carried out His mission perfectly as He crushed death on its home ground and thus redeemed humanity.

The French mystic Marthe Robin described what dwelled in Our Lady's heart at that very hour:

"Mary's sorrow was infinite. However, one should not imagine her suffering resembling an ocean of bitterness where no ray from Above shines through. Far from it! Her perfect happiness is found in her great sorrow as she fulfils the Father's will right to the end. Through her love and offering she greatly contributes to God's eternal redeeming plan, as, united with Jesus, she brings forth a new humanity to divine life. She also anticipated the coming Resurrection and the universal exaltation of the Divine Crucified."[72]

Jesus gave us His Mother on the Cross. She is neither a mere symbol nor a sweet substitute mother. She is a true mom indeed, a woman conceiving a child, bearing him in her womb, giving birth to her child and accompanying him in his solicitude. Of course, our earthly mother has already given us life. However, this body we received from her is going to die one day. Conversely, through the Blessed Mother, we are born to everlasting life which is the life in the Spirit. Its source is in God our Creator and will fully unfold in Eternal Life. As Saint Bernard of Clairvaux wrote, "When we are on earth, we are still unborn. We are born when we enter Heaven. While on earth, we are carried in the womb of the Mother of God."

Thus, Mary is as much a true Mother, on a divine level, as our earthly mother is our true mother on a natural level. Mary has given us infinitely more than our earthly mother. She has brought us forth to everlasting life, a divinely beautiful and happy life.

With Mary and like her, the Church follows the Lamb everywhere He goes; really, everywhere. The Church carried by Mary in her womb will inevitably come to a point where it must experience the death of Christ, before Christ triumphs. It is the night of Holy Saturday. It is the silence of God.

Therefore, in the near future, if the Church looks crushed

---

[72] *La douloureuse Passion du Sauveur* (The Sorrowful Passion of Our Savior), ed. Foyer de Charité. www.martherobin.com.

down like Her Master; if it seems destroyed, even annihilated like Him; if we witness confusion and retreat among Clergy members; if our churches are requisitioned or attacked; if our securities fall, and finally if we can only see darkness around us, one thing will always remain: we will find the most secure refuge in the motherly mantle of Mary, who became our Mother at the Cross.[73] This means living with her, in her, through her and obeying her directions as she invites us to do.[74] Never could the fiery features of the Devil enter the Virgin's mantle because this mantle is the very cloud of the Holy Spirit which covered her with Its shadow from the Annunciation onwards and has never left her since, as it is written, "The power of the most High will cover you with its shadow," (Lk 1: 35). Therefore, happy and blessed are those who welcome Mary as their Mother, the storms will not confound them.[75]

---

[73] On January 13, 1864, Venerable Father Louis Cestac, founder of Mary's Servants' Order, was struck by a vision where demons wrought inexpressible havoc on earth. At the same time, he saw the Virgin Mary who told him that evil spirits were indeed raging in the world. It was time to invoke her as Queen of Angels and to request her to send the Holy Legions to defeat the powers of Hell. Father Cestac answered, "My Mother, you who are so good, could you not send them without us asking you to do so?" But she replied, "No, prayer is the condition set up by God Himself to obtain graces." Father responded, "Then, My Mother, would you yourself teach me how to pray?"

This is the prayer he received from Our Lady: "August Queen of Heaven, Sovereign Mistress of the Angels, thou, who from the beginning hast received from God the power and the mission to crush the head of Satan, we humbly implore thee: send thy holy legions so that under thy command, they may drive the devils away, everywhere, fight them, subduing their boldness and thrust them down into the abyss. Who is like unto God? O good and tender Mother, thou will always be our love and our hope. O divine Mother, send Thy holy angels to defend us and drive far away from us the cruel enemy. Holy Angels and Archangels defend us, keep us."

[74] Our Lady told us in Medjugorje on 25th January 2001: "Those who pray are not afraid of the future. Those who fast don't fear evil."

[75] Text inspired by The "Triumph of the Heart", a magazine edited by The Family of Mary, www.de-vrouwe.info Sept/Oct 2016. Source: Ildebrando A. Santangelo, Il ritorno di Gesù, Adrano/Catania, p. 14 and following.

Not without Michael the Archangel

The book of Daniel is the first book of Scriptures to mention the name Michael: "At that time Michael, the archangel, who stands guard over your nation, will arise. Then there will be a time of anguish greater than any since nations first came into existence," (Dan 12:1).

Some two thousand four hundred years later, the great Marian Pope Leo XIII (1800 – 1903) received confirmation that we have indeed entered those prophesied times. In fact, on October 13, 1884, that is exactly 33 years before the miracle of the sun in Fatima, a prophetic vision was granted to Leo XIII, a man who was very moderate and cautious by nature. He confided this vision to his Confessor who, in turn, considered it a spiritual legacy and handed it down to Cardinal Pietro Boetto who published it after World War II.

Pope Leo XIII's vision happened just after celebrating Mass. A scene suddenly unfolded in front of him and it seems that he was the only witness. His face furrowed with fright and astonishment and turned completely white. Immediately after the vision, he walked back to his desk and, with the stroke of his pen, wrote two of the most powerful prayers the Church offers us today: "O my God, You Who are our Help" and "St Michael the Archangel, Prince of the Heavenly Hosts". What did the Pope actually see?

According to his own testimony, he saw the earth opening up like a pomegranate. Myriads of demons came out of an abyssal fissure. They invaded the whole earth, while spreading lies everywhere and bringing about uprisings, wars and revolutions. A huge widespread mist covered the earth. The number of casualties was so great that the earth appeared soaked in blood. At that moment, he watched as it appeared a gang of evil spirits were throwing themselves on the Church, represented by St Peter's Basilica. This shook the Church so badly that it looked as if it was on the verge of collapsing. At that moment of the vision, the Holy Father cried aloud: "But isn't there anything to save the Church?"

Suddenly, Saint Michael the Archangel came down from Heaven and began to wage war against the evil spirits. He was victorious. One by one, the demons retreated back into the abyssal crack of the earth, which closed in on itself. As the earth absorbed the blood that was shed, the mist lifted to give place to the dawn of a beautiful new day. Then a voice could be heard, "All this will start under the pontificate of one of the next Popes – and Russia will be the cause of it."

The veracity of Leo XIII's vision can't be doubted. In his letter during Lent 1946, Cardinal Nasalli Rocca, Archbishop of Bologna, wrote: "This prayer was written by Leo XIII himself. The words: 'Thrust into Hell Satan and all the evil spirits who prowl around the world, seeking the ruin of souls' bear a historical meaning. Leo XIII really did see the diabolical spirits gathered above the Eternal City of Rome. This vision spurred him to write this supplication, which he willed to be prayed by the whole Church. Pope Leo XIII himself said it with a trembling but strong voice. The walls of Saint Peter's basilica at the Vatican have resonated many times with this prayer."

In 1886, Pope Leo XIII had a letter sent to every diocese in the world requesting this prayer be said, kneeling down, after every mass. However, the liturgical reform of 1969-1970 didn't take this powerful supplication into account.

Pope John-Paul II also believed Pope Leo's vision to be authentic. As Cardinal, he was already convinced that "we are facing the greatest challenge ever experienced in all history of humanity." A few decades later, he added: "Let prayer strengthen us to face our spiritual battles… The book of Revelation refers to that kind of battle when it presents the figure of Saint Michael to us. (Rev, 12:7) This would have surely been the scene that Pope Leo XIII had in mind when, at the end of the last century, he introduced this particular prayer to Saint Michael to the whole Church:

> 'St. Michael the Archangel, defend us in battle. Be our safeguard against the wickedness and snares of the Devil. May God rebuke him, we

> humbly pray. And do thou, O Prince of the heavenly hosts, by the power of God, thrust into hell Satan, and all the evil spirits, who prowl about the world, seeking the ruin of souls. Amen.'

"Although the recitation of this prayer doesn't conclude Eucharistic celebrations anymore, I invite everyone to remember it and to pray it to obtain help in the battle against the powers of darkness and secularization," (John-Paul II, April 24, 1994, Saint Peter's Square, Vatican City, Rome).

Returning to Jerusalem

We know that the Blessed Mother has great confidence in the small prayer groups set up throughout the world. "Prayer groups are strong and I can see, little children, that through them the Holy Spirit is working in the world," (June 24, 2004).

If the Church is set to plunge into a great trial like its Master did (as some countries have already started to experience), then we must admit that the smaller we are, the less visible to the enemy we will be. The young Ratzinger had already spoken about a poor Church, deprived of its assets and privileges, persecuted but devout.[76] That Church's "power" will be supplanted by a great spiritual authority. Jesus didn't have anywhere to lay his head. Neither did he have earthly power nor material goods. However, what authority shone through His teaching and His witness!

In other words, the Church is invited to return to Jerusalem. Not on the actual site of the Holy City but on its own footsteps, those of the first Christians. Although they didn't hold influential positions, their lives as followers of Christ were led so closely by the Holy Spirit that the world was flooded with their light. The mystic Marthe Robin saw "small islands of

---

[76] See Chapter 45 "The forgotten prophecy of Ratzinger" in *Peace Will Have the Last Word*, by Sister Emmanuel Maillard, ed. Children of Medjugorje, 2015.

fervor" from which will emerge a purified Church. It will stand renewed, humble and strong like its Master, while being faithful to the Holy Spirit, its Founder. Its fervent prayer and real experience of brotherly love will enable the Church to adapt to the distress present today. The true message of peace, consolation and love will shine through for every person of goodwill to acknowledge. Just as we read today, in the Acts of the Apostles, how beautiful such a Church is and thus prepare its beginnings in our own hearts.

Studying the Torah in Jerusalem, © Photo Feu et Lumière

44
Our Stoles Were Wet with Tears

Confession in Medjugorje, © Photo Bernard Gallagher

Early in August, 1984, the Blessed Mother revealed to the visionaries the exact date she was born. When the Church celebrated the nativity of Mary on September 8, it was using a liturgical date, not a historical one. According to the visionaries of Medjugorje, the Virgin Mary was born on the 5th of August, and so, in 1984, she would have been celebrating her 2000th birthday, and, of course … without a wrinkle on her beautiful face! The day before this date, the prayer group gathered together once more, and fifteen year old Jelena Vasilj, the leader of the group, had an unusual experience. For two years, this young girl from the village had the gift of seeing Our Lady, not in an apparition, as in the case of the six visionaries, but in her heart, together with Jesus. She also received inner locutions which corroborated and enriched the messages received by the visionaries. These messages were intended for the edification of the prayer group that Mary had formed under the leadership of Jelena, and which was comprised mostly of adolescents.

On August 4, 1984, in the small, plain prayer room of the Vasilj family, those young people were sitting on the floor, praying the rosary with all their heart. Jelena began to recite the Our Father, when, suddenly, she saw Satan who was preventing her, at all cost, from praying. She was so young and already had to face the enemy of the entire human race. She tried in vain to pronounce the words of the Our Father. Satan was rolling around on the floor and visibly upset though, and begged Jelena to ask Our Lady not to give her blessing to the world the following day. But Jelena had been trained in the school of Mary, and so she ignored his words.

It was then that Our Lady manifested herself to Jelena, offering her the most beautiful smile. "He knows why he is asking that," she said. "Because the Most-High has allowed me to bless the world tomorrow with my solemn blessing. Satan knows that on that particular day he will be bonded and will be unable to act."

Jelena finished her Our Father in peace and rejoiced in anticipation of this very special day. We can well imagine that, for the celebration of His mother's birthday, Jesus would suspend for a time the impact of the Enemy on souls and that he would permit these souls to come to Him freely and without any obstacle.

The next day, grace flowed out so profusely that all who found themselves in Medjugorje that day experienced Heaven on earth. The 70 priests present in the village on that day heard confessions all day long, because villagers and pilgrims alike felt compelled to make their peace with God through the Sacrament of Reconciliation. The anointing of the Holy Spirit was so strong that people sobbed out their sins to the priest. The priests testified that their stoles were wet with tears and that they joined their own tears with those of their penitents. People who had come as tourists to the Adriatic coast felt irresistibly moved to come to Medjugorje and joined the line of penitents, crying out their own sins as well, confessing and receiving the peace of God's forgiveness. How many souls found grace again that day! The harvest was spectacular!

How can we not link the promise that Satan would be tightly bound that day with the astonishing fruits of the blessing felt by everyone? How can we not notice that on the very day Satan was silenced, bounded and unable to act, the flow of Divine Mercy spilled out over all the inhabitants and visitors of Medjugorje, near and far? Why should we be astonished that our mortal enemy detests mercy, when mercy makes us fall into the arms of God and not into his clutches? Why should we be amazed that all the obstacles that prevented us from welcoming God's mercy were surmounted the moment Satan was silenced? Isn't it he who through his insidious arguments inside our consciences, has us believe that sin is absolutely normal, absolutely human? Isn't it his soothing and cunning voice which suggests to us that we don't need to abandon sin, much less to throw it into the flaming furnace of the heart of Jesus in the Sacrament of Confession?

Let's not wait for Our Lady's 3000th birthday to embrace mercy!

Confessions in Medjugorje in the 80s. Archives

45
THE ILLUMINATION OF CONSCIENCE

For a long time, faced with the degradation of our society, where, as Our Lady says, "everything is collapsing," I have often asked the Lord about His vision of our future. Very simply I point out: "I don't see how You are going to get out of this!" And, in my humble way, I keep an eye out for any hints of an answer from Him.

Although I don't receive any visions or messages, all I have to do is open my eyes to see that we are witnessing today an altogether remarkable spiritual phenomenon, which is touching more and more people, regardless of their culture or religion. I greet this phenomenon with happiness, because it seems to me to be an enormous gift from Heaven.

We can call this phenomenon a "warning" or an "illumination of consciences." It doesn't really matter what name we give it.

When I went to see the Venerable Marthe Robin, I recounted the story of my conversion, and told her as well about the multitude of gifts and charisms to be found at the heart of these Renewal of the Spirit groups in Paris, where I had experienced my conversion. I thought I was sharing with her the miraculous, the fantastic, the never-before-seen. She answered me in the most natural tone of voice in the world: "That's nothing compared to what the Lord is preparing!"

Whenever Marthe talked about the future, she alluded to the arrival of a "New Pentecost of Love." She had an unshakeable faith in this promise that had been made to her by

Christ. Would this Pentecost be a handful of men gathered in a Cenacle like the first Pentecost in Jerusalem? Probably not. We have every reason to believe that it will be different, totally unexpected, and of considerable breadth. Marthe suffered deeply when she saw the development of apostasy. She even went as far as saying, on the subject of the Church in France: "There will no longer be anything left, except little islands of fervor." These little islands, humble and poor, often hidden from the eyes of the enemy, are the building blocks of this New Pentecost of Love.

The thousands of prayer groups, generated by Medjugorje throughout the entire world, are certainly part of these little islands of fervor.

Saint Louis-Marie Grignion of Montfort prophesied about the "Apostles of the Last Days" and described them in a way that would make the first Apostles jealous! They will evangelize with the authority of Christ and the power of the Holy Spirit.[77]

At La Salette, in 1846, Our Lady described herself this way: "Finally, I call on the Apostles of the Last Days, the faithful disciples of Jesus Christ, who have lived in scorn of the world and of themselves, in poverty and in humility, in contempt and in silence, in prayer and in mortification, in chastity and in union with God, in suffering, and unknown to the world. It is time for them to come out and fill the world with light. Go, and reveal yourselves to be my cherished children. I am with you and in you, so long as your faith is the light which guides you in these days of unhappiness. May your zeal make you hungry for the glory and honor of Jesus Christ. Fight, Children of Light, you, the few who can see. For now is the time of all times, the end of all ends."

Figliola, a great French mystic of the 20th century, received some revelations from Christ about the Church, in particular

---

[77] See the pages on The Apostles of the Last Days in 'The Secret of Mary'.

about France.[78] She spoke, also, about the "Church of Light" that Jesus was preparing in secret, and of a "New Pentecost" at the end of a great apostasy. She had seen in advance several people chosen by God who would be leaders of this Church of Light. She even invited some of them to come find her, which perhaps indicates that this New Pentecost is near and concerns our generation. I contend that this reality of the illumination of consciences has begun, in a manner that is still tenuous, but real and undeniable.

Symptoms Common to These Experiences

The illumination of consciences is always unexpected and surprising. Even when a person is living in sin, he suddenly sees himself in the light of God, the way Jesus Himself sees him. He experiences the reality of his soul with an acuity he never possessed before. He feels, as never before, God's immense love for him. This love, which is all gentleness and mercy, overwhelms him. The revelation goes beyond all he could imagine, and he can't find words to describe it.

In a flash, he also sees, passing before his eyes, the story of his life in all its tiniest details, and, because of God's love, he suffers terribly from the evil he has committed against God, against others, and against himself. He is humiliated and cries with abandon over his sins in genuine contrition, sometimes for several days (depending on the level of tears or compunction). He develops an absolute horror of his sin and an intense desire to confess it as soon as possible.

After this experience, the person radically changes his life, and puts it back in order without compromise, leaving the first place in his life to God and to His love. He is thirsty for His word and for the Sacraments. The opinion of others, who

[78] Figliola (1888-1976). See "Chemins de lumière" and "Qui est Figliola ?" Ed. Tequi, 1999. Pope Benedict XVI refers often with sadness to "the slow apostasy of the West."

sometimes criticize him, no longer holds sway; he is determined. He experiences a great desire for God and aspires to be with Him, so much so that his nostalgia for Heaven becomes a painful burning. He prays a great deal in a heartfelt way, having tasted the goodness of the Lord. Because he is thirsty for the salvation of souls, he wants to evangelize them and remains resolute in the face of human opinion.

Here are a Few Examples:

Patrick Latta, a Canadian, who has been living in Medjugorje since 1993, himself declares: "I had one foot in Hell, and I didn't even know it!" In his business as a car dealer, the money flowed easily. He was selling more than 50 cars a week. Money was the center of his life, and God was completely absent. He had many affairs. In short, he was living like an atheist, although he was baptized a Catholic in his infancy. One day, he was getting ready to throw a bunch of papers into the trash, when one of them fell into his hands. It was a message from Our Lady in Medjugorje, sent by his Croatian brother-in-law and left on the refrigerator. It read, "I came to you to say that God exists." Patrick froze in place. He began to sob and couldn't stop himself. That went on for days. He told me: "In an instant, I knew that God existed, that the Bible was true, that Mary was real, that God was love…" His life changed completely. He gives a powerful testimony about the love of God and Mary! How many hearts he has touched![79]

Samuel Jintoni and I met in 2015, and I know his family well. This young father of a Catholic family in Kota Kinabalu, Malaysia, led a life of sin. Deep down, he had a good heart, but he had connected with a bad group of friends and was very belligerent. In 2014, after being attacked by testicular cancer, which metastasized to the lungs and liver, he felt greatly

---

[79] Patrick's complete testimony can be found on pp. 56-57 of *Medjugorje, Triumph of the Heart* by Sister Emmanuel Maillard, 1996. See appendix 2.

confused, and all peace left him. Contradictory feelings were at war within him, and the anguish was growing day by day. He decided to participate in morning prayers at his parents' house, but he told them: "I can't find any peace! I have to forgive all those who have done me harm; I'm making a list of them in my head, but it's hard. I can't get to the point of forgiving them. I just get more angry with them." In his despair, he addressed this prayer to Jesus, "Why can't I find peace? What's blocking me? Free me, Lord!"

Later, Samuel had to undergo an MRI at the hospital. When he found himself inside such a fearsome machine, narrow and closed up like a tomb, a place where he was not exactly confident, a light suddenly flashed before his eyes, and he saw his entire life of sin as a young man. It was extremely painful to him. Everything flashed in front of him "like a video clip", as he expressed it. He saw himself watching this video clip and was profoundly ashamed and broken. He saw that he was a complete wreck, and the suffering he experienced knowing that he caused so much pain to himself and others was intolerable. But, then and there, he received the grace to repent very sincerely of all those horrible sins, and he asked God for forgiveness. He made the most beautiful confession of his life and understood at that moment that he himself had to give forgiveness on two levels: he had to forgive himself and he had to forgive those who had hurt him. Among other things, he had been the victim of a false accusation by a young man after a theft, which put him in prison unjustly for a number of days. He had the grace to forgive, finally, with all his heart.

Then, all at once, still enclosed in the machine, he saw Jesus on the Cross; He was bloody, his flesh in shreds, suffering atrociously. Samuel was overwhelmed by it and began to sob. All of a sudden the MRI machine that he was in disappeared from his eyes, and was replaced by a beautiful blue sky. He heard the voice of Jesus, who was speaking to him from high on the Cross, "Your faith has saved you!" An ocean of Divine peace flowed through him, an indescribable peace that he had never known. From that day on, Samuel was profoundly transformed. His friends didn't recognize him. They came to him to receive the shower of peace he radiated! His cancer continued to spread through his body, but not a single complaint came from his mouth.

A little later, since the hospital could do no more for him, Samuel returned to his home, and there he gathered his whole family around him to share his experience. They all cried, from both pain and joy: from the pain of recognizing that he was going to die, and from joy in seeing the incredible work God had achieved in him. They had asked for this in prayer for many years! Samuel left to be with the Lord on March 7, 2016, shortly after his testimony to his loved ones. He was twenty-nine. Two days after his death, his aunt saw him in a dream. At that time she had serious financial problems. She saw Samuel come to her and tell her with great love, "In life, we have to do our best. We are nothing without God. If you must love, love! Life is so short! Don't worry about money, love! Give the best of yourself!"

We could make a long list of people who have experienced an illumination of conscience.

Marino Respreto, a notorious criminal, whose testimony can be found on the internet.

I have also known a number of Jewish persons, practicing or not, who have become Messianic Jews after encountering Christ in the middle of a living experience with him. They never hesitate to proclaim him as Lord, even in Israel, where they were mostly rejected by their fellow citizens. It would take a completely different book all of its own to give all the examples of those who have experienced an illumination of conscience!

That's not to mention those who have had near-death experiences, and then testified about it:

Gloria Polo for example (see Chapter 5): I have met her several times. When you consider the horrific mess she was in before she was struck by lightning, it's impossible, looking at her life today, to comprehend that this is the same person. She has truly gone through a metamorphosis! After hearing her story, most people run to the confessionals to make the confessions of their lives!

Father James Manjakhal who is originally from India, and now known world-wide for his fiery teachings and his gift of healing, also tells his story of transformation after a near-death experience. In Africa, during a mission, he was poisoned by a sorceress jealous over his success with the people. He didn't die from it, but remained in a deep coma for one full year. When he came out of the coma, he recounted all he had experienced: a special visit to Heaven, Hell, and Purgatory. He also received enlightenment and extraordinary knowledge about the realities of the Most High. He testified about this in his book, *I Have Seen Eternity*.[80]

Might we say that **the Good Thief**, also, benefited from an illumination of his conscience, at that moment when the sky became dark, and when all those gathered at Golgotha began, strangely, to beat their breasts? At the moment when he looked at Jesus with the eyes of His heart? For my part, I believe it, even if we only truly find out in Heaven, like Father Steven, whose story is found in Chapter 30.

Why Some and Not Others?

That remains a mystery and God's secret. When the visionaries of Medjugorje asked the Blessed Mother: "Why us?" she answered, "Such is the will of God!" However, I contend that this remarkable grace is actually multiplying before our eyes. Our Lady doesn't give it a particular name. To my knowledge, in her messages at Medjugorje, she has not talked about any "illumination of conscience." But she has made it happen

[80] Available in many languages including English (original version) at the publishing house Verbum Dei www.jmanjackal.net/eng/engeternity.htm – Emailing: childjesus@yahoo.com or charisjyothi@gmail.com

in many pilgrims!

For those of us who are lucky enough – or rather, who have the grace – to know Jesus and His Mother, it is urgent that we prepare ourselves to live this new Pentecost of Love. It can come upon the world at the moment we least expect it! I imagine that considerable crowds will come to ask for help, as at the first Pentecost, when thousands of people asked the apostles: "What shall we do?" (Acts 2:37).

Those who are in a state of grace will be profoundly happy to meet their beloved Savior and abandon themselves to Him. They will be affirmed in their faith. For others, it will be a chance to make a choice between God and darkness. It will be for them the test of truth. Many will repent and convert. They will need to be listened to, supported, consoled, put at peace, strengthened, encouraged, and evangelized. Others will be trapped in their rejection of God, because we have all received free will.

We are, therefore, called to pray a good deal, to adore and to listen to God in inner silence, so to receive His peace and the graces necessary to go through this "trial of Mercy" in a positive way. To permit ourselves to be instructed and formed, notably through Mary. Saint Faustina recalls, "In the evening, when I was praying, the Virgin Mary told me, 'Your life must resemble mine: gentle, hidden, constantly in union with God, interceding for humanity and preparing the world for the second coming of God.'

For Mary, in Mary, with Mary!

For the apostles, Our Lady was the image of the Church in prayer. She was with them in the Upper Room in Jerusalem, waiting for the Holy Spirit promised by Jesus, the Paraclete whom the Father would send. It was she who animated the whole first ten days of the story between the Ascension and Pentecost. And, as the new precursor, it is she, once more, who is preparing today's world for this New Pentecost, calling all her children to come back to God, to find the state of grace again, and to put God first in their lives. Her maternal interventions are multiplying today in visible ways! Lourdes, Fatima, Medjugorje… It's the whole Gospel retold in the words of the Mother. It's the urgent invitation of a mother who sees that time is short and that there's not a minute to spare.

This movement of the illumination of consciences, or of warning, will introduce us, little by little, into the Civilization of Love, which John-Paul II talks about, into the New Evangelization, into the Pentecost of Love, into the springtime of the Church, into the Triumph of the Immaculate Heart of Mary!

46
Scandalous Mercy!

As you have seen, the mercy of God is nothing like human justice; not even like basic morality. One final story might illustrate this. It's a totally unique story, because it came directly out of my imagination. Imagination? Well, yes and no! Something similar may have actually happened. And who knows, maybe some readers will be able to identify with the main character.

Let's go back two thousand years to that Friday on which the story of humanity was changed dramatically, a Friday on which the very culmination of mercy occurred.

Avigaël quickened her steps in Jerusalem, which was teeming with people who were there for *Pesach*, Passover (Friday), *Chag Hamotzi*, the Feast of Unleavened Bread (Saturday), and *Yom Habbikkurim*, Feast of the First fruits (Sunday). It was the Middle East, with its sounds, its colors, and its fragrances! On these tiny, narrow streets, men and animals were intertwined with children calling out to one another. Little did they know what would happen that day!

On this Easter in the year 33 of our Era, the atmosphere was charged with serious questions: was he going to come to the festival? Avigaël's heart was torn between love and hate. She loved this Jesus of Nazareth, this "Yeshua" whom she admired as a great prophet. After all, hadn't he cured her cousin Aaron of paralysis and given her little sister back her sight? For more than a year, she had followed him everywhere so that she could capture every word that came out of his mouth. She knew him well, because like him, she also came from

Galilee. Moreover, people said he was the Son of God, and Avigaël was deeply convinced of this. No one could have done the works he did unless God had been with him. No one could have spoken as he spoke, combining gentleness with power, humility with authority. It was magnificent! And when his eyes met yours… It was Heaven itself flowing inside you and moving you. The Scribes and the Pharisees could say what they wanted, but there was no mistaking that look.

Lately, Avigaël noticed the presence of Myriam, the mother of the prophet Yeshua, even though she was quite unassuming. They had become friends during long walks following Jesus on the shore of Lake Tiberius. She was aware of the immense goodness emanating from this mother, so simple, so beautiful, and so pure. She was a woman who could always find comforting words to say, giving the smile that restored hope. Yes, the mother of the prophet was a woman who had a good heart in whom Avigaël loved to confide.

But, then, several days ago, not far from the little hamlet of Cana, in Galilee, Avigaël's daughter was raped and savagely murdered at the age of only 16 by a highway thug, and her mother's heart was ravaged with pain. OK, she had wonderful sons, but Rachel was her only daughter. After the funeral, she hurried to Jerusalem for the Feast of the Passover. She had learned that the criminal had been arrested and condemned to death. He was going to be crucified this very Friday along with another criminal. Avigaël told herself: "Good. That's just what he deserves!" She didn't want to miss such a spectacle and headed toward Golgotha, where her daughter's murderer would be in agony for long hours before dying on a cross. "I'm glad about that!" she repeated to herself with a satisfaction that still didn't calm her pain and anguish.

It was around noon and the trumpets of the Temple resounded mightily, because it was time for the Pascal lamb to be slain. As she approached Golgotha, Avigaël noticed something unexpected: a very noble woman of forty or so, whom she thought she recognized, was standing there. It was Myriam, the mother of the prophet! Avigaël couldn't imagine what on earth she could be doing there, next to the Roman soldiers. She seemed so sad. Alongside her was a young man, supporting her. He was just as sad as she was. "My God," Avigaël thought. "They haven't condemned my Jesus, too? No, that can't be!"

But, yes, it was Him. As her eyes ascended to meet the eyes of the criminals hanging there, she recognized Him, Jesus, crucified between those two thieves, one of which was her daughter's rapist. It was really Him!

Avigaël was devastated. He meant everything to her and gave such great hope for her nation! How could they have condemned such an innocent man? They must be out of their minds! She drew nearer, and, all of a sudden, her blood froze in her veins. Catching sight of the criminal on the left, she was stunned and murmured as though in a trance, 'That's my daughter's murderer! The horrible Dismas! The horrible assassin!" She moved nearer still and positioned herself not far from Jesus' mother, behind her. Conflicting emotions were at battle within her; she was torn between her love for Jesus and her hatred of her daughter's murderer. She heard the voice of Jesus cry out: "Father, forgive them; for they know not what they do!" But, since she was concentrating wholly on the assassin, Dismas, and on her hatred toward him, she paid no attention to those words.

What followed was for her intolerable, scandalous and unthinkable. Was what she heard right? Dismas murmured something. After being moved by the divine gaze of Jesus, this criminal began to defend Jesus to the other thief who was insulting Him. Dismas' breathing became distressed from the pain of the crucifixion, but Avigaël captured the essence of his words. She absolutely didn't expect this: Dismas just admitted that he deserved this terrible death, given the evil he had done. How bizarre! He made amends honorably! And the response of Jesus confounded her even more: "This very day you will be with me in Paradise!"

'WHAT??? This criminal? This sadist? Am I hallucinating?' Her entire being screamed in horror, "That man, Dismas, in

Paradise this very day?" What a scandal! How is it possible? The world had turned upside down!

Avigaël stood there frozen, stupefied. Her body did not respond anymore. She became inert. This was too violent a shock!

But her Jesus had foreseen everything. He knew. From all eternity, he knew, he saw, he prepared. He knew that at the foot of the Cross, another mother besides His own had lost her child under atrocious circumstances. He addressed Myriam, His mother: "Woman, behold your son!" Then His disciple John: "Behold your mother!" With these words he was giving His mother not only to John but also to Avigaël, and to all people until the end of time.

Myriam became Mother at the foot of this Cross, at the foot of this triple crucifixion which united in the same fate a God and two evil doers. Jesus had accomplished everything. He now gave up his last breath by letting out a loud cry, a cry that even a man in good health could not emit. Satan was rubbing his hands together, sure of his victory: he had finally put to death his worst enemy! But he didn't know that by doing so, by killing the Author of Life, it was he who lost everything, and lost it forever. Death was vanquished on his own land, the adversary was crushed at the very moment that he believed he had achieved victory!

Myriam looked on. For her as well, they had just killed her one and only beloved child, Jesus. She had only him. Overcome with grief, she stood there and watched in silent prayer. And then, as though moved from the inside, overflowing with that universal and maternal anointing which had just been conferred upon her by her Divine Son, she turned around. Avigaël was standing there, rigid, devastated, her mouth contorted. One look was enough, but – oh, the miracle – the Mother of the Crucified came towards her, holding out her arms!

"Who is this, arising like the dawn, as beautiful as the moon, as resplendent as the sun?" (Song of Solomon, 6:10).

Avigaël's limbs relaxed again. The two women embraced at length. Silence. Tears of peace and pain intermingling. Not a word was said. Little by little, as though a purifying water flowed through her, Avigaël understood. From then on, there would no longer remain that hatred inside her alongside the love. A spark of mercy had suddenly arisen deep within her. Surrendering herself to the heart of Myriam, she finally laid down her agitated soul. Only love remained. Myriam's heart burned like a torch. How could that flame permit a single ounce of hatred towards Dismas, the criminal, to remain in Avigaël? Revolt, frustration, hatred, despair: all that garbage melted like snow in the sun. At one with the heart of Myriam, Avigaël forgave the unforgivable…

Jesus had done all things well. At the moment of his last cry, when the veil of the Temple tore and the rocks split open, wasn't it fitting that He gave his own mother to His ravaged Avigaël and threw her the life line of mercy? And what mercy! Scandalous mercy!

Appendix I

LITANY OF DIVINE MERCY

Saint Faustina was excellent at praising Divine Mercy. She let this litany flow from her heart and she added a promise: "The love of God is the flower – Mercy the fruit. Let the doubting soul read these considerations on Divine Mercy and become trusting:

Divine Mercy, gushing forth from the bosom of the Father,
I trust in You.
Divine Mercy, greatest attribute of God,
I trust in You.
Divine Mercy, incomprehensible mystery,
Divine Mercy, fount gushing forth from the mystery of the Most Blessed Trinity
Divine Mercy, unfathomable by any intellect human or angelic,
Divine Mercy, from which wells forth all life and happiness,
Divine Mercy, better than the heavens,
Divine Mercy, source of miracles and wonders,
Divine Mercy, encompassing the whole universe,
Divine Mercy, descending to earth in the Person of the Incarnate Word,
Divine Mercy which flowed out from the open wound of the Heart of Jesus,
Divine Mercy enclosed in the Heart of Jesus for us and especially for sinners,
Divine Mercy unfathomed in the institution of the Sacred Heart,
Divine Mercy, in the founding of the Holy Church,
Divine Mercy, in the sacrament of Holy Baptism,
Divine Mercy, in our justification through Jesus Christ,

Divine Mercy, accompanying us through our whole life,
Divine Mercy, embracing us especially at the hour of death,
Divine Mercy, endowing us with immortal life,
Divine Mercy, accompanying us every moment of our life,
Divine Mercy, shielding us from the fire of hell,
Divine Mercy, in the conversion of hardened sinners,
Divine Mercy, astonishment for angels, incomprehensible to saints,
Divine Mercy, unfathomed in all the mysteries of God,
Divine Mercy, lifting us out of every misery,
Divine Mercy, source of our happiness and joy,
Divine Mercy, in calling us forth from nothingness to existence,
Divine Mercy, embracing all the works of His hands,
Divine Mercy, crown of all God's handy work,
Divine Mercy, in which we are all immersed,
Divine Mercy, sweet relief for anguished hearts,
Divine Mercy, only hope of despairing souls,
Divine Mercy, repose of hearts, peace amidst fear,
Divine Mercy, delight and ecstasy of holy souls,
Divine Mercy, inspiring hope against all hope,

Eternal God, in whom mercy is endless and the treasury of compassion inexhaustible, look kindly upon us and increase Your mercy in us, that in difficult moments we may neither despair nor become despondent, but with great confidence submit ourselves to Your Holy Will, which is Love and Mercy itself."

Appendix II

OTHER BOOKS FROM THE AUTHOR

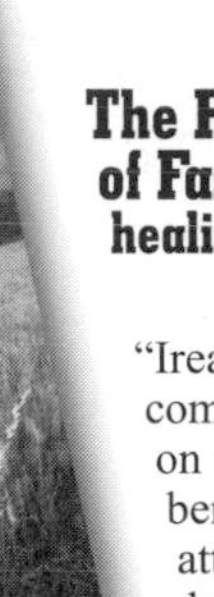

The Forgotten Power of Fasting
healing, liberation, joy...

"Iread your book from cover to cover. Your words completely captivated me and have convinced me on the importance of fasting. I knew already the benefits of fasting, but I wasn't aware of all its attributes, that you explain so well. Reading this book one discovers fasting.

As we know, Our Lady in Medjugorje continuously insists on the importance of fasting, but we avoid putting into practice something when it means we have to make a sacrifice. We struggle to convince ourselves to actually fast.

The arguments you present, and the examples that you give in this book, show very clearly the reason why Our Lady insists so persistently on something so precious for the soul and the body, for the apostolate on earth and for the souls in Purgatory. I thank you for emphasizing such an important topic, very often mentioned in Sacred Scripture, so precious for the living and for the intercession of the dead.

The final part of your work, with the words from the saints, will convince even the most reluctant.

This book will be nothing less than a true discovery of fasting to whoever reads it.

Don Gabriele Amorth

Euro 7.00
Sister Emmanuel
© 1995 Children of Medjugorje
www.sremmanuel.org

Medjugorje, Triumph of the Heart

A revised edition of *Medjugorje, the 90s*, *Medjugorje, Triumph of the Heart* has become a Medjugorje classic over the years. It not only inspires pilgrims to dig deeper into their own pilgrimage experience but Sister Emmanuel also offers a pure echo of Medjugorje, the eventful village where the Mother of God has been appearing since 1981. She shares at length some of the personal stories of the villagers, the visionaries, and the pilgrims who flock there by the thousands, receiving great healings. Eight years of awe has inspired this book. It has been translated into 22 languages. These 89 stories offer a glimpse into the miracles of Mary's motherly love.

US $ 12.95
Sister Emmanuel

www.sremmanuel.org

Children, Help My Heart To Triumph!

At the height of the Bosnian War, Sister Emmanuel remained in Medjugorje with a few members of her community. During that time, memories of her father, a Prisoner of War during WWII, continually surfaced. Remembering how much he suffered, she felt a need to do something to spiritually help those on the front lines. Sister Emmanuel describes a call that she received at that time to appeal to the children for their sacrifices in order to alleviate the war. *Children, Help My Heart To Triumph* was written in response to that call. It describes for children how to make a 9-day novena of little sacrifices. Included is a coloring book that they can color and mail to Medjugorje where they will be presented at one of Our Lady's apparitions.

US $ 11.99
Sister Emmanuel

Reprinted 2012 Includes Coloring Book
www.sremmanuel.org

The Amazing Secret of the Souls in Purgatory

It is not often that a book touches the soul so deeply. *The Amazing Secret of the Souls in Purgatory* is such a book. Maria Simma, deceased in March of 2003, lived a humble life in the mountains of Austria. When she was twenty-five, Maria was graced with a very special charism – the charism of being visited by the many souls in Purgatory – and being able to communicate with them! Maria shares, in her own words, some amazing secrets about the souls in Purgatory. She answers questions such as: What is Purgatory? How do souls get there? Who decides if a soul goes to Purgatory? How can we help get souls released from Purgatory?

US $ 8.99
© 1997 Queenship Publishing
www.queenship.org
www.sremmanuel.org

The Hidden Child of Medjugorje

"Reading "Medjugorje, the 90s" had left me dazzled and so deeply touched that it had literally pulled me to Medjugorje. I just had to see with my own eyes the spiritual wonders retold in that book. Now with "The Hidden Child," the ember of love for Mary has received a new breath of air – a Pentecostal wind. Sr. Emmanuel is indeed one of Mary's best voices! Congratulations for this jewel of a testimonial! I wouldn't be surprised if the Gospa herself turned out to be Sister's most avid reader."
Msgr. Denis Croteau, OMI

"Books are like seashells; at first they all look alike. However, they are far from being identical and their value varies greatly. Some of them are packed with riches and so well written, that they hide rare pearls within. Sister Emmanuel's book is one of those; it contains the most beautiful pearls, and with them enriches the reader. Through her accounts and anecdotes, the reader is pleased to meet people of great worth and to be filled with the teachings of so many events. Through this book, one will explore more fully a way still too little known: the way of the Queen of Peace."
Fr. Jozo Zovko, OFM

US $ 15.99
Sister Emmanuel
© 2010 Children of Medjugorje, Inc.
www.sremmanuel.org

Maryam of Bethlehem, the Little Arab

Who is this little Arab? Maryam Baouardy is a daughter of Galilee. Her life? A succession of supernatural manifestations worthy of Catherine of Sienna. Maryam shares the keys of holiness, including ways to defeat Satan himself. This is a book you don't want to miss?

US $ 5.00
Sister Emmanuel

www.sremmanuel.org
Available in E-Book

The Beautiful Story of Medjugorje As Told to Children from 7 to 97

In this book, you will follow the experiences of six little shepherds, their shock when they saw the "Lady" appearing to them in 1981. You will see how Vicka and Jokov actually experienced the reality of life beyond this world, when Our Lady took them with her on the most extraordinary journey to Heaven, Purgatory and Hell.

You will learn how brave they were under persecution. You will be excited to know the messages they share from a Mother who thinks only of helping us, who loves each one of us so much – including you in a very special way! You will read about the powerful healings of bodies and souls happening there, as in Lourdes.

This is an adventure story, except that this story is true and is happening right now for you!

US $ 5.00
Sister Emmanuel

www.sremmanuel.org
Available in E-Book

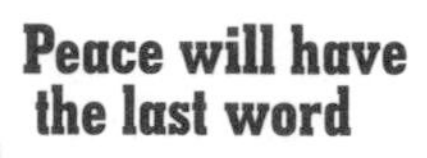

The mercy of God is scandalous, it even borders on the extreme! In her engaging and lively style, Sister Emmanuel recounts real life stories and testimonies that take the reader's heart on a journey of God's mercy, passing through the prisons of New York, and into the confessionals of the Saints!

In these pages, a mosaic of photos and parables, the reader encounters the very depths of the human heart and is transported into the midst of scenes and situations that are as captivating as they are diverse. Through them we witness that much-desired peace that comes from Above, gaining victory over emptiness, futility and fear.

Here are words that many no longer dare to speak, and yet, they have the power to help rebuild a degenerating society. This book is a shot in the arm, an injection of hope that will hasten the time when, in the hearts of all, peace will have the last word!

US $ 13.99
Sister Emmanuel

www.sremmanuel.org

About The Author

Sister Emmanuel Maillard was born in France in 1947. After completing a degree in Literature and History of Fine Arts at the Sorbonne University in Paris, she studied theology with Cardinal Daniélou. In 1973, she had a powerful experience of the love of Jesus and she decided to consecrate her life to God. In 1976 she joined the Community of the Beatitudes in France, which she is still part of. In 1989, she received a call from the Blessed Mother and she was sent by her community to Medjugorje where she still lives. Since 1992 and from there she has been travelling around the world to evangelize and bring hope to a society that often looks for happiness where it gets lost.

Her books have been translated into several languages and have touched the hearts of many readers around the world, quickly becoming best-sellers. Her talks and testimonies have also been publicized through CDs, TV shows, Internet and other media.

One can find the list of her works on ***www.sremmanuel.org***

In order to receive her monthly Newsletter, please register at:
commentscom@childrenofmedjugorje.com

To get it in French (original version), ***gospa.fr@gmail.com***

In Spanish, ***gisele_riverti@mensajerosdelareinadelapaz.org***

In German, ***commentscom@childrenofmedjugorje.com***

In Italian, ***vannalvisepg@gmail.com***

In Flemish, ***gclaes@scarlet.be***

In Croatian, ***djeca.medjugorja@gmail.com***

In Arabic, ***friendsofmary@live.com***

In Portuguese, ***medjugorje.portugal@gmail.com***

In Chinese, ***teresamedj@gmail.com***